Cantor William Sharlin

ALSO BY JONATHAN L. FRIEDMANN

*Music in Our Lives: Why We Listen,
How It Works* (2015)

*Music in the Hebrew Bible: Understanding References
in the Torah, Nevi'im and Ketuvim* (2014)

*Music in Biblical Life: The Roles
of Song in Ancient Israel* (2013)

*Synagogue Song: An Introduction to Concepts,
Theories and Customs* (2012)

* * *

COMPILED BY
JONATHAN L. FRIEDMANN

*Music, Theology and Worship:
Selected Writings, 1841–1896* (2011)

*The Value of Sacred Music: An Anthology
of Essential Writings, 1801–1918* (2009)

*Music in Jewish Thought:
Selected Writings, 1890–1920* (2009)

ALL FROM MCFARLAND

Cantor William Sharlin
Musical Revolutionary of Reform Judaism

Jonathan L. Friedmann

McFarland & Company, Inc., Publishers
Jefferson, North Carolina

All photographs are from the Sharlin family. Permission to use them was granted by Lisa Sharlin Klein.

LIBRARY OF CONGRESS CATALOGUING-IN-PUBLICATION DATA

Names: Friedmann, Jonathan L., 1980– author.
Title: Cantor William Sharlin : musical revolutionary of Reform Judaism / Jonathan L. Friedmann.
Description: Jefferson, North Carolina : McFarland & Company, 2019 | Includes bibliographical references and index.
Identifiers: LCCN 2019002419 | ISBN 9781476677064 (paperback : acid free paper) ∞
Subjects: LCSH: Sharlin, William. | Cantors (Judaism)—United States—Biography. | Reform Judaism—United States.
Classification: LCC ML420.S533 F74 2019 | DDC 296.4/62092 [B] —dc23
LC record available at https://lccn.loc.gov/2019002419

BRITISH LIBRARY CATALOGUING DATA ARE AVAILABLE

ISBN (print) 978-1-4766-7706-4
ISBN (ebook) 978-1-4766-3558-3

© 2019 Jonathan L. Friedmann. All rights reserved

No part of this book may be reproduced or transmitted in any form or by any means, electronic or mechanical, including photocopying or recording, or by any information storage and retrieval system, without permission in writing from the publisher.

Front cover image: William Sharlin teaching songs at camp, 1980s (courtesy of the Sharlin Family)

Printed in the United States of America

McFarland & Company, Inc., Publishers
 Box 611, Jefferson, North Carolina 28640
  www.mcfarlandpub.com

Table of Contents

Preface   1
Introduction   5

1. Beginnings   9
2. School of Sacred Music, New York   21
3. Hebrew Union College, Cincinnati   35
4. Leo Baeck Temple, Los Angeles   53
5. Department of Sacred Music, Los Angeles   92
6. Saratoga, California   121

Epilogue   134
Appendix: The Writings of Cantor William Sharlin— An Annotated Bibliography   143
Chapter Notes   155
Bibliography   174
Index   181

Preface

Cantor William Sharlin (1920–2012) was a leading figure in twentieth-century synagogue music. A rarity in his profession, he was simultaneously an inspiring cantor and teacher, virtuosic composer and pianist, first-rate scholar and intellectual. To use one of his favorite metaphors, these were the streams that flowed through him. His nearly forty-year career as cantor at Leo Baeck Temple, Los Angeles, witnessed the emergence of sharply divergent musical styles in the synagogue. Although he cautioned that "alien musical forms" could pose a threat to the sincerity of worship, he was aware of the need to breathe new life into ancient prayers. An accomplished and widely performed composer, William wrote new melodies for Jewish liturgy—vibrant and original—that somehow retained an unmistakable link to the past.

His formative years were spent in yeshivot in New York and Jerusalem. He later studied piano and composition at Manhattan School of Music and entered the Reform cantorate. He was both fond and critical of his Orthodox upbringing, both in favor and cautious of Reform innovations. He stood between tradition and post-modernity, bridging the old and the new in his compositions and approach to prayer. His music ranges from subtle to complex, playful to sublime. Every note is precious; every measure is intricate.

I was introduced to his music during my high school years. Several of his pieces were mainstays of the High Holiday repertoire at Temple Israel in Long Beach, California, where I sang in the choir. As a cellist

Preface

and budding composer, I was keenly interested in the harmonic coloration and melodic creativity in the pieces we sang. His music soared above the rest, superior in my perception to the celebrated works of nineteenth-century masters and the music of twentieth-century contemporaries.

My first voice teacher arranged for me to audition for William in 2002, when I was twenty-two years old and vocally unpolished. He heard some potential and took me on as his last student. Thus commenced ten years of arduous training. He was an old-school taskmaster who would not let a poorly executed note escape his scorn. Some lessons were spent singing two measures over and over for the better part of an hour. He also had a philosophical side. Our meetings usually culminated in deep conversations, during which we discussed the history and current state of synagogue song. I remained his student until he passed away in 2012 at the age of ninety-two.

Although William was a fixture in my life and a primary influence on my career, I have striven to present this biography from a place of objectivity (as much as such a thing is possible). The good is presented alongside the blemishes, and, for the most part, I have refrained from interjecting my personal feelings. At the same time, even the most rigorously researched book bears the imprint of the author's interests, experiences, and perspectives. This is certainly true of the present volume. In an effort to keep my own emotions in check and remain true to the historical record, I have included only that information which sheds light on William's musical world. Relevant reminiscences from colleagues and family members flesh out the conversation. When interviews are utilized, I have done my best to adhere to standards of accuracy and impartiality.

The framework for this biography is derived from seven interviews I conducted with Cantor Sharlin in May and June of 2007. His wife, Jacqueline Drucker Sharlin (1926–2016), initiated the interviews when she learned that William, then eighty-seven, had entered the early stages of dementia. It was a time-sensitive assignment that had me laboring over hours of tape, wading through repetitions, piecing together thought fragments, and carving out a chronology. Inevitably, there were misremem-

Preface

bered events and the occasional blurring of people and places. The result was an illuminating 18,500-word story, which captured memories before they faded and convictions while they were still strongly held. What is more, William's oral history preserved the essence of his personality—his wit, charm, and intelligence—which I hope also shines in this book.

William requested during those interviews that I not include negative comments about individuals. It is no secret that he, like other passionate artists engaged in a small and close-knit field, had conflicts with a number of colleagues. He was no stranger to heated disagreements with rabbis and fellow cantors, composers, and musicians. Yet, when it came to putting his life on paper, such things seemed tangential and petty. That request is honored here as well.

In addition to those foundational interviews, information has been drawn from recordings, bulletins, clippings, concert programs, published and unpublished essays, library collections, and William's personal papers. As if predicting that he would someday be the subject of a biography, he preserved a remarkably detailed (if disorganized) archive of himself. Stored away in cluttered drawers were school transcripts, fan mail, correspondences with colleagues, letters from publishers, lecture notes, musical manuscripts, handwritten essays, travel diaries, and more. I am grateful to Jacqui Sharlin for granting me full access to those documents.

I am indebted to the interviewees who offered insights into various aspects of William's life and work: Jacqui Sharlin *z"l*, Lisa Sharlin Klein, Sheldon Merel, Marcie Merel *z"l*, Shirl Lee Pitesky, Mark Saltzman, Joel Stern, Bill Cutter, Perryne Anker, Alan Weiner, Amy Simon-Weiner, and William himself. Deepest appreciation is owed to my wife, Elvia, whose endless patience, steadfast support, and honest critique have made this book possible.

A quick note on organization: The first half of the book is presented in sequential order (Chapters 1–3). It chronicles William's life from childhood to his graduate fellowship in Cincinnati. When he arrived in Los Angeles, his career branched in three main avenues: synagogue, teaching, and Jewish camping. Each of these areas is treated separately and within its own chronological framework, even as they ran parallel (Chapters 4–6). The threads are pulled together in the final chapter.

Introduction

A photograph of Cantor William Sharlin sits on my desk (see next page). His right foot is perched on a chair and a guitar is resting on his knee. His right hand is gesturing to a group of Jewish youngsters crowded into a dining hall. His attire is casual yet respectable. His demeanor is loose yet dignified. He has the spectacles, male pattern baldness, and full mustache of an intellectual. He is in the middle of saying something important. It is the 1980s, and the sixty-something cantor is a beloved figure in the Jewish camping movement. In the minutes before and after the picture is taken, he is cracking jokes, moving energetically around the hall, and encouraging the children to sing along. But in the captured frame, he is all business. He is explaining the significance of the song at hand—the deeper meaning of its words and melody.

The seamless coexistence of the playful and the serious was a hallmark of Cantor Sharlin's multifaceted life as cantor, song leader, composer, teacher, pianist, and scholar. He had fun but was never frivolous. He appreciated group song but avoided trivialities. He strummed the guitar but never allowed it to compromise his musical integrity. He was a citizen of the modern world but upheld the high standards of an earlier time.

William's career is in some ways the story of the professionalization of the American cantorate. He was a member of the first graduating class of the first cantorial school in America, the School of Sacred Music at Hebrew Union College–Jewish Institute of Religion (HUC), and a

Introduction

William teaching songs at camp, 1980s.

Introduction

founding member of the American Conference of Cantors. He is recognized as the first professional Jewish camp song leader, and the first to play a guitar in the synagogue. He was one of only a handful of cantors with an advanced degree in composition (Manhattan School of Music). He developed the Department of Sacred Music at HUC in Los Angeles and taught there for forty years. He raised the profile of the cantorate and Jewish music in California—areas historically dominated by the East Coast establishment. He trained women as cantors before they were allowed into the seminary. His four decades at Leo Baeck Temple (LBT) were among the most musically inventive in the history of the synagogue.

William was grateful for his mixed background of Orthodox and secular. Born into an insular religious family in New York in 1920, he spent his early years immersed in Judaic study. In the mid-1930s his family settled in Jerusalem, where he entered the Jerusalem Conservatory to study piano. This initiated a chain of events that would lead him further into the world of general music, away from parochial tribalism, into the rarefied realms of composition and musicology, and on an idiosyncratic pursuit of the sacred. Although he led worship services, internalized the language of the prayer book, and was fully committed to the Reform cantorate, he almost never spoke of God or piety in the conventional sense. He found holiness in intense musical experiences. He was devoted to song.

William was acutely aware of his own biography. During an unscripted introduction to a concert of his work at the 1989 Western Region Biennial of the Union of American Hebrew Congregations (now the Union for Reform Judaism), he described the harmonious tension within himself:

> I was blessed with polarities, and I say that because I think my musical work is some kind of a synthesis to reconcile the polarities—to work the polarities together, to have these polarities be productive. The first third of my life I lived as an isolated little yeshiva boy in New York. I didn't know the rest of the world. The next third, I left that early world and moved into the universal world of music—and that was a marvelous discovery. And the third third—there'll be a fourth third—I brought those two worlds together. I feel very fortunate about having these two worlds

Introduction

to live with all of these years.... I am a man who straddles two worlds: I am a Jew, and I am a universalist. I am a tribal Jew, and I am also a humanist. I am a mystic and I am also a rationalist. This doesn't bother me. I love these two worlds. I live in the world of the "Three Bs" [Bach, Beethoven and Brahms] (and you can add an M for Mozart); but I also live in the world of that other B, Broadway. It's there somehow or other. I live in the past, and I also live in modernity. And it's these two challenging worlds that I think have moved me my entire life.

1

Beginnings

William Sharlin came into the world on January 7, 1920. He was preceded in birth by three siblings: Edward, Rachel, and Hillel. Their father, Isaac, was a native of Jerusalem. He delivered mail on a mule for the Turkish government in Palestine. Chaya (Ida), their mother, was a third-generation Palestinian Jew from Hebron.

Isaac Sharlin arrived in New York in 1915. He came alone to investigate the possibility of relocating the family, which at the time consisted of Chaya and the two eldest children, Edward and Rachel, ages four and two. Isaac secured a job with a New York–based Jewish organization, and Chaya, with the two children, made her way through Europe to the American consulate in Switzerland. They boarded a ship in Bordeaux, France, and arrived in New York in 1917. Eventually Isaac's entire family came to the United States—his parents, brothers, and sisters. They were all clustered together in Harlem. Chaya's family remained in Palestine, and subsequently Israel.

William and his older brother Hillel were born in New York, about a year and a half apart. William's birth name was Wolf (Hebrew: Ze'ev; Yiddish: Velvel). He never asked his father when or why his name was changed; such intimate questions were unnatural in their authoritarian household. William described his upbringing as "normative, strict Orthodox," and his father as "the ultimate and only authority ... his approval meant everything."[1] There was no such thing as a family discussion.

The Sharlins lived in a modest apartment in Harlem on 113th Street, between Madison and Fifth avenues, which was then home to a sizable Jewish community. Isaac had difficulty finding steady work. His education was poor and he constantly shuffled between jobs.[2] The situation was exacerbated by his unwavering adherence to a strict Jewish lifestyle, which included maintaining a Yiddish-speaking home.[3] He refused to entertain compromises like working on Shabbat. His unwillingness to Americanize extended to the children. When Hillel was a teenager, Isaac searched hard to find him a job that was closed on Shabbat. He eventually found him lowly employment as a rag collector.

Chaya was more resourceful. While her husband ruled the home and struggled to earn a paycheck, she was busy designing infant wear. Her efforts slowly grew into a respectable business. At its peak, she had about ten seamstresses working for her, and converted the first floor of their two-story apartment into a small workshop. Isaac assisted by hiring salesmen to peddle the clothes around the city.

William attended yeshivot throughout his youth. He remembered that time fondly, both for instilling him with Hebrew and Judaic literacy, and for consciously and unconsciously enriching his later contributions to the Reform synagogue. William's career exhibited a sophisticated and often-subtle merging of tradition and innovation. He described the intersection in a 2006 interview:

> I have emerged out of a very Orthodox background, which is, in a way, a blessing for me because I've internalized that whole world even though I am living in a different world. I can fuse the two worlds together and I know that when I sing *hazzanut*, even in my Reform synagogue, I know that there are many people who are moved by what I do—I want to emotionalize them. They open themselves up more. I find that to be a good device to bring them into what is normally a strange or foreign entity.[4]

William credited Orthodoxy with shaping key elements of his persona: it made him a Hebraist, enabled him to exude authenticity in prayer (even when he did not believe its literalness), and infused his compositions with traditional flavors. In his later years, he reminisced that had his father expressed a different attitude toward Jewishness, he may have continued to live an Orthodox life. But the family's linkage with Judaism was never joyous. His father had little enthusiasm for their

1. Beginnings

traditional lifestyle; he was observant out of respect for his own upbringing.

In elementary school, William and Hillel studied together in a combination class at Yeshiva D'Harlem on 114th Street. Though he was a respectful student and remained so throughout his school years, William's most vivid childhood memories were ones of mischievousness—early signals of his gradual shift to universalism and Reform Judaism. For instance, when he was eight or nine, his class celebrated the completion of a major portion of the Torah. They had a modest party, to which the Sharlin brothers brought a bottle of sweet wine. The bottle was half full after the party, and the boys carried the remaining wine home. On their walk they became "thirsty." When they arrived home, their mother saw them swaying from side to side with an empty bottle. She calmly took them to bed.

Another incident occurred during William's high school years. By that time, the two boys had distanced themselves from their father's rigid Jewishness, though Hillel was much further on that course (William was still a yeshiva student). They no longer observed Shabbat as strictly as their father demanded and had begun toying with forbidden notions. One afternoon the brothers secretly ate *treyf* hot dogs from a sidewalk stand. William felt little guilt: "I had begun to see myself as both a universalist and a Jew, and this manner of eating seemed a natural extension of my developing persona. I think my father knew this about me, but he never brought it up."[5]

Still, as a small child, the indoctrination and isolation of home and school made excursions outside of his insular community uneasy experiences. His father was intensely suspect of the outside world, both non–Jewish and Jewish. The family had few friends and William felt physically alone and emotionally unsure. When he passed a church, he was fearful to look inside and "be in touch with that alien tradition."[6] At Christmastime he turned away from the trees displayed in peoples' windows. Yet he held a quiet fascination for those restricted horizons. He and his siblings attended afterschool activities at a Jewish-run building on 110th Street, overlooking Central Park. William often sat on the rooftop, gazing in wonder at the secular goings-on.

Cantor William Sharlin

The extended Sharlin family began migrating to the Bronx when William was in his early teens. Harlem had undergone demographic changes. William and Hillel were once stopped by a group of Puerto Rican teenagers as they walked home from school. Puerto Ricans were new arrivals to Harlem, and there were tensions between them and the Jewish population. The brothers were taunted for being Jews. They stood in fear and silence until Hillel piped up, "We are Spanish Jews." As soon as he professed their invented Hispanic roots, the boys left them alone.[7]

The grandparents were the first to make the move to the Bronx. It is possible that Isaac's father, a carpenter and devout Jew, had found new employment. Most of the other family members followed, one by one. Just two of Isaac's sisters parted ways. One was married to a freethinking and marginally religious Jew who had no interest in preserving the traditional family cluster. They settled in Borough Park. The other sister, who was very observant and involved in Jewish charities, also moved to Brooklyn. The rest of the family settled within walking distance of the grandparents' home.

The Sharlin family piano traveled with them to the Bronx. For the most part, William's parents did not bother with cultural activities. Their existence centered on making a living and upholding ritual observance. Nevertheless, Rachel convinced them to purchase the instrument. She had a teacher and practiced the piano regularly.

The eighty-eight keys called out to William. He spent considerable time at the piano each day after classes at Yeshiva D'Bronx. Without any lessons, he deciphered the structure of music and taught himself to read written notes. He remained a sight-reading whiz throughout his life, plowing through sheets of music on a daily basis. He had a hobby of arranging four-part music to sing with his three siblings on Jewish holidays. Rachel encouraged William to take up lessons, beginning around age thirteen. It was not a successful venture.

> Whenever my teacher would give me a new piece to study, I would rush home to sit down at the piano. I couldn't wait to sight-read the piece; I needed to play it right away—slowly perhaps, but right away. This habit quickly became a problem for me. Because of my urge to instantly learn a piece, I did not have a careful transition into sight-reading, and my impatience prevented me from exploring proper technique.[8]

1. Beginnings

William was the only Sharlin sibling to continue yeshiva through high school. The decision resulted more from his father's insistence than his personal desire. Even so, his infatuation with the Hebrew language made the hour-long bus rides to the Talmudical Academy at Yeshiva University High School tolerable.

As the youngest of three independent-minded sons, William was Isaac's last hope. Edward, who was eight years his elder, was the first to drift away from Orthodoxy. After synagogue one Friday night, the family sat down for their weekly Shabbat dinner. Edward was absent. They ate in worried silence. When he finally came home at a very late hour, Isaac picked up a dish and threatened to throw it at him. This only exacerbated Edward's aversion to his father's traditionalism. A few years later Hillel announced that he wanted to attend a public school. Isaac's response was uncharacteristically passive; Hillel's wish was granted. Perhaps there was lasting trauma from how things were handled with Edward.

Jerusalem

William's parents moved the family to Palestine in 1935. Chaya's father had passed away in Jerusalem. She had not seen her family in many years and was filled with grief and

The Sharlin family, c. 1930. Top row from left: Isaac, Edward, Chaya, and Rachel. Bottom row from left: Hillel, William.

guilt. It was also the middle of the Great Depression, and the clothing business was quickly failing. Isaac found himself with little to do; the family was barely surviving. Edward, who had graduated college, helped with some of the expenses, but the situation became untenable. The parents, William, Hillel, and Rachel headed east for Jerusalem.

This was an enormous blow for the grandparents in the Bronx. William's grandmother had been the matriarch and center of the family. Despite this and other heartaches that followed, William counted his Jerusalem years among the highlights of his life. They lived about two blocks from Meah Shearim, Jerusalem's old ultra–Orthodox neighborhood. Isaac went into business with Chaya's nephew, who owned a sandwich shop on Jaffa Road. William entered the Bet Midrash L'Morim Mizrachi (Mizrachi Teachers Seminary) in Jerusalem. After school he would stop by the shop to help squeeze orange juice. Chaya learned how to make American-style doughnuts, and family lore has it that she introduced doughnuts to the city.[9] About a year after arriving in Jerusalem, Chaya discovered that she had cancer. Her condition rapidly declined and she passed away in 1936. William was just sixteen years old. Chaya died on a Saturday morning. The family waited until Shabbat ended to visit her body in the hospital. In an unusual break from the norm, her funeral was held later that night. "It was close to midnight when we boarded a school bus with my mother's body on a stretcher," William remembered.[10]

The odd scene can be attributed to the dangers of the time. It was during the 1936 Jerusalem riots, when Arab rebels were smuggling arms into the Old City. Violence had erupted in April of that year, after six prominent Arab leaders joined forces to protest Zionist advances in Palestine. They aimed to rid the region of British colonial rule, achieve independence, and put a stop to Jewish immigration. Occasionally, a Jew was shot along the border of the Arab quarter. British soldiers accompanied the Sharlin family to the Mount of Olives and stood guard as they conducted the funeral. "My mother's body was wrapped in a simple shroud and laid on flat stones," William explained. "Additional stones were placed on top of her, and she became one with the hill."[11]

William recalled another incident during the riots, which he admitted may not have actually happened (or did not happen exactly how he

1. Beginnings

described it). It was, perhaps, an imaginative story written for a school exercise. Still, it gives an impression of life in Jerusalem during those uncertain days. After his mother's passing, the family moved into an uncle's apartment next to the Old City. The Haganah used the residence as a command center to conduct underground military operations. Hillel had joined the Haganah and William saw him around the city standing guard in his hat and uniform. One day William observed a suspicious Arab man walking in their neighborhood. He told a Haganah soldier who was fluent in Arabic. The soldier quickly dressed himself in Arab garb and approached the man, who informed him that he was carrying a bomb. Fortunately, there was a British police station close by. Officers were notified, and they arrested the suspicious man.

William used music to help cope with the instability and the death of his mother. He supplemented yeshiva studies with classes at the Palestine Conservatoire of Music and Dramatic Art in Jerusalem (a.k.a. Jerusalem Conservatory), where he composed his earliest formal pieces. Isaac was not as resilient. He could hardly bear his wife's death. He never mentioned her name after her passing. William and his siblings took their father's lead: the devastating loss of their mother would remain a silent subject.

William was his mother's caretaker during her final months. She suffered terrible seizures, and he did everything he could to hold her steady and keep her warm. After she died, he would wander into the closet where her garments still hung, holding the fabric and smelling her lingering aroma.

Manhattan School of Music

Before long Rachel moved back to the Bronx, where she was engaged to be married. Although the marriage never came to be, Isaac soon followed, leaving William and Hillel under their uncle's care in Jerusalem. William continued his studies, and Hillel helped support him with a job at Barkley's Bank. William returned to the Bronx in 1939 and enrolled at the Bet Midrash L'Morim (Teachers Seminary) of Yeshiva University

High School. Hillel came home a year later. The family took up residence at 1520 Crotona Park East.

William's transcripts from Palestine contained significant gaps, especially in American history and civics.[12] According to the 1940 U.S. census records, he had completed the equivalent of three years of high school, despite being twenty years old.[13] He took make-up classes at Morris Evening High School and received a diploma in the spring of 1940. Rachel again encouraged him to pursue piano, which he did—this time diligently.

William entered the Manhattan School of Music (MSM) in the 1939–40 academic year, while he was still enrolled at the high school. His "early enrollment" was more commonplace then than it would be in later years. MSM was founded in 1917–18 as the Neighborhood Music School in Manhattan's Upper East Side (first at the Union Settlement on East 104th Street, and later on East 105th Street), a progressive-era settlement house aimed at facilitating the cultural assimilation and Americanization of recent immigrants. The founder, pianist Janet D. Schenck, devoted herself to bringing high-quality, low-cost musical training to immigrant children.

In the decades that followed, the school drew in more students, hired more instructors, built larger facilities, broadened its programs, expanded its outreach, and diversified its mission. The name was changed to Manhattan School of Music in 1938, and a college-equivalent program was established in 1941. The charter was amended in 1943 to authorize the granting of bachelor of music degrees. MSM began offering master of music degrees in 1947.[14]

William enrolled during the period of transition. His age (19–20) put him with students in the College Department, or Upper School, but his academic records put him in the Preparatory Program, or Lower School (pre-school to high school). MSM was his first concentrated immersion in the world of classical music. He often obtained unclaimed tickets to symphony concerts reserved for wealthy patrons of the school and interacted with musicians involved in that still-alien realm. The opportunities for cultural enrichment gave him an ever-widening musical experience and ever-broadening view of a world beyond Judaism.

1. Beginnings

However, there were some sources of frustration. His training was less structured than he would have liked. He recalled: "[C]omposition studies were under the direction of a figure—I hesitate to call him a teacher—who was halfway known in the world of music. He didn't teach a class *per se*. Instead, we simply approached him with our compositions, essentially to prove that we were working on the craft. He never guided me; he just looked over the pieces and gave his approval."[15] That figure was Vittorio Giannini, the head of the composition department.[16] Fortunately for William, he was a meticulous student with an aptitude for self-teaching. It was almost inconsequential that his instructor was not fully in touch with what he was doing. The freedom allowed him to develop his own compositional voice.

One experience was seared into William's memory. Early in his studies he was included in a program featuring student pieces. He had memorized one of his ambitious piano works and reluctantly agreed to play it. He was not a performer by background or disposition; he was an introverted and timid young man from a sheltered home. During the performance, his mind suddenly went blank and he was unable to continue. All he could do was begin the piece again from the top, hoping that when he returned to that point, he would remember how to continue on. He was able to finish the piece, but regretted not asking someone else to play it.

America's entrance into World War II depleted the student body of the nation's colleges. MSM was no exception. The older students enlisted or were drafted.[17] William enlisted in the United States Army on December 12, 1942, and his academic career was put on hold until the spring of 1946.[18] Although he earnestly desired to serve abroad, poor eyesight restricted him to "limited service." He was stationed outside of the Pentagon in Arlington, Virginia, where he had the unglamorous tasks of guard duty and "kitchen patrol." He also occasionally trained Army doctors in the use of firearms.

For all of its regimentation, the military proved to be liberating. It was William's first taste of life outside of the restrictive confines of his family's apartment, and it gave him the independence to discover himself. He learned to drive a car and got into jazz music. He lived and worked with people of assorted backgrounds and faiths.[19] It was his "release."[20] He quickly befriended LeBrie, a young Army recruiter of French-Canadian heritage. LeBrie was especially drawn to William's piano playing. A nearby housing complex for Pentagon secretaries had a social hall with an upright piano. LeBrie encouraged William to sit down and play, mainly to attract young ladies. The two "made friends with a number of girls on and off—sometimes serious, other times not so serious."[21]

Even during those forays into freedom, William felt the constant pull of family. Once while on leave, he visited his grandmother in the Bronx. The first thing she asked him was, "Do you eat everything?"—meaning, "Are you keeping kosher?" With some hesitation, he divulged that keeping kosher was not an option at the base; he ate what he was given. To his surprise, she responded, "It's all right." William attributed his grandmother's tolerance to the unique relationship they had developed over the years. William explained: "One day in my late teens, my grandmother kept nudging me about something and I couldn't take it. I lost control and yelled at her. I was shocked by my own actions; I did not know I was capable of doing such a thing. After that, instead of seeing my grandmother as an enemy, we became very close."[22]

He recounted another incident with his grandmother. She stayed in bed for a prolonged period, allegedly due to a bad back. She constantly complained of debilitating pain, and a doctor made frequent house calls. William happened to peek inside her bedroom: "I expected to see her resting in her bed, but she was sitting on a stool in front of a mirror, fixing her hair. I stood there speechless.... I kept this encounter a secret. I refused to let anyone know about my grandmother's little game."[23] His grandmother's inability to get out of bed was likely linked to depression. The disorder was prevalent in the Sharlin family, and would afflict William as the years progressed.[24]

Toward the end of his Army service, a personnel office was set up at the base. For reasons unknown to him, William was made assistant to the director. In that capacity, he helped soldiers obtain necessary information prior to being discharged, and arranged meetings with counselors as needed.

1. Beginnings

He returned to MSM in the fall of 1946. As noted, the school had only begun granting bachelor's degrees in 1943, during his enlistment. When he finally graduated in 1949, he received both a B.M. and M.M.[25] His thesis was entitled "German Keyboard and Instrumental Ensemble Music in the 16th Century," a period to which he paid frequent tribute in his compositions. His choral music often features the canon, a term first applied to music in the sixteenth century and a dominant device among Renaissance composers. One voice begins a melody and another voice repeats that melody (usually note for note) a few beats later, giving the impression of "running after the leading."[26] In William's music, the canon usually occurs in two or three voices.

The clearest example is an adaptation of an anonymous sixteenth-century twelve-bar melody, set as a three-part canon and sung to the greeting, *Shalom Aleychem*.[27] Another homage to the Renaissance, though not a canon, is his setting of a Shabbat poem of the same name, *Shalom Aleychem*. Written for mixed a cappella choir and reminiscent of Italian Jewish composer Salamone Rossi (c. 1570–1630), it is William's most widely performed piece.[28] He composed it in his head while driving. It was a "half hour of missing time" resulting in a synthesis of Renaissance (style) and Hasidism (spirit).[29]

Other pieces inspired by that period include, in whole or in part, *Eliyahu, Yom Zeh L'Yisrael II*, and his arrangement of Gershon Ehpros' melody for *Esa Einai*.[30] Unlike the *Shalom Aleychem* settings, these pieces hybridize Renaissance flavors with modernist tendencies, hints of Broadway, sections of *hazzanut*, and motivic figurations, creating a rich texture that is best described as "quintessential Sharlin."

William had aspirations of becoming a college or university professor, but the small amount of student teaching he did at MSM discouraged him from that goal. There was little stimulation in teaching music theory to performance-oriented students who reluctantly trudged through the material.

Fortuitously, he caught wind of the newly formed School of Sacred Music (SSM) at New York's Hebrew Union College (HUC).[31] It is unclear how William learned of the school. In a personal remembrance, he mentioned taking "sporadic courses" at SSM while he was finishing up his master's degree, but there is no official record of this.[32] William entered HUC as a "special student," a designation usually given to female students who pursued degrees in Jewish music, but whose gender made them ineligible for the cantorate.[33] William retained "special" status from October 1949 to February 1950, when he became a fulltime second-year student in the fledgling cantorial program, the first of its kind in the United States.

2

School of Sacred Music, New York

The idea for a cantorial school in the United States was hatched long before the opening of the School of Sacred Music (SSM). On March 22, 1904, the Society of American Cantors, an organization of full- and part-time cantors, used its annual meeting to discuss plans for a New York–based school for cantorial training.[1] Founded in 1895 by Alois Kaiser of Oheb Shalom, Baltimore, the society had three central aims: elevating the cantor's profession, building cohesion among its members, and raising musical standards in American synagogues. Membership was open to all affiliations, though in practice it only attracted cantors serving non–Orthodox congregations.

The society's seminal accomplishment was selecting and arranging music for the *Union Hymnal* (1897), the first standardized songbook of the American Reform movement.[2] The 1904 proposal was an attempted next step in the evolution of the American cantorate. It coincided with the centennial anniversary of the birth of Salomon Sulzer, the Viennese father of the modern cantorate, and included this exhortation: "Brethren, if you have your cause and the cause of Judaism at heart, you cannot more befittingly commemorate this centennial birthday of the great master than by establishing a school for cantors where young men of musical ability shall be trained in every branch that is requisite for a modern cantor."[3]

Cantor William Sharlin

The call was renewed in 1924 by the Jewish Cantors Ministers Association of America (a.k.a. Hazzanim Farband), a loose federation of mostly East Coast cantors. Despite being the largest cantorial organization of its day, funds and interest were lacking.[4] Its failure to launch a school was symptomatic of frustrations within the association, which, according to several former members, was never more than a patronage club.[5]

The campaign was revived in the 1930s by a different segment of the Jewish musical world: scholars and composers affiliated with *Mailamm* (American Palestine Music Association, 1932–1939) and the association that replaced it, the Jewish Music Forum (est. 1939). They advocated for the general improvement of Jewish music in America, rather than the cantorate *per se*, and envisioned an institute equipped to train Jewish musicologists, composers, and performers. They understood the crucial role of an academy in giving stature and recognition to the cantorial profession.[6]

These concerns headlined the Jewish Music Forum's symposium held on June 20, 1944. Musicologist Eric Werner sent a letter to the symposium expressing his support, and afterward circulated a "Memorandum Re Organization for Liturgical Music of Judaism" to colleagues at HUC, where he was a professor of Jewish music. His arguments swayed the Board of Governors to sponsor a planning meeting in 1945 for a "Society for the Advancement of Jewish Liturgical Music." The group assembled at Congregation Shearith Israel, the Spanish and Portuguese Synagogue of New York. Its goal was to found a non-denominational cantorial school that would serve *Klal Yisrael*—all the movements of Judaism.[7] To that end, it included cantors and rabbis from the Reform, Conservative, and Orthodox movements, along with Spanish-Portuguese rabbi David Cardozo, who served as president, and a handful of Jewish composers and musicologists.[8]

However, because three quarters of the budget came from the Reform movement, there were misgivings and eventual divides. Rabbi Cardozo balked at the affiliation with HUC.[9] Yeshiva University (Orthodox) was quick to reject the school plan. The Jewish Theological Seminary (Conservative) made alternative arrangements for its own program.[10] Con-

2. School of Sacred Music, New York

servative cantors began their own movement-centered organization, the Cantors Assembly, in 1947.[11] According to Neil Levin, who has written a history of music at the Jewish Theological Seminary, "From the beginning [the traditionalists] could not accept the notion that a single all-embracing school acceptable to the Reform movement could also meet their objective—only the less so if actually housed at Hebrew Union College."[12]

HUC's Board of Governors persisted and unilaterally approved Eric Werner's proposal. The School of Sacred Music (SSM) opened in the fall of 1948, originally as The Hebrew Union School of Education and Sacred Music. (Hebrew Union College merged with Stephen Wise's Jewish Institute of Religion in 1950, forming HUC-JIR.) Three arguments in particular motivated the decision. First was the indication that a growing number of Reform congregations were willing to hire professional cantors—a significant shift from the choir and organ dominated "classical" synagogues of previous decades. This coincided with a gradual reintroduction of "authentic" music into the Reform movement, and a gradual move away from the hymnals that had constituted the movement's musical-aesthetic foundation.[13] Second was the painful realization that, in the aftermath of the Holocaust and World War II, trained experts were needed to salvage the continuity of Jewish musical heritage. American cantors would need to assume leadership of synagogue music, which had its historical center in the European continent. Third was the shortage of trained educators in American synagogues, particularly in booming suburban communities. The cantorial curriculum initially consisted of a three-year program leading to cantorial investiture and certification as "cantor-educator."[14] (The nature and length of the program, as well as the type of degree and certification it awarded, would continue to evolve as the decades progressed. The program is currently five years culminating with a master's degree and cantorial ordination.[15])

Eric Werner conceptualized and oversaw the program, which placed most of the teaching and curricular development in the hands of fellow scholars, rather than cantors.[16] Werner was on the faculty of HUC in Cincinnati, the historic nucleus of the HUC system. However, from the outset, New York was seen as the only viable location for a cantorial program. Three reasons can be given for this. First, New York was home to many European cantors, whose artistic legacy SSM wished to emulate and advance. Second, the city had numerous composers, music scholars, and voice teachers from which to draw potential faculty members and private instructors. Third, Reform leaders were becoming aware of the importance of New York as a national center of Jewish life.[17]

With Werner's fulltime commitment in Cincinnati, HUC brought in Abraham N. Franzblau as dean of SSM. Franzblau was trained in Orthodox yeshivot. He obtained a Ph.D. in psychology from Columbia University, writing on the relationship between religious attitudes and moral behavior. His affiliation with HUC spanned over thirty years, first as head of the School for Teachers (1923–1931), and later as a professor of education in Cincinnati. In 1947 he became dean of the School of Education in New York, and in that capacity absorbed the affiliated SSM.[18] Franzblau procured an official charter for SSM from the Board of Regents of the State of New York. HUC president Nelson Glueck authorized the school as one of his first acts of office.[19] Meanwhile, Werner helped to recruit faculty members and solidify the curriculum.

At first SSM retained its original vision of training cantors of all denominations. The inaugural class of sixteen students had backgrounds ranging from yeshiva to opera.[20] An early press release highlighted the eclectic assemblage: "Of the regular students who will undertake the full three-year program, two will receive training for service in Orthodox congregations, eight in Conservative congregations, five in Reform congregations and one for service in either a Conservative or Reform service."[21] The school also admitted three "special students," a euphemism for women who took classes but were not eligible for the all-male cantorate.[22]

The program itself had a strong (though not explicit) basis in the *Lehrerseminare* of late nineteenth- and early twentieth-century Central Europe, consisting of a multi-year study program culminating in state-recognized cantorial status.[23] The replication of this model on American soil came somewhat naturally, as several key founders of the school, including Werner, were themselves transplants from Central Europe.

Music classes in the early years were held three days per week.

2. School of Sacred Music, New York

Hebrew and Jewish education classes met two evenings per week. Some of the students complained that the educator-training component was "forced" upon them.[24] That sentiment was strongest among musically focused students, who entered the school with performance backgrounds and saw the cantorate as a viable alternative to show business.[25]

The original curriculum included an array of courses stressing liturgical proficiency and musical acumen: Jewish liturgy, Jewish music history, conducting, choral ensemble, harmony, cantillation, *nusach*, *hazzanut*, and Eastern European folk music. To these were added vocal coaching, courses in musicianship and theory, and divided modules of "traditional" and "Reform" repertoires. The latter courses marked denominational lines in a way the program had previously avoided. The diet of "traditional" material ensured that students had grounding in cantorial heritage. However, greater emphasis was placed on music and customs peculiar to the Reform movement. This narrowed focus coincided with the development of the Cantors Institute at the Conservative Jewish Theological Seminary (1952) and the Cantorial Training Institute at the Orthodox Yeshiva University (1954). SSM eventually became solely affiliated with the Reform movement.

In the early days, the school was motivated by the question of "what is Jewish music," and specifically "what is *good* Jewish music."[26] Werner, for one, pursued the thorny (and some would say untenable) task of separating the "spurious" from the "authentic" in synagogue music.[27] He was well aware of the historical diversity of music in Jewish communities; but as a classical musician, he insisted upon elevated musical standards that included a rejection of "impurities," an embrace of customary chant patterns, and overall artistic sophistication.

Understandably, the initial years were fraught with significant challenges. As an essentially unprecedented enterprise, there was rampant disorganization, off-the-cuff decision-making, and numerous trials and errors. Students had to find their own vocal coaches, and the school did not assist in job placement.[28] Virtually every applicant was admitted, even those with glaring weaknesses. Students were largely responsible for patching together their own "core" repertoires.[29] Moreover, instructors were generally hired because of their stature in the community, not because they were effective teachers. A good teacher was a lucky exception.[30]

This last predicament bears some fleshing out. Three well-regarded recruits for the part-time faculty were quickly dismissed due to poor student reviews: Lazar Saminsky, Israel Goldfarb, and Jacob Weinberg. Others were switched to courses where they could (presumably) be more effective. Yet, even with the administration's attentiveness to student complaints, two of the worst offenders were, according to some, the men in charge. Rabbi Wolli Kaelter, William's good friend and a graduate of HUC, described Franzblau as "the poorest model imaginable for effective pedagogy.... [H]is instruction in educational methodology was absolutely worthless, all jumbled and quite unusable."[31] Of Werner he wrote: "He was a fine musicologist and a very peculiar person who prided himself on having fought duels and was willing to challenge anyone. He was a brilliant man but no pedagogue, to be sure." Another graduate confirmed that assessment, albeit in softer terms: "Werner was a great scholar, but not a great teacher. He would lecture and then point at a student and say, 'What do you think?' He seemed to take pleasure in pinning his students down."[32]

Throughout the growing pains and program shifts, Dr. Werner remained committed to his ideal of the American cantor as a figure straddling theory and practice.[33] Perhaps no student, past or present, fit that description better than William. He would complete the program in just two years, receiving exemptions from a range of courses, including conducting, harmony, and sight singing. He graduated with high honors and was invested as a cantor-educator. He was a star representative of SSM's first graduating class and North America's first crop of academy-certified cantors.

The inaugural graduation ceremony took place on Sunday, June 17, 1951. The ten graduating students led a service, with the rest of the student body forming a supporting choir.[34] Prominent Reform leaders addressed the gathering in enthusiastic terms. President Nelson Glueck portrayed the graduates as part of a chain reaching back to ancient times. He painted a romantic picture drawn from his background as a Near Eastern archaeologist and rabbinic homileticist:

2. School of Sacred Music, New York

> The music of Israel has long caught and perpetuated much of the meaning of the past and much of the promise of the future. Some years ago, while excavating Solomon's seaport of Ezion-Geber, I found the mouthpiece of a flute which one of our ancestors had used. Three millennia have passed by since, but tonight we are linked to this ancestor.[35]

Werner, who invested the graduates, was similarly sentimental in his twenty-fifth anniversary tribute to the inaugural class, written in 1976. The message was supposed to be read at the annual meeting of the SSM Cantorial Alumni Association, but did not reach its destination in time. It was published in the organization's periodical, *Shalshelet*:

> First graduating class of the SSM celebrating its 25th anniversary—My old friends, it's hard to believe, for it was not only last month that we sat together in the small classroom or in the auditorium—But it is a fact, good or bad. I am with you all in spirit today and greet you affectionately from the halls of the Hebrew University in Jerusalem. Each of you is like a son to me. I embrace all of you in faithful friendship.[36]

Path to the Cantorate

Given his high marks as a cantorial student, it is surprising that William initially had no desire to become a cantor. His only "professional" singing before entering the school was with a choir in the Catskills, under the direction of Jack Barash. William did not fancy himself a singer. He expected to be a music director at a large Jewish center, which at the time had full musical programs. As a student, he wished to dig deeper into synagogue song. Although he had experiential familiarity with synagogue customs from his observant youth, he lacked exposure to contemporary idioms.

Despite his vocal insecurities, William enrolled in a repertoire class full of cantorial students. He formed a quick bond with one of his classmates, Sheldon Merel, a fellow bachelor who was also living at home. The two spent much of their free time together, visiting each other's families on opposite sides of the Bronx, and occasionally going on double dates. William was a reserved and somewhat lonely man from a segregated upbringing. Sheldon was a gregarious go-getter with a background in vocal performance. He knew his way around the secular world.

Cantor William Sharlin

William claimed that Sheldon single-handedly pushed him onto the pulpit. Sheldon disagrees: "Although I was but one among many of our classmates at HUC who had encouraged Bill to take a pulpit after graduation from cantorial school, he always credited me as the 'nudge' who helped change the course of his career." For his part, Sheldon looked to William as a mentor. "I entered the college as a neophyte in Jewish music.... I will always be indebted to him for introducing me to the art of *chazzanut* and synagogue ritual."[37]

Sheldon Merel was born in Chicago in 1924.[38] He moved to New York with his parents and older brother, Maynard, in 1933. His mother was heavily involved in Hadassah, but the family was basically secular. Although he had a bar mitzvah at a Conservative synagogue, his first memorable Jewish experience came at the 92nd Street YMHA (Young Men's Hebrew Association), where he had his debut "singing engagement."

After graduating high school in 1941, Sheldon was admitted into the College of the City of New York (CCNY)—just a few months before the U.S. entered World War II. After studying engineering for about a year and a half, he enrolled in the New York State Maritime Academy to avoid being drafted. He graduated eighteen months later as an ensign in the U.S. Naval Reserve and a licensed engineer in the U.S. Maritime Service. As a merchant mariner, he sailed Liberty Ships in the North Atlantic, Mediterranean, and Caribbean seas. These slow-moving ships traveled in large convoys, carrying essential cargo to the Allies. They were easy targets for German submarines, and nearly 80 percent were sunk. The death toll among merchant seamen was second only to that of the Marines. Yet, because they were not considered part of the military, they did not receive benefits for themselves or their families.

Sheldon left the maritime service in 1946 with an honorable discharge. But, without G.I. benefits, he was ineligible for a free college education. He returned to CCNY, where he transferred to the business college. He supported himself working as a night relief engineer on merchant ships in New York harbor. At age twenty-one, he decided to pursue his love of singing and take his first voice lesson. He was soon performing in student shows at CCNY, gaining acclaim on campus. He also

2. School of Sacred Music, New York

found summer employment in the Catskill Mountains (Borsht Belt) as a singing master of ceremonies.

Sheldon graduated in 1947. Soon after he and his brother Maynard opened Merel Brothers Recording Studio on 42nd Street in NYC. The brothers were contracted to record Jewish weddings and bar mitzvahs. Sheldon paid close attention to the virtuoso cantors who sometimes officiated at those events.

One fortuitous day, a cantor named Gershon Ephros came to the studio to record a series of Torah and Haftarah portions. The session engineer played a demo recording of Sheldon for the cantor. Impressed, he encouraged Sheldon to apply to the first cantorial school in North America, which was opening at HUC. As it happened, Cantor Ephros was a noted anthologist of cantorial music and a faculty member at the new school.

Sheldon had given some thought to a cantorial career, but was uncomfortable with the informality of the training. Student cantors typically apprenticed with an expert for an indefinite period and for an undetermined fee. That "old world" pattern did not sit well with his modern sensibilities. But the concept of a cantorial *school* brought an air of credibility to the vocation.

The link between institution and legitimacy was crucial for SSM. According to Mark Slobin, whose chronicle of the American cantorate is the most comprehensive to date, professionalization was an utmost concern in the years following World War II.[39] Unlike American Reform rabbis, who established the Central Conference of American Rabbis in 1889, their cantorial counterparts—few as they were—had no organization through which to safeguard, regulate, or legitimize the work they did. Poor wages, job insecurity, disunity, shoddy standards, and marginalization were tremendous hindrances to their livelihood. The establishment of a school would ensure a level of systematic knowledge, occupational competency, communal authority, and public recognition.

Sheldon was admitted to SSM in 1949 as part of the second cantorial class. The admissions standards were not particularly high. "I got by with my voice and good looks," he reflects, "because I had not much else."[40] William also enrolled in 1949. By the spring of 1950, William was committed to the cantorial program, largely thanks to Sheldon's prodding. When William matriculated he was placed with the first class and graduated a year early. His fast track was a tribute to his extensive musical and yeshiva training—a combination unique among his peers.

As noted, students came to SSM with varied backgrounds. Some were more competent and/or experienced than others. William may have been the only one who was truly well rounded. Sheldon recalls "*shul* hopping" to Shabbat services in New York with five other students. In addition to Sheldon and William, the group included: Jacob Bornstein, who had a weak voice and poor musicianship, but expansive Judaic knowledge; Morris Greenfield, who could sing *hazzanut* but had no formal vocal training; Saul Altschuler, an accomplished lyric tenor with minimal Jewish literacy; and Saul Sanders, the oldest student by about twenty years, who possessed a natural voice and came from an Orthodox environment.[41]

The group kept track of where big-name cantors were officiating around the city. For instance, Saul Sanders learned that the son of Richard Tucker was having his bar mitzvah in Brooklyn. They sat in the congregation and waited for Tucker to appear. As was customary, the synagogue's *sheliach tzibbur* began the service, and then handed it over to the "showcase" cantor. As the Torah service began, Cantor Tucker emerged in full glory, awing the congregation with his powerful tenor voice.[42]

They also frequented Cantor Moshe Ganchoff's Shabbat morning services. Ganchoff was regarded as a top-notch improviser of *hazzanut*, and was dubbed "the cantor's cantor." (In later years, William would also be honored with that title.[43]) After the *sheliach tzibbur* chanted the preliminary prayers, Ganchoff came in with *Shokhayn Ad*. He never sang the prayer the same way twice. Ganchoff was hired to teach at SSM. William had the privilege of transcribing some of his liturgical creations, as the cantor's notating skills were not always on par with his impressive improvisations.[44]

William and Saul Sanders' mutual affection for *hazzanut* is enshrined in a setting of *Ahavat Olam* for Shabbat evening, which they composed at SSM. It is possibly William's first original liturgical piece.[45] Set in F

2. School of Sacred Music, New York

minor for solo cantor, it displays rhythmic subtleties, naturalistic melismata, gradually ascending lines, word-born drama, melodic sensitivity, classical structure, modernist tendencies, and sparse accompaniment—all of which would become hallmarks of William's compositions.

William and Sheldon also enjoyed extra-curricular collaborations. William was the campus's resident accompanist and arranger. He accompanied Sheldon at local events, such as the celebration of the fifth anniversary of the Menorah Group of Hadassah on April 3, 1951.[46] He did the same for other students and even some professors. "Those were the days before William 'found his voice,'" Sheldon recalls. "I loved that guy. We were like brothers in those days and, of course, he was my teacher, mentor and accompanist, and coach."[47] When Sheldon married his bride Marcie in 1952, the couple did not ask William to be the officiating cantor. Those duties went to Cantor Larry Erlich, another SSM graduate. William instead played the organ, which was more in his comfort zone.

On Sheldon's advice, William began voice lessons with a Jewish opera singer. "This teacher would sometimes put on concerts of Jewish music at Central Park," William remembered. "[A]s payment for lessons I helped him—musically, not vocally—with these performances. Overall, I wouldn't say he was a great teacher. Many singers teach voice to make a steady income, but are not really gifted in the art of instruction. At any rate, he was my teacher, and he did introduce me to the complexities and nuances demanded of high-level vocal performance."[48] This somewhat unsatisfactory experience initiated a cold relationship between William and vocal teachers. He tended to dwell on his teachers' shortcomings, large or small, and preferred learning from books. Over the years he amassed an enormous collection of technical manuals on vocal technique. Quoting Sheldon: "He worked on himself. He had a great ear, and was so intelligent that he was able to do it himself."[49]

William never had a student pulpit. Because the school did not handle placements, student initiative was absolutely essential. Given William's lack of vocal confidence and ambivalence about the cantorate, it is understandable why he did not pursue that opportunity. But most of his classmates did, and many who entered Reform congregations pioneered their own positions. It was an era of "first cantors" for many

Reform synagogues, both longstanding communities and new ones springing up with the suburban expansion.

Sheldon's story is illustrative. He served as student cantor of the Rye Street Synagogue in his second and third years at SSM. After graduating in 1952, he went to Temple Beth El in South Bend, Indiana, where he was the congregation's first cantor. In 1956 he was hired at Temple Sinai in Oakland and worked as the cantor-educator, filling the job title strategically concocted by SSM. By 1969 he was worn out as an educator and desperately longed to devote more time to music. He accepted a position as cantor and music director of the 2,500-family Holy Blossom Temple in Toronto, Ontario. In 1979 he went to Congregation Beth Israel in San Diego.[50] William installed him at the synagogue, and returned a few years later as composer-in-residence.

The Katchko Anthologies

William made a seminal contribution to the craft during his student days. The opportunity came by way of Theodore Katchko, a classmate and the son of renowned cantor Adolph Katchko of Anshe Chesed, New York. Adolph Katchko was both a master cantor and a preserver of European synagogue musical customs. The school was already using some of Katchko's music, along with sundry other materials; but students were basically left searching for music on their own. Werner blamed the scattered state of music on American Jewish communities: "The American Cantor has had ... to steer between the extremes of sacrificing both taste and tradition for the plaudits of the masses, or of clinging to a local *minhag*, or a *nusach* transmitted to him by some individual cantor, and thus slavishly following a narrow pseudo-tradition."[51] To remedy the deficiency and preserve a "chain of tradition," Cantor Katchko's chants for the liturgical year were collected as the *Thesaurus of Cantorial Liturgy* (1951–52). Theodore Katchko served as project liaison. William and fellow student Wolf Hecker edited and prepared the transcriptions, which required occasional hospital visits to the aging cantor.

The Katchko anthologies became the standard curriculum and

2. School of Sacred Music, New York

"exclusive property" of SSM. The school had tentative plans to publish "portions of it from time to time," but ultimately decided to guard the material as part of its unique identity.[52] That remained the case for over thirty years.[53] According to William, "They zealously guarded these treasures from cantors who could have benefited from the wealth of material they contained. [Later on, the] president of the HUC became aware of the policy and condemned it as a sin against God."[54] The change occurred in 1986 under the leadership of President Alfred Gottschalk.

The public volumes, published in three parts,[55] include a heavily abridged version of Eric Werner's biting Preface, complete with ellipses and paraphrases.[56] Invectives against the state of Jewish music in America are absent, either because the editors felt the problems had been solved, or (more plausibly) because of discomfort with Werner's confrontational tone. Additionally, in what appears to be a re-writing of history, the later version erases key pieces of the original plan. From the 1952 Preface: "The entire work is now the exclusive property of the School for teaching purposes, and through publication of portions of it from time to time, it is hoped to make it available ultimately to cantors and congregations everywhere, thus serving '*K'lal Yisroel*' in accordance with the goal of the school." Embarrassed by the length of time that had transpired since the original project, the 1986 edition truncates the statement in a manner that is incomprehensible without reference to the original: "The entire work is now the exclusive property of the School for teaching purposes, thus serving '*K'lal Yisroel*' in accordance with the goal of the School." Precisely how a volume that is the "exclusive property" of a denominational program serves "the whole of Israel" (*K'lal Yisroel*) is a puzzle.

More important is a note that appears at the beginning of the 1952 edition: "We wish to acknowledge our indebtedness to Cantor-Educators Wolf Hecker and William Sharlin, graduates of the school, who handled all publication and distribution arrangements, and edited the Hebrew text for proper accentuation."[57]

The Katchko anthologies inspired SSM to undertake the "Out-of-Print Classics of Cantorial Liturgy" in the 1950s. It was an ambitious effort to republish thirty-five foundational synagogue collections (in twenty-five volumes). The first was Abraham Baer's *Ba'al Tefillah* (1877), a collection of 1,511 transcribed liturgical chants for the Jewish year in German (*deutsche Weise*; or *minhag Ashkenaz*), Polish (*polnische Weise*; or *minhag Poland*), and Portuguese (*minhag Sepharad*) variations, along with new works (*neue Weise*) and older cantorial selections (*alte Weise*). Subsequent reprints included works by nineteenth-century Central and Eastern Europe composers—Salomon Sulzer, Louis Lewandowski, Eduard Birnbaum, Eliezer Gerovitsch, Samuel Naumbourg, Abraham Dunajewsky, Hirsch Weintraub, and David Nowakowsky—and sixteenth-century Italian composer Salamone Rossi.

The books were not part of the school's curriculum, and their practical value was somewhat limited. A review by composer Chemjo Vinaver sums up the issues:

> Unfortunately the job was done by photo-offset, so that what we get here is an unedited, unselective collection that "faithfully" reproduces everything in the original editions, including textual errors, misprints, and a bewildering variety of transliterations in German, Russian, French, and Polish styles. How is the American cantor or choirmaster, for whose use this set was designed and who hungers for a reliable guide to authentic Jewish music, to find his way through such a maze of compositions of varying merit?[58]

In Werner's defense, he viewed the reprints as scholarly resources and a means of securing SSM as a center of Jewish music: "Since the study of Jewish folk-lore, the acme of which is the chant of the Synagogue, is now a serious musicological discipline, frequently undertaken in scholarly fashion, the interest in source and reference works has naturally increased."[59]

The Katchko project was William's debut as a cantor-scholar. He would never be "just" a singer, though he took singing as seriously as one could. He was to become a master composer, exacting teacher, and assiduous researcher, constantly striving to discover and elucidate the nuances and complexities of synagogue music, both in historical and present tense contexts.

3

Hebrew Union College, Cincinnati

As William neared the end of cantorial school, he was still undecided on a career path. Although Sheldon Merel and others encouraged him to pursue the pulpit, he remained a reluctant cantor. Fortunately, Professor Eric Werner recognized his unique gifts as a scholar-composer, and requested his musical assistance at HUC's Cincinnati campus. William accepted a doctoral fellowship.

Notices appeared in several New York area newspapers. *The New York Post Home News*, a Bronx daily, ran an announcement on June 27, 1951:

> A Bronxite was invested as cantor-educator at the first graduation exercises of the Hebrew Union School of Sacred Music, 40 W. 68th St. He is William Sharlin, 1520 Crotona Park E., who holds B. Mus. and M. Mus. Degrees from the Manhattan School of Music. Also awarded a graduate fellowship at the Cincinnati School of the Hebrew Union College–Jewish Institute of Religion, Cantor Sharlin is a candidate for a Ph.D. in music.

Similar pieces ran in the *American Jewish Review* (New York), *Jewish Record* (Elizabeth, N.J.), and *Jewish Post* (Paterson, N.J.). *The Enquirer* in Cincinnati, Ohio also published a notice: "Cantor William Charlin [*sic*], New York, has been awarded a graduate fellowship at the Hebrew Union College–Jewish Institute of Religion. He graduated this week from the Hebrew Union School of Sacred Music, New York."

William was interviewed by a few professors when he arrived in

Cincinnati. One asked him to demonstrate German fluency. That was not a problem: he came from a Yiddish-speaking home, took German courses at Columbia University, and wrote his MSM thesis on sixteenth-century German music.[1] Another probed him on a different subject. Before he could answer, a third professor objected, claiming the question was irrelevant. They argued back and forth as William sat nervously. In the end, he received a three-year fellowship, which included a teaching appointment and studies toward a Ph.D. in Jewish music.[2]

Eric Werner immediately took William under his wing.[3] Eric was born in Ludenberg, near Vienna, and studied musicology and composition in esteemed European academies. He received a doctorate from the University of Strasbourg in 1928. His dissertation (in Latin[4]) compared Western Christian and Jewish cantillation motives. The possible intersections between the sacred chants of Jews and Christians consumed much of Eric's research. His extensive bibliography contains over a half dozen articles on the subject,[5] along with an influential (though now largely outdated[6]) two-volume treatise, *The Sacred Bridge: The Interdependence of Liturgy and Music in Synagogue and Church During the First Millennium* (1959; 1984). He also authored eight volumes and scores of articles on topics ranging from Richard Wagner to musical practices in the American synagogue, along with a number of liturgical and instrumental works.[7]

Eric and his wife Elisabeth came to the United States in 1938 seeking refuge from the Nazis. In 1939 he was appointed to the faculty of HUC in Cincinnati as successor to Professor Abraham Z. Idelsohn, the esteemed founder of Jewish musicology who died the previous year. Like his predecessor, Eric was a strongly opinionated and almost supernaturally gifted scholar. His high expectations for his students were rarely satisfied. He was drawn to William, an erudite musician with a classical Jewish background and advanced musical training. Eric invited William to his home on several occasions. After a meal the two would sit at the piano and play symphonic works by Gustav Mahler arranged for four hands. William was also Eric's go-to proofreader and uncredited ghostwriter. Eric inscribed article offprints to William with variations of the Hebrew dedication, "L'talmidi, b'yedidut"—"To my student, in friend-

3. Hebrew Union College, Cincinnati

ship."[8] Decades later, the octogenarian scholar wrote in William's copy of *The Sacred Bridge, Volume II* (1984): "To Bill Sharlin, my dear friend, far or near—you are here."

The image of an affectionate teacher often found contrast in the classroom. Musicologist Judith K. Eisenstein, who began work on a Ph.D. at SSM, summed up the consensus experience in a reflective essay. She described Eric's "merciless tongue-lashing over inexcusable gaps in our knowledge," and how he was "rendered awesome in wrath" at the hint of intellectual laziness, shoddy research, or banal taste. Yet, he exuded a "generous expression of delight with the smallest new insight by a student: a neat philological juxtaposition, or a discovery of a thematic relationship in a musical work which he—by heaven knows what strange accident—had not noticed."[9]

In later years, William's own demeanor and teaching style would elicit similar, though not as extreme, impressions: stern but encouraging, critical but forgiving, passionate but warm, humorous but serious, playful but biting. Perhaps the best example of Eric's mixed persona is his satirical essay, "O, Once There Was a Magic-Kabalistic Song."[10] Written in the jocular spirit of the Purim holiday, the article presents an exaggeratedly detailed origin myth for the well-known children's song, "O, Once There Was a Wicked, Wicked Man" (a reference to Haman, the villain of the Book of Esther). With clear self-deprecation, Eric pokes fun at the minutia and abstruseness of historical musicology, including this confounding gem: "Of deep significance is the fact that the first two lines consist of 10 + 7 syllables (and notes), a symbolization of the fight between the decadic system and the 'seven up' system, so characteristic of the struggle between Babylonian economists (decadists—erroneously referred to as 'decadent') and astrologers (centered in the village of Unk-o-la and fascinated by the seven planets)."[11] Bitterness is woven into the humor: harshly sarcastic jabs at populist trends, lightweight scholars, fluffy publications, and *New York Times* music critic Harold Schonberg. A sardonic footnote reads: "The learned essays on synagogue music, as they appear in the newspaper *Reform Judaism*, are indeed an ever-flowing source of facts and theories, hitherto unknown to older scholars, such as C. Sachs, A. Z. Idelsohn, E. Birnbaum, and similar ignorant fossils."[12]

William occasionally took similar forays into satire—although, as a congregational leader, he was not permitted the same leniency of academic freedom. An example is a tabulation of contradictory observations from his article, "Comments Made to the Cantor."[13] The article pokes fun at the diversity of musical opinions in American synagogues, while lambasting the lack of commitment among liberal Jews. The list displays whimsy and (soft) criticism.

> "The service was beautiful. I don't know why I don't come more often."
> "I would come more often if there were more variety in the service."
> "Why didn't the choir sing tonight? I miss them."
> "I prefer it when you do the chanting without the choir and lead us in singing. It's more personal."
> "The truth is that I'm uncomfortable when the Torah is exhibited so directly at us, and people actually touch and kiss it."
> "Why did you change the tune for *L'cha Dodi*? I just got used to the other one."
> "It's refreshing to hear you introduce new music in the service. Keep it up."
> "Why can't we have more congregational singing?"
> "I don't come to temple to hear the congregation sing. I want to hear the cantor and the choir."
> "I like those warm, intimate services when you pack us up in front."
> "Please! I feel more comfortable sitting in the back row."
> "The guitar adds warmth to the service."
> "It doesn't belong."
> "Why do we rush through the service?"
> "One hour is all I can take."
> "I feel self-conscious singing at the service when no one around me is singing."
> "I wish so-and-so wouldn't sing so loud."
> "We're getting too Orthodox."
> "We're too Reform."

Oconomowoc, Wisconsin

Before leaving for Cincinnati, William was invited to be the music director at a summer camp for disabled children in New Jersey. The person scheduled for the job backed out at the last minute and the camp was frantic to find a replacement. Evidently someone knew about him

3. Hebrew Union College, Cincinnati

and recommended him for the position. He accepted, bought a twenty-five-dollar guitar, and committed to spending a month at the camp.

He quickly discovered that the camp specialists—in music, dance, art, and so on—did more than just teach their subjects. They were also caretakers for the campers, some of whom required a great deal of attention. William helped the children in mundane activities, like eating, dressing, bathing, and using the toilet. The camp posed a musical challenge as well. It was not a Jewish institute, and William had little experience singing (let alone leading) English-language songs. He compiled a list of songs the campers knew and liked—material that was, by and large, new for him. He gradually eased into the role, and over the course of the month became attached to the kids. He was most touched by the interpersonal bonding the music fostered.

When the session ended, William and the other counselors accompanied the campers to a ferryboat, not knowing what would happen next. Their parents were waiting for them on the other side of the Hudson River. A few of the counselors wondered out loud whether the children would even remember the camp experience. Most were heading back to the relative staleness of the special facilities they lived in. The excitement of summer camp was sure to dissolve into the routines of assisted living.

That experience paved the way for decades of involvement in youth camping. Early in his fellowship, William noticed a group of HUC students taking pots and pans out of the cafeteria kitchen and loading them onto a truck. They were packing for a weekend trip to a National Federation of Temple Youth (NFTY) conclave near the campus. Conceived by the National Federation of Temple Sisterhoods, NFTY was founded in 1939 as the youth movement of American Reform Judaism. It began by offering college students alternatives to synagogue. When NFTY entered the camp scene in 1951, it started catering to younger Jews.

William was friendly with Rabbi Samuel Cook, the organizer of the conclave trip and the head of Reform camping. As William stood watching the students load the truck, Samuel approached him and asked if he would like to come along. He agreed, grabbed his twenty-five-dollar guitar, and joined the caravan.

William initially saw himself as an interested observer. He led a few song sessions, but was mainly curious to see how the conclave was run. His participation swayed Cook, who hired him to lead group singing at the NFTY Leadership Institute, held at the brand-new camping facility in Oconomowoc, Wisconsin (later renamed the Olin-Sang-Ruby Union Institute).[14]

William developed an important principle at the Wisconsin camp: if you don't love what you teach, don't teach it. He was not simply a song leader; he was a communicator of music. With wholehearted singing and playing, he breathed life into Jewish values, stories and customs. This was precisely the role Cook had envisioned for music at the camp. The program was designed to fill youngsters with a sense of pride—a goal readily furthered by song. William's spirited sessions encouraged the campers to take ownership of their Jewish heritage and identity.[15]

A camp highlight was "a walk through history," during which counselors reenacted scenes from the Bible and Jewish history. The children marched through the campsite, encountering various skits along the way. William was stationed up in a tree with his friend Joseph Glaser, preparing to act out the revelation on Mount Sinai. Joseph had a small bottle of alcohol with him, and they took a few sips. William would never have done this on his own; but Joseph had the ability to bring him into otherwise unthinkable situations. The two were in a somewhat altered state when the children came by. The experience inspired William to write a playful song that remains a NFTY staple:

> Some day you are liable
> To open up the Bible
> And you'll be quite amazed to see
> That out from the pages
> Come Prophets from the ages
> Telling all about our ancient history.
> > The five books of Moses
> > With clarity discloses
> > Many laws that are right and true
> > Doing justice for others
> > And loving men as brothers
> > That is what the Lord requires of you.
> Jeremiah, Obadiah
> Zechariah, Micah, Jonah
> Amos, too!

3. Hebrew Union College, Cincinnati

> Some day you'll wake from slumber
> And find a goodly number
> Of these Prophets so bold and wise
> If you stop, look and listen
> You'll know what you are missing
> You and I, if we try
> Very hard, we'll know why ...
> They were truly such wonderful guys!

William's main venue was the dining hall, where he ran around, strumming his guitar. He introduced songs by way of conversation. He read verses and asked for interpretations. When they finished singing, he posed questions, like "What do you think this sounds like?" or "How did that make you feel?" This method was not a calculated plan, but an intuitive extension of his love for what he was doing.

His effusiveness had an impact. One of the camp rabbis wrote a poem about him called "The Man with the Golden Feet." Marc Shapiro, a camper who went on to be a rabbi and song leader, shared this memory: "[T]he way he moved around the dining hall and the kind of sound he elicited from people; and the high, the sense that music at camp was an art, not just the day camp 'let's sing songs' ... Sharlin wanted us to sing well, he wanted us to have a good time, he wanted it to be a vehicle for Jewish expression."[16]

The campers sometimes had to learn a half-dozen songs or more. Even so, William avoided song sheets, which he considered obstacles to full participation. Instead, he wrote lyrics in transliteration on chalkboards hung around the dining room. After a few repetitions he erased the words, one by one. This method aided the rapid internalization of texts and helped transform a series of syllables into meaningful music. "By doing all of this," William explained, "the kids were brought into a real experience. They became engaged in a dialogue with the song, with me, with each other, and with their own Jewish identities. Most gratifying for me were the camp bus trips. Quite spontaneously, the students would begin singing the songs I had taught them—they memorized them all."[17]

The musical repertoire was somewhat of a mixed bag. Hebrew material was primarily drawn from Israeli pioneer songs and a few liturgical pieces. Because the majority of campers did not understand the language, texts were often simplified. American folk song elements were added to complement the group's aesthetics. Some pieces came from Samuel Cook's wife, Ray, who was an active composer of children's songs.[18] Others were plucked from standard campfire fare, like "Joshua Fit de Battle of Jericho" and "Blue-Tail Fly,"[19] and Broadway tunes, like "Oh What a Beautiful Morning."[20]

William also had a dependable resource, *"Git on Board": Collection of Folk Songs Arranged for Mixed Chorus and Solo Voice* (1950), with over seventy songs in six categories: Early Days in America; Songs of American Humor; Work Songs; Songs of Negro Origin; Significant Songs of Our Day; and Rounds.[21] Songs in that book, such as "Pick a Bale o'Cotton," "Go Down Moses" and "Lift Ev'ry Voice and Sing," resonated with the Reform Jewish ethos. The prevailing feeling was that civil rights were a common cause for Jews and blacks. Taken as a whole, the camp music served a triple purpose: strengthening bonds, affirming Jewishness, and promoting a political consciousness.

This type of "prophetic Judaism" was among the first things William encountered in Cincinnati. The HUC campus was divided between those with a strictly Jewish focus and those with a more universal worldview. Over time, these divisions sharpened, especially among the faculty. William was at home with the traditionalists—they respected his background and musical sensibilities—yet he gravitated toward the universalists. That environment helped him to navigate and consolidate the two worlds he occupied. His personal interests increasingly turned toward broader themes of social justice, peace, and love; but his musical vision retained the indelible imprint of Jewish identity.

Advancing the Profession

Along with his camp activities, William devoted considerable energy to furthering the cantorate. He was founding president of the SSM alumni association (est. 1952), an independent network with a grassroots ethos. He urged the association to create a "two-way relationship with

3. Hebrew Union College, Cincinnati

the School of Sacred Music."[22] To that end, he helped create the *H.U.S.S.M. Alumni Bulletin*. The first issue was published in October of 1952, and included greetings from Drs. Franzblau and Glueck, information on repertoire, and alumni news.[23]

He also spearheaded the formation of the American Conference of Certified Cantors (ACCC). The organization was primarily established for SSM alumni, and leadership positions were held by graduates of the school. However, it was not exclusively affiliated with the Reform movement. To gain stature, the leadership handpicked established cantors whose names would bring credibility to the venture. As an early member recalls, "We didn't ask for credentials. They were successful cantors, and that's what mattered."[24] They represented an array of denominational affiliations, and their involvement reinvigorated SSM's original mission of trans-denominationalism.

The decision to bypass movement particularism contrasted with the Cantors Assembly (est. 1947), which began under the Conservative movement's United Synagogue of America.[25] According its founding statement, the ACCC was "the official organization of all cantors, who have met the requirements and standards of the Board of Cantorial Certification."[26] Standards were agreed upon through negotiations between SSM and Hazzanim Farband, a predominantly Orthodox group.[27] Its mission was "the proper organization and control of cantorial placement, the creation and distribution of better cantorial and choral materials for the synagogue, plans for establishing retirement and pension funds and other benefits, and any and all other matters which serve the interest of the cantorate."[28]

William headed the group of charter members, consisting of two dozen SSM alumni—including Cantors Sheldon Merel, Joseph Portnoy, George Weinflash, and Harold Orbach—and several "old-time" cantors, including Walter Davidson and Samuel Kelemer.[29] Among the group's first projects was the *Special Songster of New Materials for Congregational and Solo Singing*. The twenty-two-page booklet featured specially commissioned works by leading synagogue composers of the day: A. W. Binder, Gershon Ephros, Frederick Picket, Hugo Ch. Adler, Moshe Nathanson, Pinchas Jassinowski, Lazar Weiner, Adolph Katchko, and

Max Helfman. It was distributed at the ACCC's first convention on June 8–11, 1953, in New York City.[30]

In 1969 the ACCC dropped a "C" and became the American Conference of Cantors (ACC). This change signaled the organization's formal affiliation with the Reform movement's Union of American Hebrew Congregations (UAHC).

Campus Activities

William organized and directed the rabbinic student choir at HUC Cincinnati. His showcase was Saturday mornings, when students and faculty members gathered for Shabbat services. He led the all-male group in the chapel choir loft (women did not enter the Reform rabbinate until 1972[31]). The experience pushed William to write music for Jewish worship—mostly arrangements for the choir and settings for the organ. This was a practical sort of writing; he was not yet thinking seriously about synagogue composition.

At the time, Rabbi Leo Baeck was also teaching at the school. His dormitory was across the hall from William's. Born in Germany in 1873, Baeck was the son of an Orthodox rabbi. He received a yeshiva education and secular training in the Lissa Gymnasium. The dual focus continued throughout his student days. In 1897 he received a rabbinical degree and a doctorate from the University of Berlin. He served as rabbi of Berlin's Oranienburger Synagogue, and was considered among the foremost Jewish scholars in Europe. He was made leader of the council of German Jews, established by Hitler in 1933, and was later head of the council of elders in Theresienstadt. Both were transparent shams designed to give the appearance of Jewish autonomy and mask Nazi atrocities. Some criticized Baeck as a Nazi collaborator; but he used the positions to promote Jewish learning as a means of resistance. He refused all invitations from synagogues or universities abroad, and swore to remain in Germany with the last Jewish *minyan*. He was deported to the Theresienstadt concentration camp in 1943, where he provided hope and comfort for its suffering Jews. He moved to London after the liberation, and then to Cincinnati in 1948.

3. Hebrew Union College, Cincinnati

Rabbi Baeck was about fifty years older than William. Despite the age difference, the two became friends and lunched together at the HUC cafeteria. William learned firsthand of Baeck's tremendous warmth: "He was always open to students seeking help with their studies or personal matters. He had such patience and understanding. This was one of his greatest gifts."[32]

The impression was bolstered during a memorable trip. Baeck's grandson-in-law, also a rabbi, was being installed at a congregation in a nearby state, and the elder rabbi was invited to speak. He asked William to accompany him as his cantor. They rode on a train together for nearly four hours. William refrained from initiating deep theological discussions, fearing an awkward mismatch of intellects. Instead, Baeck indulged William in musical conversation, which helped ease his anxieties during that long ride.

William's fellowship ended in 1954. He passed his candidacy examinations on May 28, 1953, but his dissertation was far from complete. He had written just two chapters of the paper, entitled "The History of Hasidic Music." Only the first chapter is extant: a historical overview of the Hasidic movement. He kept his handwritten notes and the proposed table of contents, preserving the rudiments of what could have been an illuminating twelve-chapter tome.[33]

The topic was natural for William, given his traditional background and interest in music's ecstatic potential. However, Hasidism was a subject Eric Werner greatly detested. Eric had little patience for its populist mysticism, which he dismissed as a frivolous distraction from the rigorous search for knowledge and truth.[34] Moreover, as a refined Central European, he could hardly tolerate the emotive and often derivative Eastern European songs of Hasidic devotion. He considered the music "cheap," "unoriginal," and "not genuine."[35] Typical of his scholarly attacks is a passage from his weighty opus, *A Voice Still Heard*, in which he chides Hasidism's disregard for the penitential function of the *Ahavah Rabbah* synagogue mode, characterized by the flattened second and an augmented interval between the second and third scale degrees: "Today that mode is the most hackneyed of them all, and, what is worse, has almost totally lost its original association with penitence and supplication.

Indeed, the Hasidim loved it so much that about 85 percent of their songs are in the *Ahabah Rabah* mode—even those with very gay or satiric texts."[36]

William never divulged why his dissertation was left unfinished. He rarely mentioned that he worked toward the degree, and presumably regretted not seeing it through. While he did not blame Eric for impeding the paper, he did say: "God bless Eric. He was not of great help to me. Of course, it was a foreign subject for him."[37]

Whatever the circumstances, it can be surmised that William's interests were drawn elsewhere, and that Eric was not insistent that he complete the degree. Nevertheless, Hasidic songs continued to fascinate William throughout his long career. He had strong affection for the classical *niggunim* of Eastern Europe, and reservations about the modern appropriations and distortions of Neo-Hasidism and its mainstream inheritors. Classical Hasidic songs held a special place in his vast music library. Research on the topic marked chronological points in his career—Beginning: "Chassidism," a lecture from the mid–1950s; Middle: "Davening and Congregational Singing," read at the 1973 Pacific Area Reform Rabbis Convention; End: "Chasidic Music," a lecture-demonstration presented at Metivta: Center for Contemplative Judaism, Los Angeles in 1998.

Eric remained close with William until his death in 1988. Although they diverged on Hasidism, several of Eric's other passions reverberate in William's writings. Most prominent are theories about musical assimilation, criticisms of populist trends, musical convergences of Jews and Christians, an interest in biblical cantillation, and looking to the past to help explain the present.[38] William honored Eric's comradeship at his mentor's eighty-fifth birthday celebration, held at HUC New York in the summer of 1986. His comments are presented here in full.

> Some thirty-eight years ago I drifted into the halls of the School of Sacred Music, not having any clear direction of where to go with my life. Fortunately for me, the one experience that helped set me on a firm course into the world of synagogue music, Eric, was my meeting with you. For you represented to me both the intellectual and spiritual anchor that I needed then, and I hasten to add, I still need—that we all need—this very day.
>
> Though I have been on the West Coast some 33 years, and have had only

3. Hebrew Union College, Cincinnati

sporadic meetings with you during that period, I want you to know that there have been many, many times when the image of you and your highest idealism have confronted me and have helped keep me (for the most part) on straight paths. For you were then, and continue to be, a part of my conscience—a conscience nurtured by the force of your integrity. I say this, particularly now, when the synagogue is too often submitting itself, passively, to secularization and trivialization—at a time when even the best of us, tired of all the searching and groping for solutions to serious problems, might be tempted to choose the path of least resistance, to succumb to immediacies, to quick fixes, to the popular. It is especially at such times that your presence persists, exerting influence on me and, I would hope, on the many others who are fortunate to know you.

Let's face it, Eric, you are a rare entity in the life of our musical heritage. Some scholars dig below the surface but may have little concern with what takes place above ground. You have demonstrated, profoundly, not only your passionate and adventurous curiosity of how, why and what took place in the deep past, but also how you care critically and lovingly for what is taking place in your own time. You love the search, but you also love the thing itself.

You have brought to light a number of sacred bridges that have expanded our understanding of the history of liturgical music—but permit me to turn a phrase, Eric, playfully yet seriously. I see you not only as the author of *The Sacred Bridge*, but also and significantly as a *bridge to the sacred*. For it is your noble spirit and unbroken dedication to that which is highest in our tradition that have helped me, and others, to bridge the gap between the ordinary and the sacred.

Your scholarly works are not just sitting on shelves—they are alive in our thinking and teaching. Your fine musical creations have enriched our literature. And you yourself continue to keep the spark of the sacred within us.

The ripe number of eighty-five happens also to be ripe for a bit of Gematria. The letters *Pe* and *He* seem to leap out to us, to speak to us, in the here and now. Needless to say, you have been the *Peh*, the spokesman for that which had to be said, and you have never hesitated to say it *Poh*, in the here and now.

For all that you have said, for all that you have given and for all that you are, we give honor and thanks to you. May God bless you and give you the strength to continue to stand tall, and walk tall into the future. Amen.

William again paid public homage to Eric on November 24, 2002, that time posthumously. HUC New York hosted "Building Sacred Bridges: Conference and Concert in memory of Dr. Eric Werner," an event cosponsored by the Leo Baeck Institute (New York) and the SSM Cantorial Alumni Association. The event reflected on the life and legacy of Dr. Werner, who passed away on January 30, 1988, two days shy of his eighty-seventh birthday. The conference included academic papers by musicologists Mark Kligman, Eliyahu Schleifer, and Kay Kaufman Shelemay, as well as remembrances from colleagues and former students. William, then eighty-two, sang Eric's setting of *Kedushah* for Shabbat. Dr. Schleifer, professor of music at HUC's Jerusalem campus, praised his "pure, easy-flowing voice."[39]

Entering the Cantorate

Toward the end of his fellowship, William was informed that The Temple (Congregation Tifereth Israel), a historic synagogue in Cleveland, was looking for a cantor. They had a world-renowned rabbi, Abba Hillel Silver, whose charisma and oratorical skills attracted scores of Jews and non–Jews to his services. Born in Lithuania and ordained at HUC, Rabbi Silver gave persuasive sermons on the topic of Zionism, and helped found a number of local and national Jewish organizations.

Silver's son, Daniel, then the synagogue's junior rabbi, knew of William from his camp work. The Temple was functioning without a cantor, and Daniel asked William if he was interested in the new position. William agreed to audition. He used leftover funds from his annual honorarium to make the weekend trip.

William sang in the Friday evening service with a quartet up in a choir loft. He was not permitted to sing from the pulpit. After the service, he joined Abba Hillel Silver for Shabbat dinner at his home. He was surprised to discover that the ostentatious rabbi's abode resembled an Eastern European *shtetl* dwelling. "Few people realize that Rabbi Silver had a *shtiebel* background in Lithuania," William said, "and that he was a simple man in many ways. At heart, he was an old-fashioned Jew—very different from the elegant and progressive man who stood on the *bimah* in a striped suit."[40]

On Sunday morning, when The Temple held Shabbat morning services, William was again asked to sing in the loft. He realized that being cantor of that congregation meant never being seen. The pulpit was solely the domain of the rabbi and his powerful sermons. As it turned

3. Hebrew Union College, Cincinnati

out, The Temple was mainly interested in having William simulate the camp experience for children in the religious school. "I had to turn down the job," he recalled. "I would not give up the pulpit." There were evidently no hard feelings. William was invited back to the synagogue on December of 1956 to "sing the Cantorial parts of the Service, and also solos before and after the Address."[41]

During the spring term of 1954, HUC president and rabbi-archaeologist Nelson Glueck petitioned to create a permanent academic post for William in New York. This caught William by surprise. Although he admired Glueck's work and had warm relations with him, William felt he was not fully dedicated to the HUC position. Glueck typically spent half the year in Israel surveying ancient sites in and around the Negev. As William put it, "his heart and mind were in the Holy Land, and in the arena of archaeology."[42]

That being said, Rabbi Glueck managed to stay involved with the student body. For example, he once caught word that students were planning a good-natured gathering to poke fun at the faculty. He was most interested in Joseph Glaser's much-heralded impersonation of him. Glueck enjoyed it immensely. "That was the kind of man he was," William remembered, "serious about archaeology, but not too serious about himself."[43] William played the piano for the event, accompanying songs addressed to the faculty, like "Go Home, Go Home. Why Did You Come to Ohio?"

Glueck sent the petition to SSM dean Abraham Franzblau, dated April 6, 1954:

> I am very concerned about Bill Sharlin. I should hate to lose his services, direct or indirect, for the benefit of our school. I have the highest regard for his abilities and character and hope very strongly that you will be able to utilize him creatively in our School of Music and to find an adequate cantorial position for him in New York. He has, I think, absorbed our general philosophy which is important for cantors as well as for rabbis. I should be very pleased if a proper position were found for him within our School of Music.

It is unknown whether or not Franzblau offered him a job. Regardless, by that time William had turned his focus to congregational work. He was taking voice classes at the Cincinnati Conservatory, and was increasingly drawn to the cantorate. As events unfolded, William did land a teaching position at HUC, albeit at its Los Angeles campus (see Chapter 5).

The invitation to come to Los Angeles came from Jack Skirball, a colorful rabbi-entrepreneur. Jack served on the board of UAHC and headed the (informal) cantor search committee at Leo Baeck Temple (LBT)—a small synagogue named for the beloved rabbi. He was ordained at HUC in 1921 and afterward served congregations in Cleveland, Ohio and Evansville, Indiana while studying sociology at the University of Chicago. In 1933 he became manager of the Educational Films Corporation, most famous for producing *Birth of a Baby* (1938), the first motion picture showing the actual birth of a child.[44] He later founded Skirball Productions and produced Alfred Hitchcock's *Saboteur* (1942) and *Shadow of a Doubt* (1943), among others. In the 1950s his interests shifted to real estate. He developed a number of bowling alleys and masterminded Vacation Village in San Diego, a model for resort hotels across America.

Although he never returned to the pulpit, Jack remained a fixture in the Reform movement. He served as regional president for UAHC, helped develop the HUC campus in Los Angeles, and established museums and galleries for the HUC system.[45] The Skirball Cultural Center in Los Angeles also bears his name.[46]

Jack traveled on behalf of LBT in search of a new cantor. The temple had been making use of "non-cantors"—singers who could adequately navigate the liturgy, but were not trained professionals (a common situation in that era).[47] Jack appeared on the Cincinnati campus one day, seemingly out of the blue. He struck up a conversation with William, during which he offered him a part-time cantor position and a part-time teaching position at the newly formed Department of Sacred Music at HUC Los Angeles.

William also received a letter during Jack's visit. It was an invitation to meet Rabbi Leonard Beerman (1921–2014), the founding rabbi of LBT. Leonard informed William of his attendance at an upcoming meeting of the Central Conference of American Rabbis in Pike, New Hampshire.[48] Arrangements were made for William to borrow a car and drive to the June gathering.

3. Hebrew Union College, Cincinnati

Leonard Beerman was born in Altoona, Pennsylvania, in 1921, and spent his youth in Illinois and Michigan. Early on, he was sensitized to the plight of the poor and the out-of-work. Although he was too young to understand the Depression, he could see its effects in south-central Michigan. He developed a conviction that would define his rabbinate: "the sense of responsibility for one another."[49]

Leonard returned to Altoona midway through high school. He attended Pennsylvania State College (now University), but dropped out in 1941 to work as an unskilled laborer in a machine gun factory. The intense anti–Semitism he experienced on the assembly line marked a turning point in his life. He reenrolled in college, graduated in 1942, and served in the U.S. Marine Corps from 1942 to 1943, partly to test whether his pacifistic views were just a cover for a lack of courage.[50] He entered the rabbinical school at HUC, and took a year off to enroll at Hebrew University of Jerusalem and serve in the Haganah (1947–48). He was ordained in 1949. His rabbinic mission was one of social justice, racial equality, human and civil rights, peace advocacy, and community service.[51]

During their meeting at the New Hampshire conference, Leonard hardly spoke about LBT. He was more interested in hearing William play the piano. They searched around and found a piano in the corner of a hotel lobby. "I started playing a medley of show tunes," William recalled. "[Leonard] shouted, 'That's it! I want this man!'"[52] That was the extent of William's cantorial interview. Leonard never even asked him to sing.

When news of William's impending departure reached the Cincinnati campus, the Student Association drafted a declaration:

WHEREAS William Sharlin has been our deeply cherished friend these several years;

WHEREAS he has directed our College Choir with spirit and with great skill, bringing beauty and inspiration to our Chapel Service;

WHEREAS he has gained the affection and the respect of the entire Student Association;

WHEREAS William Sharlin is leaving our midst to take up his duties in another part of the country as a Cantor and Educator, there to enrich the hearts of many by his noble spirit and broad outlook;

THEREFORE The Student Association of the Hebrew Union College expresses herewith its best wishes for the coming year; its hope that they will be years of consecration and reward and happiness.

Cantor William Sharlin

William viewed the Los Angeles move with a mixture of worry and excitement: "I came out of a background that was not particularly adventuresome, and to travel to the West Coast in itself was a magical thing, even at that age [thirty-four].... It was a major decision, and always major decisions were very difficult for me."[53] When he left Cincinnati, Rabbi Morris Hershman took over as director of the HUC choir and song leader at the Wisconsin camp. Like William, Morris was a trained musician. He sang in the student choir under William, and received special instruction from William in conducting, song leading, and guitar.

4

Leo Baeck Temple, Los Angeles

Leo Baeck Temple (LBT) had its beginnings in 1947, when a small group of families founded Temple Beth Aaron. Shortly thereafter, members of the fledgling congregation heard Rabbi Leo Baeck speak locally on his experiences during the Holocaust. Inspired by his heroism, decency, compassion, and gentle manner, they voted to rename the young synagogue in his honor.

In 1949 Rabbi Leonard Beerman became the temple's first professional leader. The membership immediately began to flourish, and funds were accumulated to purchase a permanent home. LBT procured the former Canadian Legion Hall at 434 South San Vicente Boulevard. The main hall was converted into a sanctuary, the garage became a social hall, and the second-story apartments were reconfigured as offices and classrooms. Rabbi Leo Baeck was the guest of honor at the dedication ceremony in 1952.

By 1954, the 250-family congregation was poised to hire a cantor. Leonard sent William two letters in May and June of that year in anticipation of his arrival. The casual tone and flexible job description reflect the relative simplicity of the time. Leonard wrote, "I am confident that if even half the good things we have heard about each other are true our relationship will be idyllic."[1] It was an accurate prediction. The expectations were relaxed:

Cantor William Sharlin

> There is no finality about this, but we thought of your role as being one in which you would be in charge of the entire musical program of our congregation—serving as Cantor for Friday evening services (we have no Shabbos morning service), festivals, and holy days; organizing a volunteer choir from the members of the congregation; and being in charge of music in our Religious School as well. I understand from Mr. Skirball that you expressed a desire not to assume responsibility for the Religious School and as you see, in keeping with that, the duties outlined above refer only to the field of music.[2]

William eased into the role with help from the temple's leadership. A past president, who was too old to drive, sold William his lightly used Pontiac for around two hundred dollars. A board member found him an apartment on Burton Way for sixty dollars per month. His part-time salary was $3,000 per year; it was raised to $4,500 just six months later. The looseness of the arrangement was a sign of things to come. Throughout his career at LBT, William received a part-time salary despite putting in fulltime hours. He worked without a written contract for several years before a business-minded congregant advised him to have one drawn up.[3]

In the early days, Leonard and his family had William over for Shabbat dinner each week. Leonard and his wife Martha knew something of the culture shock he was going through. Like William, their arrival at Leo Baeck Temple was their first trip West.[4] He greatly appreciated (and badly needed) their outstretched arms, as he was not, in his own words, "a gregarious cantor," "an active hand-shaker," or interested in "earning points" with the congregation.[5] The welcoming environment made it easy for him to turn down generous offers from two other synagogues.[6]

William was admittedly nervous the first time he led services at LBT. He possessed a sensitive, though not yet professional voice. Moreover, he was not accustomed to the frontal performance demanded of him. Although he had sung at congregations during the High Holidays while in the Midwest, his natural environments were playing behind the keyboard, conducting with his back to the audience, and writing behind-the-scenes in the composer's studio. At the conclusion of his shaky debut service, Leonard praised him in front of the congregation. Being extolled

4. Leo Baeck Temple, Los Angeles

in that public manner, especially for a job not so well done, made William visibly uncomfortable.

The rough start prompted William to find a voice teacher in Los Angeles. After a handful of lessons he was told, "That's it, you've got it!" He knew that was not the case. From that moment until almost the day he died, he would continue to practice daily, absorb vocal techniques from books and articles, and attend workshops and master classes. He was never completely satisfied with his own singing or anyone else's. He conditioned his students to adopt a patient and never-ending pursuit of perfection. He insisted that they repeat each measure of a piece until it approached a higher plane, and then repeat it again. "Trust the process" was his oft-reiterated motto.

William considered this approach his utmost responsibility to himself, his congregation, his students, and the congregations his students served. He constantly searched for ways to "move up and up and up," and equated vocal development with spiritual development.[7] For him, the ultimate goal was to marry devotional intention with technical tools, so that the cantor would be fully engaged in the sacred duty (self-gratification) and thereby inspire others to enter the experience (communal-gratification). As he put it: "You can't teach people to pray, but you can expose them to someone who does."[8]

It did not take long for William to blossom on the *bimah*. It was a platform where the introverted intellectual was transformed into a warm and engaging leader. He had an innate sense of how to bring people together. He encouraged congregants to fill in seats in the front, and set up chairs in smaller venues to ensure an intimate arrangement. One Friday evening when the sanctuary was less than full, William asked everyone to stand up: "Move, please, to the center aisle and find a seat in the front." They did. Pleased with himself, William announced, "It is the job of the cantor to move people."[9]

The temple's membership continued to grow, and it became necessary to rent larger facilities for the religious school, High Holiday services, and other major events.[10] The expansion also augmented William's workload and responsibilities. By the end of the 1950s, this included some musical experimentation.

Cantor William Sharlin

A Musical Partnership

William forged a strong and lasting partnership with LBT's organist, Shirl Lee Pitesky. Shirl Lee was a fellow perfectionist, and she welcomed the challenging literature William brought into the services. She admired his ability to play the piano in a variety of styles, and he admired her deep grounding in classical music. Shortly after they began working together, William took Shirl Lee out to a bar to listen to pop music. Nothing romantic came of it: she was not a drinker and there was a ten-year gap between them. She was then a junior at UCLA majoring in music and minoring in education. However, the two gelled musically, leading services together through the entirety of William's career.

Shirl Lee was born in Chicago in 1930. Her parents fled Russia during the Revolution and ended up in Constantinople, where her brother was born. Some time later, sponsors arranged for them to settle in the Windy City. On a Shabbat morning during her sixteenth year, Shirl Lee visited KAM (Kehilath Anshe Ma'arav; now KAM Isaiah Israel) in Chicago's Kenwood neighborhood. She auditioned for Max Janowski, the congregation's esteemed organist and a major composer in the Reform movement. Janowski sat her at the organ and put a Bach Chorale Prelude in front of her. When she finished playing he said: "Yes, I will have you as my student."[11]

Janowski was pleased to have a Jewish pupil. Most synagogues had Christian organists whose main employment was at a church. Jewish organists, however, did not play in churches—a fact owing as much to prejudice as to a shortage of Jews who played the instrument. His hope was that more Jewish musicians would take up the organ and fill synagogue positions. Janowski encouraged Shirl Lee to pursue that path: "When I was studying with him, he requested that I teach the junior choir on Sunday mornings. In addition, he asked and assisted me to arrange and compose music for them, which I did."[12] That led to other opportunities.

> When I was a student at the College of Jewish Studies [now Spertus Institute of Jewish Studies], Hyman Resnick, who was director of Jewish music at the college, hired me as a music teacher for various Hebrew schools across the

4. Leo Baeck Temple, Los Angeles

north and northwest sides of Chicago. I must have done this for several years while attending the college and being music director and pianist/organist at Beth Emet in Evanston, Illinois.[13]

After graduating from the College of Jewish Studies, Shirl Lee received a partial scholarship to study at Northwestern, which had a Jewish quota at the time. In her sophomore year she was invited to the Brandeis Arts Institute in Simi Valley, California, directed by the influential and charismatic synagogue composer Max Helfman. The summer camp program, which ran from 1948 to 1952, aimed at training the next generation of Jewish cultural leaders. Many campers went on to meet that goal, including Jack Gottlieb, Gershon Kingsley, Chuck Feldman, Raymond Smolover, Yehudi Wyner, and Sheldon Merel.

Shirl Lee relocated to Los Angeles after two years at Northwestern. The move was prompted by her father's heart condition, which forced him to retire. Her brother, Leon H. Guide, lived in Pico Rivera in southeastern Los Angeles County, and encouraged them to come to California.[14]

Leon was conductor of the community orchestra at Wilshire Boulevard Temple, and assistant director at Hess Kramer, the temple's Malibu summer camp. He brought Shirl Lee in as music counselor at the camp, where she led songs from the piano. She also enrolled at UCLA to finish her degree and took a job at University Synagogue in Brentwood. When that job ended, Leon contacted Alfred Wolf, a Wilshire Boulevard Temple rabbi and head of the UAHC. He explained that his sister needed work. Wolf informed him that Rabbi Leonard Beerman was looking for an organist at LBT. Leonard's wife, who had accompanied services on a small Hammond organ, was pregnant with their second child and was no longer up to the task. Shirl Lee was hired.

LBT had been using a bass-baritone cantorial soloist, but as the congregation grew in size and stature, Leonard decided they needed a full-fledged cantor. That is when he found William. Shirl Lee realized right away "what a unique experience it was to work with somebody who was so wonderful—who was so correct about what worked and what didn't work. It was a happy combination of two *real* musicians."[15] William often improvised sections of the service, and Shirl Lee was right there with him, anticipating where he was going and adding harmonic support to his melismatic turns. She played interludes connecting one piece to the next, creating an atmosphere of "meditation, peace, good will, and quietude."[16] She admired William's musicianship, how diligently he worked on his voice, how well he understood his own physiology. They depended on each other for the right cues at the right times. They acted as a single musical entity.

During their first years together, the congregation used volunteer musicians. A junior choir of religious school students, trained by Shirl Lee, sang at family services three or four times per years. A string quartet drawn from two musically talented member families accompanied William on special occasions, such as Shabbat services coinciding with Passover.[17] A volunteer adult choir, directed by William, was added to the mix, populated largely by former junior choristers. Shabbat services were held on Friday nights and only rarely on Saturday mornings (e.g., a bar/bat mitzvah). During High Holidays, the temple used a professional quartet, minus the volunteer singers, and William later expanded that quartet to twelve professional singers.

Shirl Lee retired after over sixty years as fulltime organist. Her career with LBT pre-dated William's appointment by at least a year, and she fondly remembers being a founding member of the LBT musical cadre. She always took special pride in being the authority on how William's music should be performed.

Settling Down

William's expanded workload, and the increased compensation that came with it, coincided with his marriage to Jacqueline (Jacqui) Drucker in 1958. William was nearing forty. Although he had dated, most of his relationships were not very serious. He went to a psychotherapist to help him determine why he resisted settling down (and to see if he was even marriageable). Blooming late was in the Sharlin family makeup. William's brother Hillel, the happy-go-lucky sibling, did not marry until his fifties. Rachel, the sister, never married and was at times a very difficult and

4. Leo Baeck Temple, Los Angeles

moody person. Edward, the eldest and "most normal" of the group, was happily married but passed away at a young age. They each struggled to leave their father's psychological grip. Even as mature adults, they acted like obedient children in his presence.[18] Their maturation was, it seems, stunted by their upbringing. Bouts with depression were not uncommon.

William's most significant love interest had been Shirley Kaiser, a non–Jew. Shirley was the director of the prestigious School for Nursery Years, where Leonard's children attended. At a certain point, William began bringing Shirley to LBT services. An elderly woman approached him after a service, warning him not to make a mistake. "Don't fool around this way. You're going to start a lot of trouble."[19] It was clear that marrying a non–Jew would pose major problems, both for the congregation and for William personally. With some difficulty, they ended their relationship.

Rabbi Isaiah (Shai) Zeldin was aware of William's dilemma. In addition to being colleagues at HUC in Los Angeles—Rabbi Zeldin was dean and William headed the music program—William spent many Shabbat afternoons at the Zeldin residence. In his capacity as regional director of UAHC, Zeldin traveled to synagogues throughout the West, drumming up support for the Union and interest in Reform Judaism. One such location was a start-up synagogue in Phoenix, Arizona. After the presentation, a woman asked Zeldin if he knew of any single Jewish men in the Los Angeles area.[20] She was looking to find a match for her niece, who recently moved there from San Francisco. Her niece was Jacqui Drucker, a talented concert pianist. "It just so happens that I do," he replied. "Someone just came to LA from Cincinnati."[21]

William's musical interests and problematic romance made him a good candidate. However, Jacqui was not consulted before her aunt spoke on her behalf, and news of the impending blind date annoyed her. She was doubly peeved when she found out her date was a cantor. Although she considered herself liberal and open-minded, she harbored a bias against "that work."[22] She came from a Labor Zionist home, where religion was anathema. Her main focus was the piano, which she practiced many hours each day.[23] She thought it was odd when her aunt and uncle joined the Phoenix synagogue, making them the only religiously affiliated members of the extended family. Nevertheless, being a "good girl," she concealed her feelings, and resolved to make the best of it.[24]

Jacqui was a student of E. Robert Schmitz, a prominent Franco-American pianist, composer, and pedagogue who resided in San Francisco. Schmitz was something of a controversial figure. He made numerous enemies in the musical establishment with his "rational approach" to piano technique. He balked at the traditional model that determined a "good teacher" by pedigree: a teacher's status was based less on competency than on who his teacher was, who taught his teacher, who taught his teacher's teacher, and so on. "If you go far enough back," Jacqui explained, "you end up in a time of a different instrument—the harpsichord and forte-piano—and smaller halls, which required a different type of technique. That approach is not appropriate for contemporary music."[25]

A World War I injury left shrapnel in Schmitz's hands and put him in the hospital for two years. Much of that time was spent contemplating the physical act of playing. He developed a technique that saved his own career and made him a leading figure in the performance and promotion of contemporary music. He insisted that proper playing on the modern piano required not just the fingers and wrists, but also deliberate use of the weight of the arms.

In the mid–1940s Jacqui went to live in the Schmitz home in the Presidio. The opportunity came with "blessings and trials."[26] The arrangement was advantageous for her lower-income family, and put her in contact with illustrious guests, including Igor Stravinsky. On the negative side, Madame Germaine Schmitz was an exceedingly difficult person to live with, and Jacqui felt pressured to become a "star," which was not necessarily a role she envisioned for herself.

Her association with Schmitz led her to Reuben Rinder, the beloved cantor of Temple Emanu-El of San Francisco and a scout of musical talent in the city's Jewish community.[27] He is credited with "discovering" violinists Yehudi Menuhin and Isaac Stern and pianist Leon Fleischer as young boys, and attracted a network of philanthropists who helped foster a Jewish musical renaissance. Most notably, this led to the com-

4. Leo Baeck Temple, Los Angeles

missioning of the sacred services of Ernest Bloch and Darius Milhaud, widely considered the crowning achievements of twentieth-century synagogue music.[28]

Jacqui attended the first Shabbat dinner of her young life at the Rinder household. To her surprise, Cantor Rinder had to explain what a *challah* was to the mostly Jewish guests—a ritual bread that even she, a thoroughly secular Jew, knew something about. Rinder tried to bring her into his musical fold and made a few calls for sponsors on her behalf, but to no avail.

In August of 1948 Schmitz organized the North American Prize Contest, an international contemporary music competition held in San Francisco.[29] Jacqui, aged twenty-two, was among several of Schmitz's students who participated. Because the competition came on the heels of World War II, it did not include European or Asian pianists. Competitors were drawn exclusively from North and South America. Even so, the skill level was very high, and the jury consisted of such notables as Darius Milhaud and Alfred Frankenstein, the city's foremost music critic.

The competition began with a composition phase, for which new works were written for solo piano. The winner was New York–based Neo-Classical composer Louise Talma. The second phase was the public performance. The pianists were required to present a full program of contemporary music that included Talma's winning piece, *Sonata No. 1* (in three movements). Jacqui had just two months to master the immensely challenging program. She won first prize and was awarded one thousand dollars.

Seeking to capitalize on the victory, Schmitz arranged for Jacqui to play at Carnegie Hall. Schmitz was active in New York in addition to San Francisco. His greatest fan was Virgil Thomson, the venerated composer and music critic for the *New York Herald-Tribune*. Thomson placed Schmitz above such luminaries as Sergei Rachmaninoff and Vladimir Horowitz. The status gave him access to exclusive halls that were notoriously difficult to book.

Jacqui, who had practiced tirelessly for the competition, had little time to ready herself for the October Carnegie Hall concert. She was consumed with self-doubt. Her prior performances mostly took place in small and relatively "safe" halls. The prestigious and pressure-packed New York stage was far beyond anything she had done. She begged her family not to attend, but they came anyway at a considerable expense.

Jacqui was disoriented by the enormous space of the stage, and had trouble hearing herself. The hall, known for its fine acoustics, had recently been used as a set for a Deanna Durbin film. A dampening coat of paint and other acoustically damaging changes remained.[30]

The opening of the concert went well. Jacqui began with a New York premiere of six of J. S. Bach's two-part inventions (Cm, F, Am, A, E, and G). Next was Bach's *Fantasia and Fugue in G Minor*, transcribed from the organ by Franz Liszt. After getting through the exposition of the fugue, her memory went blank and panic set in. She had no idea where to go next, so she started back at the beginning. She had trouble regaining her composure for the remainder of the program, although the rest of the pieces were well executed.[31] "I was supposedly a star," she remembered, "but I was not equipped to handle it."[32]

It is hard to ignore the similarities between Jacqui's Carnegie Hall concert and William's memory from the Manhattan School of Music, described in Chapter 1. William also told of playing a difficult piece on the piano (one of his own), blanking out, and having to return to the beginning. It could be that William's story, told in his late eighties, was a projected memory. He may have empathized with Jacqui's experience so much that he made it his own.

In spite of the perception of failure, Schmitz arranged for Jacqui to meet his manager. The manager was willing to take her on as an investment in the future. It was common for promising musicians to struggle in their initial efforts. Isaac Stern, for instance, received scathing reviews after his first high-profile concert. Had it not been for the support of a wealthy old woman and other benefactors at Temple Emanu-El, he may have never had the confidence to continue on.[33] The manager's offer was conditional. He wanted a large sum of money upfront to cover a tour and Jacqui's development, but her family was without funds.

Things were difficult for Jacqui when she returned to San Francisco. Schmitz was planning her next steps, but she was overwhelmed by all

4. Leo Baeck Temple, Los Angeles

that had happened. She began to look for a way out. She had been teaching the daughter of Carole Singer of the Singer Sewing Machine Company. She asked Mrs. Singer if she knew of an older person who had a piano and needed a live-in helper/companion. She was referred to Louise Reider, a niece of the widowed matriarch of the Manischewitz Company, who spent winters in San Francisco. Louise told Jacqui that her aunt had left town earlier than expected. All hope was not lost. Sensing Jacqui's desperation, Louise and her husband Norman, founder of the psychology department of Mt. Zion Hospital in San Francisco, graciously invited Jacqui into their home, which was across the street from the Schmitz estate. Soon thereafter, E. Robert Schmitz died unexpectedly at the age of sixty. Furious that Jacqui had left their home, Madame Schmitz never spoke to her again. There were many awkward moments when they passed each other silently on the sidewalk.

Jacqui decided to make herself "indistinguishable."[34] She abandoned any idea of being a star. She taught herself to type and got a part-time job at a flower shop. Meanwhile, she had occasion to socialize with friends of the Reiders. She fell for a nearly divorced man who was twice her age: she was twenty-three and he was forty-six. He was not a distinguished looking man, but she was nevertheless enthralled. The attraction was mutual, but he insisted that he was too old for her and was not looking to start a second family. Jacqui needed to break from the accumulating drama; she had to leave San Francisco.

She moved to Los Angeles in 1956 and shared an apartment with her brother who was studying at USC. It was "cheap, beautiful, and had [her] piano."[35] She took a part-time job at the headwear union office, located in a dingy downtown building. Her father had previously worked there as a union organizer, but he and Jacqui's mother moved to St. Louis before she arrived in Los Angeles. Jacqui pursued an unremarkable path as an "artist trapped in the anonymity [she] made for herself."[36]

But she was not completely detached from the piano. She received student referrals from a couple that ran Camp Roosevelt—a liberal, middle-class camp on the Westside of the city. She took the bus to reach the nucleus of Westside students, and walked from house to house giving lessons. Eventually, she learned to drive and bought a used car.

Cantor William Sharlin

Jacqui and William were set up on their blind date around this time. They connected over music, anxieties about being in Los Angeles, and their decisions to delay marriage for career. Initially, Jacqui's aversion to his religious profession prevented her from considering a romantic relationship. They still managed to see each other quite a bit. In a typical scenario, William would find Jacqui a student, she would call to thank him, and he would ask her out for dinner. Things went on like this for the better part of two years. At one point Jacqui thought, "He's so nice, but it's all wasted on me."

When they got engaged, they decided against a big wedding. They had very little money and their families, also of limited means, lived in faraway St. Louis and New York. Instead of a grand nuptial ceremony, the couple had a modest engagement party at the home of Mischa Kallis, an art director at Universal Studios, whose oldest son was soon to marry Jacqui's first cousin. Mischa reminded Jacqui of her parents, both of whom were artistically inclined. Her father was an amateur visual artist (sculptor, illustrator, etc.) and her mother was a fine weaver. They visited Mischa regularly when they lived in Los Angeles.

The remarkable house was designed by Austrian-American architect Rudolph Schindler (completed 1946). Schindler was active in Los Angeles in the mid–twentieth century. He was known for his inventive use of complex three-dimensional forms, and for operating within tight budgets. He was considered a true maverick in the world of modern architecture, and has been the subject of exhibitions at Los Angeles' Museum of Contemporary Art and MAK Center for Art and Architecture.[37] Known as the Kallis House, it is a mid-century modern structure on a sloping lot overlooking the San Fernando Valley. Among its striking features are a butterfly roof, angled walls and ceilings, clerestory windows, leopard-spot stonework, and built-in furniture and cabinetry.[38] The Los Angeles Conservancy recognizes the house as a historic building:

> The design as a whole used other methods to create a sense of flow and unity with the landscape: it is generally linear, with constant changes in the shape, slope, and orientation of the roof to vary ceiling height, allow sunlight in some places, and block glare in others. Schindler's love of industrial materials

4. Leo Baeck Temple, Los Angeles

The wedding of William and Jacqui Sharlin, June 6, 1958. From left: Rabbi Leonard Beerman, Jacqui, William.

is reflected in his use of rough split-stake fencing in cladding on parts of the downhill façade. This material acts as a sort of camouflage to help the building blend into the hillside. The Kallis House is one of Schindler's most-cited works, beloved as a dramatic illustration of the architect's design philosophy both indoors and out.[39]

Mischa had tried to sell the house for a number of years. He could not find a buyer, in large part because the house consisted of two separate

Cantor William Sharlin

buildings joined by an open deck: a one-bedroom residence and a painter's studio atop a two-bedroom apartment. It was impractical for a family. Moreover, because the house was so modern, banks were not willing to give much of a mortgage. When the house finally went into escrow, there was a problem. The woman who was to buy it was Schindler's mistress—a mysterious and beautiful "gypsy lady" with no proof of income.[40]

William and Jacqui were not looking for a house; they were pleased with their "little jewel" of an apartment. But the price tag for the Kallis House was enticingly low. Jacqui's father gave her some money in lieu of a large wedding, and they managed to make the purchase. They rented out the lower part to help make payments, and connected the two parts when Jacqui was pregnant with their first daughter, Ilana, born in 1961. Lisa, their second daughter, was born three years later.

Temple Expansion

LBT procured a ten-acre plot in the Sepulveda Pass in the early 1960s. That area of Los Angeles, between the western part of the city and the San Fernando Valley, was considered "the middle of nowhere." But construction of the 405 Freeway commenced in 1960, and by the time the building was dedicated on April 17, 1963, it was a relatively convenient locale.

The new site attracted affluent Westside Jews who were not deeply connected to "old style" Judaism. They gravitated toward Rabbi Leonard Beerman, who

William Sharlin, 1964.

4. Leo Baeck Temple, Los Angeles

was "a modern man engrossed in the major issues of the day."[41] Because of Leonard's presence and the resonance he had—particularly among left-leaning Jews—LBT became known for universal concerns and social action. Throughout his rabbinate, he exercised a strong and consistent voice for justice and human dignity. Leonard was lucky to be in a city "not known for following everybody else. A place where somebody like [him] could come along, stir things up, and not get kicked out."[42]

He maintained that the synagogue should not be separate from society, but provide a platform for speaking out authentically on issues of the day—even when those views rubbed against the majority stance. He gave many sermons against American foreign policy and Israel's treatment of Palestinians as "second-class citizens." He survived harsh criticisms from local colleagues, notably the ardent Zionist Isaiah Zeldin. A letter to the *Los Angeles Times* printed in 1976 shows the backlash he often faced: "The rabbi is telling [Israel] to commit suicide sweetly and nicely for the sake of world opinion and peace—the peace of slavery and death."[43] He publicly refused to vote in protest of the Vietnam War, spoke about racial inequality and nuclear disarmament, embraced the local Muslim community, pushed for better wages for the working poor, met with Yasser Arafat, and was the long-time rabbi-in-residence at the left-wing All Saints Episcopal Church in Pasadena.

Leonard dreamed of humanity rising to its highest moral potential. He devoted his life to putting that dream into inspiring words and meaningful action. His call for a better world was not rooted in ancient texts, though he gained much from their wisdom. Rather, his motivation came from a sense that "life is a problem yearning for a solution." He articulated that mission in the *Leo Baeck Temple College Bulletin* (winter 1967):

> This yearning that arises out of tears, sorrow, and affliction is a strange, paradoxical expression of a fundamental optimism about the nature and direction of human life which the Jewish religion has always affirmed. It is paradoxical and strange because it is an optimism based on a clear recognition that life is dirty and brutal. Leo Baeck once spoke of this when he said that the unique quality of Judaism's optimism is that despite the prevalence of what is degrading, dehumanizing and brutal, we face the world with the will to change it, with the commandment to realize the good in it. We do not pretend that

everything comes up roses; we do not cultivate a cool detachment; we do not anesthetize ourselves against frustration and disappointment. Rather we enter life and wrestle with it determined, like Jacob, to wrest a blessing from it, and insisting that such a blessing is there waiting to be achieved. That is the optimism that emerges from our pessimism.[44]

William was in synch with Leonard's humanistic values, especially when it came to the amorphous phenomenon of "spirituality." Echoing Abraham Maslow's conception of "peak experiences,"[45] William understood spiritual inclinations as universally human and accessible through a variety of triggers, from joy and grief to music and art. He framed such experiences as profound departures, during which one temporarily shifts from the ordinary self toward an unknown otherness. It mattered little to him whether the ontological source of that otherness was within or outside of oneself. "The God-intoxicated know it," he once said, "but I tell you that even the atheist can experience it."[46] William was himself possibly an atheist.[47]

He was particularly impressed with Leonard's way of "making music" out of the reading of liturgy. He did not "just read"—he *prayed*. In so doing, he helped make the text believable even for congregants who were not internally connected to the words. Indeed, Leonard himself struggled with the concept of God. He modeled the principle that one need not believe the literalness of a prayer to understand its underlying value and poetic beauty. In William's phrase, "He communicated the loftiness of the language."[48]

During a Shabbat weekend when Leonard was out of town, William was given full charge of the service. He took the opportunity to enact one of his core convictions: "the cantor [must] have a voice to speak with, not just to sing with."[49] Echoing Leonard's "speak as if" approach, William asked the congregation to reflect on the role of myth in shaping human perception. While not "true" in a historical or scientific meaning of the term, myths help make sense of reality and point to greater lessons that can be obscured in everyday dealings and real-life scenarios. "Ritual is also a myth," William reminded the congregation. "We are expected to act out a role—to read and listen to words and ideas that someone else has written—to pray those words as if they were our own, even

4. Leo Baeck Temple, Los Angeles

when some of it or much of it is rationally problematic."[50] He later put it more succinctly: "[T]here is this great beauty, whether you believe the literalness of it or not."[51] He was also aware of the obstacle of the Hebrew language, which is unintelligible to the majority of synagogue-goers: "Let the Hebrew of the prayer book flow through you; whether you understand it or not, enjoy its sounds."[52]

William applied this experiential philosophy to the music of the service. He believed that even when the music was not of great intrinsic beauty, it could be elevated with a sense of holiness. He constantly strove to assume a state of prayerfulness. That was especially important when it came to prayer-melodies he sang hundreds of times, like the Ashkenazi folk setting of *Etz Chayim Hi*. Each time he sang the prayer, he encountered it as something new. At times, he added improvisational departures to give an element of spontaneity.

William and Leonard's shared philosophy translated to mutual affection. In 2000, on the occasion of William's eightieth birthday, Leonard wrote:

> I am full of gratitude for the friendship that has brought so much blessing to me and to all the members of my family. But it is not only friendship. It is also the image you have held for all to see. The richness of your knowledge. The quest for integrity in your work and in your life. The persistent endeavor to hold fast to the highest standards. A deep appreciation of the Jewish tradition and the people who fashioned it, in all times and places. And the insistence that we must build upon this to move on beyond it, in our music, in our very lives. And you have shown us that the more we know, the more free, the more playful, the more joyful we can become.[53]

William would also share leadership duties with Sandy (Sanford) Ragins, a Chicago-born rabbi who grew-up in Los Angeles. Sandy was a member of the first rabbinical class at the Los Angeles campus of HUC, and was ordained in Cincinnati in 1962. He earned a Ph.D. at Brandeis University in the history of ideas, while serving a synagogue in Hingham, Massachusetts. Sandy filled in for Leonard during his sabbatical in 1964. The following year Sandy became the congregation's first assistant rabbi. He returned to LBT in 1972 as the associate rabbi, and was made senior rabbi when Leonard retired in 1986. Sandy served in that capacity until his retirement in 2003.

Cantor William Sharlin

William was never as close with Sandy as he was with Leonard. Still, they sincerely respected one another. Sandy's fond remarks appeared in the 2000 tribute book alongside Leonard's:

> [William] has been my mentor and strength, one who steadies shaky young rabbis, and older ones, too; my companion on camp weekends, on college trips to Berkeley, and on the long, sad drives to and from the cemetery; a genius with an instinct for the appropriate, and a sense of theater, so that he always seems to know which music should go where and at what tempo the door of the ark should be closed; a creator who has brought so much distinction, so much dignity to his profession, to the Hebrew Union College where he has influenced generations of young cantors and rabbis, and to this synagogue community which has had the incredible good fortune to have him as cantor; William who has taught me in his quietness and in his sighing things that cannot be learned from books; William, the nudger, and persistent people mover, the *tummeler*, who has shown us all how much music we have within us, and how lovely it can be when a song is there to grace an evening.[54]

Leaders of Leo Baeck Temple, Los Angeles, 1992. From left: Rabbi Leonard Beerman, William, Rabbi Sanford Ragins.

4. Leo Baeck Temple, Los Angeles

The environment of freedom and respect enabled William to flourish as a composer, arranger, and researcher of liturgical music. He accumulated a massive library of synagogue material, much of which came from a small music store he frequented during visits to Jerusalem. He brought many of those melodies into his synagogue and other venues, and some have become staples of the North American Jewish repertoire. Through passionate study, he made himself an authority on Israeli music.[55]

William's first major event at LBT occurred six months after the move to Sepulveda Boulevard. On October 23, 1963, the temple was host to a concert presented by the HUC Department of Sacred Music entitled "Sacred Chants of Church and Synagogue." The concert brought together music from Jewish, Greek Orthodox, and Roman Catholic traditions. It was programmed in two halves: "Common Elements in the Chant" and "Choral Compositions Based on Chant."[56] William conceived of and directed the event, which had ties to Eric Werner's influential book *The Sacred Bridge*, published a few years earlier (1959).[57]

William enlisted the collaboration of Frank Desby, a professor at the University of Southern California and director of the St. Sophia Greek Orthodox Cathedral Choir, and John Biggs, a conductor with Verve and Capitol Records, choir director of the Saint Monica Church Choir in Santa Monica, and director of the John Biggs Singers. The three men were kindred spirits: scholars, composers, and conductors of sacred music. For the concert, William conducted the combined choirs of LBT and the HUC Cantors Ensemble,[58] Frank Desby conducted The Byzantine Choral, and John Biggs conducted The John Biggs Singers.

The program highlighted musical intersections between the three bodies of sacred chant. The first half included selections bearing musical resemblances: Scriptural Chant (East-European Jewish: *Shir Hashirim*, Song of Song, ch. 1; Roman Catholic: *Lave Ejus*, Song of Songs, ch. 8; Greek Orthodox: *Tade Legi Kyrios*, Isaiah, ch. 52), Psalm Chant (German Jewish: *Hallelujah*, Ps. 113; Roman Catholic: *Laudate Pueri*, Ps. 113; Greek Orthodox: *Kyrie Ekekraxa*, Ps. 140), and Antiphonal Chant (Hasidic Jewish: *Birchas Kohanim*; Roman Catholic: *Solemn Tone*; Greek Orthodox: *Great Ektenis*). The concert's second half featured chant-based works from the three liturgical traditions.[59]

John Biggs and Mark Desby included pieces they had written, but William did not. William had yet to compose any large-scale works for the synagogue, let alone chant-based material that would have fit the program. His synagogue pieces to that point were, by and large, arrangements of short songs suitable for congregations and volunteer choirs. Representative of that period is a pamphlet of sheet music published for the Twelfth Annual Convention of the American Conference of Cantors, held at the Sportsmen's Lodge in Los Angeles in the summer of 1965. The pamphlet includes William's multi-voice arrangements of Reuben Kosakoff's Psalm 148, Naomi Shemer's "Shirey Zamar Noded" (composer listed as "unknown"), an anonymous setting of "If I Am Not for Myself," and a Chabad tune for *Ma Tovu*.[60] His compositions matured when he assembled a professional vocal quartet at LBT. That development marked a shift in his writing from *Gebrauchsmusik* to more creative settings.

William was intensely involved in all aspects of "Sacred Chants of Church and Synagogue." He prepared translation sheets for audience members, and created an illustration depicting intersecting segments of ancient notation from Latin, Greek, and Hebrew sources. The striking image was included on the program cover, postcard advertisements, and a paperboard poster, which he kept on a music stand next to his piano.

Composer of Note

Particularly in the 1950s and 60s, American synagogues expected a formal cantor-choir-organ led service (the shift toward congregational melodies had not yet taken hold). "Listening music" was, more or less, an expected modality. However, it was not until the 1970s, when William was in his fifties, that he became a composer of note. He wrote sophisticated pieces for his professional quartet (soprano, alto, tenor, bass), who joined him on the *bimah* for High Holidays and some Friday evening services, and LBT gave him *carte blanche* when it came to musical repertoire. He was endlessly grateful for the freedom to "open up, and create, and use fine singers."[61]

4. Leo Baeck Temple, Los Angeles

William regularly showed up on Friday nights with new arrangements and compositions he had prepared during the week. These were usually opening songs meant to set a tone for the service. He demanded perfect execution from his quartet on first reading. "He would be very upset if it wasn't done precisely right," Shirl Lee reminisces. "If he didn't mark an accidental and the musician didn't know where to go, he'd yell at you: 'Of course you know what it is! Realize what key we're in!'"[62] The group tolerated these outbursts. They "would lay their bodies down if he wanted to run over them like a tank."[63] "Anything for William" was their unspoken motto. But the mood was not always heavy. For instance, William routinely walked out during the meditation and returned to tell the singers the score in the Lakers' game.

He was also the liturgical stage director. He felt the service should have a logical and continuous flow building to a high point or crescendo. Like a choreographer creating a ballet or opera, he would demonstrate for Leonard how to walk up to the ark, when to turn around, and so forth. This careful approach was also apparent in musical decisions. When Shirl Lee introduced organ preludes and postludes, for example, William was sometimes hesitant.[64] Everything needed to fit together. The integrity of the service was so paramount that he would have ushers prevent people from entering during certain prayers (e.g., *Bar'chu* and *Sh'ma*).[65] He also despised the announcement of page numbers. A substitute rabbi who made the mistake of saying, "now Cantor Sharlin will sing *Mi Chamocha* on page 57," would find William "standing in utter silence at his lectern—on strike—showing his displeasure."[66]

William's musical creativity was more or less an in-house secret during LBT's first decade on Sepulveda Blvd. That changed in 1972 when he was invited to compose and arrange the musical portion of the "Service of Inauguration for Alfred Gottschalk as the Fifth President of the Hebrew Union College–Jewish Institute of Religion," held at Isaac Mayer Wise Temple in Cincinnati. Rabbi Gottschalk, previously dean of the Los Angeles campus of HUC, was appointed successor to Nelson Glueck, who passed away on February 12, 1971. Gottschalk was a fan of William's "little pieces," and wanted him to write something on a grander scale. William was given a very short deadline, and Jacqui's support was crucial.[67]

Cantor William Sharlin

The service, held a year and twelve days after Glueck's death, was a celebration both of Gottschalk's appointment and of the school itself. All but one of the participants was an HUC graduate, including Gottschalk himself ('57).[68] The presenters, who had roles as shofar blower, reader, Torah carrier, and the like, were some of the Reform movement's more notable figures. The transmission of the Torah was assigned to ten people, including Rabbi Jacob R. Marcus ('20), HUC professor of American Judaism and founding director of the American Jewish Archives, Rabbi Sheldon H. Blank ('23), HUC professor of Bible, and Rabbi Sally J. Priesand, the first woman rabbi ordained at HUC ('72).

The school's rabbinics professor Rabbi Eugene Mihaly ('49) prepared the program, comprising ten parts woven around a modified Torah service: Procession; The Sounding of the Shofar; The Transmission of the Torah; Torah Service; *Mi Shebeirach* (chanted by William); Inauguration; *Rabbi Meir 'Omer* (sung by Howard Stahl '72); Adoration and *Kaddish*; Benediction; and Recessional. William's music was performed by a combination of soloists, a male student chorus, brass ensemble, harp, guitars, and organ.

In the weeks and months following the service, William received several congratulatory letters from colleagues and luminaries in the movement. Some, like Rabbi Robert Blinder of the Midwest Council of UAHC, had known of William's musicianship, but "did not suspect the level of [his] genius."[69] Others expressed excitement about this "new" composer, and a desire to spread his talent around the movement. A number of attendees requested recordings and sheet music of the pieces performed.[70] Others simply shared their awe and appreciation for William's musical presentation. Robert A. Alper, a senior rabbinical student who later became a rabbi/stand-up comic, included a humorous comment: "I thought you might be interested to know that a strange new form of competition has erupted in the Cincinnati HUC community. It seems that everyone struggles to find an even more superlative adjective to describe the music of the inauguration ceremonies."[71] Jack Skirball wrote, "Nobody applauded with more enthusiasm than I at the luncheon last Thursday. Your music and its rendition was the most inspiring service I have ever attended."[72] Joseph Glaser wrote, "It was our finest

4. Leo Baeck Temple, Los Angeles

hour! I just returned home and am in a state of absolute euphoria."[73] Gottschalk extended his gratitude:

> I wish I knew how to compose music to reciprocate in kind the magnificent spirit and feeling which you created for the service of the inauguration. You know that from the start there was no one else whom I wanted more than you to create the spirit and mood for this occasion. The music was a tour de force; it was sparkling, contemporary, Jewish, and made its point.[74]

Shortly after the inauguration, selections from the service were produced as a record and decorated score.[75] Harold Orbach ('52), a German-born cantor who studied with William at SSM, coordinated the project. The ten selected pieces are representative of William's wide musical interests and active imagination. They include unison songs, two- and three-part choruses, solos, and duets in styles ranging from accessible "sing-alongs" to esoteric modernist expositions—all accompanied by an inventive orchestration of horns, harp, organ, and guitar.[76] William's introduction to the published work describes his intentions:

> The motivating concept underlying this work is the force and flow of Jewish history: transmission, continuum, and departure. These elements (hopefully) expressed in the core opening statement of the Processional, in the development of its motifs throughout the work, and in the integration of borrowed material into the primary character and mood of the whole.
>
> This Service, while conceived for male voices, can be performed by mixed choir provided the rearrangement is sensitively considered. Likewise, it can be adapted to varying Tora [sic]-centered celebrations: confirmations, installations, and dedications.[77]

William was perhaps the most precise synagogue composer of his generation. A self-described "freak" for the canon, his music freely crosses stylistic borders and evades conventional limitations of the worship setting. At its most elegant, it seamlessly blends melodic modernism, jazz harmonies, Renaissance form, and Jewish folk material. And nothing he wrote was ever finished.

Like many artists, William was never completely satisfied with his output—or, perhaps more accurately, ceased being satisfied with it after a short duration. Well into his eighties, he compulsively made changes to vocal lines, expanded harmonic coloring, and added to piano accompaniments. Some pieces were left on the brink of indecipherability, while others bear only surface resemblance to their original conceptions. He gave this treatment to published and unpublished pieces alike, and complained when his music was reprinted without his consent, as he typically had a more recent—and, in his mind, improved—version.

This became something of a running joke at the American Conference of Cantors annual conventions, where William often presented works. Colleagues began to notice that, more often than not, the "new" pieces were actually re-arrangements of material he had already composed or arranged. It is unclear whether William meant this as a joke, a lesson in the writing process, or, as many assumed, a sincere belief that each rendering was an entirely different piece.[78]

The editing and re-editing was not done from a place of frustration. It was the inevitable byproduct of a perspective that saw written notes as temporary suggestions rather than concrete representations. For William, whatever appeared on the page was but a carefully constructed abstraction (though he was meticulous about how it was performed). Notation was the model of an artistic reality, not the reality itself.

Part of this fluidity stemmed from William's position as a composer who regularly "tested" his compositions on a live audience: his congregation. The laboratory environment elicited quick feedback and equally quick changes, when necessary. This was essential, as William sought to appease two very different constituencies: cosmopolitan Jews, who made up the majority of LBT, and old-fashioned *shul*-goers, who were smaller in number but still highly valued.

William felt a kinship with both groups: each resonated with the polar aspects of his own persona. He referred to one group as "*haimish*" (old-fashioned, folksy) and the other as "sophisticated" (modern, not grounded in Jewish folkways). The blended congregation meant there were "mixed levels of exposure to more sophisticated music as well as folksy music."[79] William described the situation in an interview:

> [We could] divide the congregation into these two categories, into people who are more "*haimish*" and would lean towards participating in singing the musical content, as against those who came for a listening experience—and even a spiritual experience—but not necessarily having the need to be very

4. Leo Baeck Temple, Los Angeles

> active musically, as they can receive music that's well performed in terms of quality and spirituality and that is sufficient for such people for their worship needs. My awareness of this culture has always led to what I thought was a reasonable balance between music of participation as well as music to offer.... Even in listening material, [I strived to] balance that category between simple and elaborate [material] that would primarily appeal to the musically knowledgeable [i.e., concert-goers].[80]

This personal initiative encapsulates William's experience at LBT. Leonard's hands-off approach to service music was motivated by respect for William's musical judgment.[81] Moreover, the laity did not play an active part in determining the content or direction of the music. As William put it, he had "no external pressure to do this or that."[82]

Perhaps most significantly, this enabled him to retain the choir modality even as trends in American Jewry were leaning toward congregational song. "Leo Baeck Temple was the perfect place for me," he stated. "There was always the possibility of introducing new music—cantorial, choral, and congregational—and I never denied the congregation. I welcomed their participation, both in listening and singing. I made sure the service was balanced, allowing for substantive *hazzanut* for cantor and choir, as well as congregational melodies. I always strived to bring the congregation into the process of prayer."[83]

William developed methods of introducing the congregation to new melodies. He was determined to teach them challenging music, rather than feed them an instantly digestible diet of simple tunes. This desire had two sources: a personal need for artistic expression, and respect for the congregation. To dumb down the music would have been suffocating for William and, he believed, disrespectful to the worshipers. His approach was patient: he did not insist that melodies be absorbed instantaneously. He engaged congregants by explaining textual meanings, pointing out musical nuances, and showing enthusiasm for the piece. Typically, he would sing a short section and invite the congregation to listen for that section during the performance. He sometimes had the choir demonstrate passages. The congregants also saw William conducting on the *bimah*, expressing with his body genuine involvement in the piece. All of this encouraged what he called "spiritual listening."[84] Linda Rabinowitch Thal, whose acquaintance with William began at summer camp and continued when she became LBT's education director, gives this account:

> Sometimes his music challenges us, stirs us, makes us reach, and makes us deal with doubt and disjunction. Sometimes it evokes our playful side, just when we are beginning to take ourselves too seriously.... And sometimes his music transports us; often just when it seems that the path of religious experience is closed off to us. At that moment, the notes of William's melody and the purity of his voice catch us, and as if wrapping ourselves like a *tallit* around our souls, they carry us to that higher realm to which we thought ourselves cut off.[85]

Congregational singing was not the norm when William began at LBT. Reform services were conducted using the *Union Prayer Book*—a book filled with richly poetic English interpretations of the liturgy, but uninviting in terms of musical participation. William was intent on bringing people in, particularly during opening songs, the blessing of candles, responses, closing hymns, and special pieces such as "May the Words" (*Yih'yu L'ratzon*). At the same time, he understood the importance of listening to presentational music: solo, choral, and organ pieces. The balance between these modalities made LBT a cut above the rest. The services "had meat to them."[86]

The musical variety at LBT was exceptional. Typically, a synagogue's musical choices are restricted to old favorites and "traditional" settings (i.e., what the congregation is accustomed to). It takes a remarkable leader and a trusting congregation to experiment in an environment that lends itself to monotony and standardization. This does not mean that all of the melodies were unpredictable; there was a healthy blend of the new and the old-reliable. Not everyone was thrilled about the dynamic musical environment. William explained:

> On a number of occasions, I would be approached by someone after a service asking, "Why did you change the melody to that prayer?" My response was always the same: "Where were you last week?" I tried to communicate that, if they had attended services in the previous weeks, they would have noticed that I was introducing the piece slowly, and that it was gradually becoming familiar to the congregation. Likewise, if they were regulars at our services, they would have surely *wanted* a variety of music.[87]

The tone of these conversations was not always in keeping with Shabbat peace and fellowship. An important temple member habitually complained to William about doing something wrong or making a poor musical change. After politely listening to the man week after week, William finally barked back: "You don't know music. You should quit expressing your opinion." The man never forgave him for that.[88]

Temple Activities

William took an active role in childhood education at LBT. He made a point of visiting every Sunday school class with guitar in hand. He travelled from room to room, leading a set of songs that included Hebrew texts, general "fun" lyrics, and songs with a social consciousness. The material was adjusted for grades one through eight. There were close parallels between these interactions and the camp experience. The students, like the campers, engaged liturgical melodies in such a way that they would, ultimately, internalize them. When William presented them with something new, he radiated high energy, hoping it would be contagious. The children occasionally shared songs they learned during Friday night and holiday services. They often sang complex three-part music.[89] William's pedagogical methods garnered notice from music educators, who solicited him as a consultant and contributor to songbooks for Jewish children.[90]

Through his involvement with the children, William noticed that some students were moving on in their religious schooling—from third to fourth grade, for example—without acquiring the necessary skills. In a typical situation, a child would stumble through the Hebrew, not able to make the proper sounds or recognize all the letters. She would move on to the next year, still stumbling, never having addressed the deficiencies. William urged the teachers, especially of the younger grades, to identify such weaknesses. Children with serious impediments were assigned tutors.

William became increasingly involved with students as they approached their *b'nei mitzvah*. He upheld high standards for liturgical singing and cantillation (ritual biblical chant based on prescribed musical patterns). He resisted making recordings for memorizing assigned

William dancing at a consecration ceremony, Leo Baeck Temple, Los Angeles, 1966.

Torah and Haftarah portions—a ubiquitous practice that does not require recognition of trope markings or enable the chanting of different texts in the future.

William innovated two methods of teaching biblical chant. The first was the use of English texts accompanied by trope markings. This allowed students to focus on the symbols and their musical interpretation, rather than laboring over the foreign letters. Once the music was sufficiently absorbed, Hebrew words were added. The second involved the trope markings themselves. The archaic Hebrew-Aramaic trope names refer to shapes and tunes. William related the symbols to English-speakers in a similar way. *Mercha* became "open parenthesis," *tipcha*

4. Leo Baeck Temple, Los Angeles

became "closed parenthesis," *munach* became "right angle," *etnachta* became "upside-down wishbone," and so on.[91]

William's system gained advocates in Jewish education circles, and became a standard teaching methodology. Cantor Helen Leneman, a student of William's and an accomplished scholar-educator, notes the advantages of the Sharlin Method: "[The students] do learn trope more quickly because relating the names directly to the shapes and sounds aids the learning process. They also do not have the additional step of mastering the more difficult Aramaic-Hebrew terms. It is an ideal system for students with Hebrew deficiencies."[92]

William also created parodies of Broadway shows for LBT's clergy, staff, and congregants to perform. They were, in some ways, an extension of the shows at HUC Cincinnati, where students poked fun at the faculty. The semi-annual productions featured humorous lyrics specific to the synagogue and Jewish life.

An example is *A Tsuris Line*—a takeoff on the popular musical *A Chorus Line*. In the original show, seventeen young dancers audition to be in a Broadway musical. In William's show, a rabbi suddenly leaves his synagogue before the High Holy Days. The congregation has no time for individual interviews with rabbinic candidates. All the candidates are brought in to lead the services together, forming a "*tsuris* line" (*tsuris* is Yiddish for troubles, worries, and suffering).

Another year, William produced a parody of *Fiddler on the Roof*. The following lyrics from that show, sung to the tune of "If I Were a Rich Man," lampoon LBT's modest beginnings and friendly competition with Stephen S. Wise Temple, led by Rabbi Zeldin.

> If we were a rich *shul* ...
> We'd line our social hall floor with another purple carpet
> To tie things together wall to wall;
> Install a P.A. system with speakers in every pew.
>> And then our Rabbis could preach a double sermon side by side
>> You could tune in on channels one or two,
>> Or dial an old favorite rerun just for you.
>
> We'd build an on and off ramp right from the freeway
> Directly to our door—oh what a sight,
> With parking attendants to ease our tired feet;
> We'd hire 300 Jewish extras

Cantor William Sharlin

To fill our sanctuary every Friday night,
Imagine, Leonard, not one empty seat!
If we were a rich *shul* ...
    We'd have our own little cemetery, halfway up the hill,
    With a catchy name like "Baeck to Mother Earth."
    Oy what a place for a family Sunday climb;
We'd hire Bateman and Eichler and maybe even Hill
Just to help us keep track of what we're worth;
And finally we'd make the cover of *Time*.
    We'd offer workshops to our sister congregations;
    They'd come pounding on the door;
    To consult and advise,
    They would plead, Leonard Beerman,
    How did you do it, Leonard Beerman?
    It would bring our friend Reb Zeldin down to size.
We could delight our Rabbis, Cantor and Exec.
With a brand-new Mercedes every year;
How else can we let them know how much we care?
    We'd even hire one more Rabbi who would only handle
    The nudnicks and the benders of the ear;
    One more Cantor just to fill that fourth red chair.
We'd build a Temple extension closer to the beach
For unusual occasions of the year;
Like a very hot weekend that falls on Yom Kippur.
    We'd acquire that cozy little place on San Vicente
    For those old members who complain
    That those were the good old days when we were poor.
Lord who made the lion and mule,
We realize that you're nobody's fool,
But at least we could have livened up
Our dreary vestibule ...
If we were a wealthy *shul*.

These performances were a welcome contrast to William's serious side. They provided him with additional creative outlets (lyricist, producer, director), and allowed him to vent frustrations in an innocuous manner.

    William's talent for Broadway was unmistakable. Musical theater held a strong attraction for him, and he sometimes regretted not pursuing it as a career.[93] He almost got his foot in the door in 1975. Gordon Davidson, founding director of the Center Theatre Group at Los Angeles' Mark Taper Forum, arranged a meeting with William and John Hirsch,

4. Leo Baeck Temple, Los Angeles

who was directing a production of *The Dybbuk*. Unfortunately, nothing came of the meeting. The show went on to receive the Los Angeles Drama Critics Circle Awards for distinguished production, direction, lighting design, and performance in a supporting role.[94]

Musical Outreach

In 1985 William was invited to write five columns on Jewish music for the short-lived *Jewish Newspaper* of Los Angeles.[95] One colorful article is "Mozart Mounts the Bimah—What a Mass!"[96] It depicts a fictional conversation between two bewildered synagogue-goers, Conni and Reyf. Reyf had just returned from her nephew's bar mitzvah (presumably at LBT). After the service she approached the cantor (presumably William[97]). She effused that his rendition of *Sim Shalom* sounded like a melody her grandfather used to sing. It was thoroughly "Jewish" to her ears. The cantor apologetically told her that it was adapted from a Mozart Mass. She was dismayed. Conni could not understand how her friend mistook it for a Jewish melody. Reyf reminded her of an earlier instance when they learned that *Ma'oz Tzur* had ties to a German Lutheran chorale. "Now don't tease me with your *Ma'oz Tzur* thing," Conni replied. "[T]here are millions of Jews who feel the same as I do. I mean—when I gaze at the Chanukah candles with my family as we sing *Ma'oz Tzur*, I almost feel myself transported back to the times of the Maccabees." From this dialogue, William concluded: what you don't know won't hurt you; the passage of time obscures musical origins; and text and context determine a song's identity.

Several years later, William was a composer-in-residence at Hebrew Congregation in Washington, D.C. (April 1992). During the lecture-demonstration, he posed a historically problematic question to the audience: "What is *Jewish* in Jewish music?" (Eric Werner called this the "eternally silly question."[98]) William's own response: "everything—and nothing." Any kind of music can *become* Jewish, but there are no exclusively Jewish elements in the music of the Jews. He emphasized the force of language in transforming the music that accompanies it: "It is the very taste, the feel, the association, and the context of that language. It's so powerful that you can put almost anything against [the Hebrew] language and you will experience it as a Jewish experience."[99] Wherever Jews have lived, they have been influenced by surrounding customs and cultures. The larger world permeated all facets of life, including the synagogue and its music. "Consciously or unconsciously, Jews heard certain music in the various countries in which they lived, and absorbed them—digested them—into whatever musical tradition was dominant in the synagogue. The pain, the passion, the pathos of our existence in the diaspora transformed what was brought in from the outside."[100] William illustrated the point with a setting of *Sim Shalom*, which had all the earmarks of a cantorial piece. He then played it on the piano and asked the audience to name the tune. "It's a Mahler song," a man replied. He was correct: it was Mahler's "Song of the Wayfarer."

The article and lecture continued the topic of musical sharing initiated at the 1963 tri-faith concert, and all three were connected to the work of Eric Werner. This was no accident. The two men were aligned in their desire to educate professionals and laypeople about the multiple and (more or less) unrestricted sources of Jewish music. Especially reminiscent is an experience Eric recounts in *A Voice Still Heard*:

> I once provided an Armenian Church song [in the *Ahavah Rabah* mode] with Yiddish words and had it sung at a cantors' convention; the assembly was completely enchanted by this "typical Jewish melody," and was prepared to introduce it into the synagogue. A week later the episode was forgotten, and they went back to their old conviction of the essential Jewishness of the *Ahabah Rabah* mode. That conviction is on a par with the belief that the German language is a dialect of Yiddish![101]

Additionally, it was probably not coincidental that William used a Mahler piece to demonstrate the character-shaping capacity of the Hebrew language. As noted, William and Eric used to play four-hand piano arrangements of Mahler symphonies, and the composer was a recurring subject in Eric's writings.[102]

William received many scholar-in-residence invitations during his career. These typically spanned entire weekends (Friday night through Sunday), and involved service leading, lectures, work with volunteer choirs, and an occasional commissioned piece.[103] Music for the choir—

4. Leo Baeck Temple, Los Angeles

William's own compositions—usually arrived well in advance of the visit. The synagogue's cantor or conductor rehearsed the ensemble in preparation for the weekend, and William took over conducting duties when he arrived. A letter from Cantor Sarah J. Sager, who hosted William at Anshe Chesed Congregation–Fairmount Temple, Cleveland, in April of 1985, describes the impact: "The gift of your music arrived long before you did, but it came alive and took on new meaning in your presence. No longer were we learning notes on a page; you taught us, truly, to sing praises to God."[104]

Choral performances were woven around musical teachings. For example, his weekend at Congregation Beth Am in Los Altos Hills, California (April 3–5, 1981) featured a Friday evening service exploring "The Ways Synagogue Music Has Evolved Over the Years." The Saturday morning program was entitled, "The Fascinating Structure of Traditional Music," and came with a provocative description: "In previous generations the mainstream of synagogue music was so stable that it Judaized what was brought in. There is no integration today." On Saturday evening, William lectured on "The Classical Hasidic Melody: Misconceptions," and on Sunday led an "open, loose-end discussion" on "What is Jewish in Jewish Music."[105] Other scholar-in-residence weekends showcased similar themes, such as "The Particular and the Universal in the Synagogue: Confessions of a Comfortable Schizophrenic," "Individual Versus Communal Participation in Worship: Can Listening Be 'Active' Participation," and "The Static (Liturgy) and Dynamic (Music) in Jewish Worship."[106] These topics populate his philosophical writings as well.[107]

William was also involved in Los Angeles' classical music scene. For example, in 1981 the Los Angeles Philharmonic held a three-day "Festival of Music Made in Los Angeles" at UCLA's Royce Hall. A few LBT members were on the organizing committee. They engaged William as narrator for Arnold Schoenberg's *A Survivor from Warsaw* (Op. 46, 1947), which headlined the concluding concert. Schoenberg's final orchestral work, the piece examines of the composer's conflicted Jewish identity, packaged as a vignette from the Warsaw Ghetto Uprising. The six-and-a-half-minute piece tells of Jews being deported to a death camp. It is pure drama, with frenetic orchestration, emotional narration, interjected Nazi orders (in German), and a defiant climactic chorus of *Sh'ma Yisrael*. Its intensity and virtuosity matched the ambitious spirit of the festival. An advertisement boasted:

> Music Composed in Los Angeles between 1934 and 1969 by an astounding number of composers headed by Stravinsky and Schoenberg. Music that sent shock waves throughout the world. Music that brings pride and glory to Los Angeles. Share this pride with the Los Angeles Philharmonic and Michael Tilson Thomas in a unique, exciting, ear-stretching, eye-opening festival. The Festival of Music in Los Angeles. The extraordinary event is not to be missed, at UCLA's Royce Hall.[108]

William absorbed himself in the labor-intensive score. He pored over the narration, carefully adhering to the rhythmic values and vocal contours to which the narration is set. "Each word I read was synched up with the orchestra," William recalled. "[I]n order to pull it off, I had to both learn my lines cold, and internalize the orchestral score. I walked back and forth through my house, repeating the words over and over until they became my own. I didn't fool around."[109] Candidly, William admitted that he was not a great fan of Schoenberg's music; but personal taste did not negate his respect for the piece and its subject matter. Additionally, Schoenberg's son and his family were members of Leo Baeck Temple. When the children had *bar mitzvah* ceremonies, William sang some of Schoenberg's more playful songs.[110]

By the time of the first performance on December 13, 1981, William was "totally at one with the piece."[111] His obsessive study and attention to detail came from his perspective as a composer. Being a meticulous notator himself, he could not cut corners in someone else's work. This attentiveness was not shared by conductor Michael Tilson Thomas, who treated William more as an orchestra member than as a soloist. He ignored William's suggestions, and insisted on making all the musical decisions. William considered many of those choices at odds with the composer's intent.

Still, the end result was a narration that stayed truer to the score than perhaps any other.[112] William's gentle and introspective tone contrasts especially with the "gold standard" recording of the Boston symphony in 1969, featuring Erich Leinsdorf in his final season as conductor and opera baritone Sherrill Milnes as narrator.[113] Milnes's loud and

4. Leo Baeck Temple, Los Angeles

extroverted performance, released on RCA's prestigious Red Seal series, is held as a model interpretation. William took the piece in another direction, exchanging outward emotionalism for intimate storytelling, and the relatively loose treatment of the score with almost mathematical precision. He softened some of the harshness of Schoenberg's kinetic orchestration.

He received stellar reviews in the press, including Martin Bernheimer of the *Los Angeles Times*, who was underwhelmed by the overall festival. Bernheimer the event as the Philharmonic trying to "assuage its bad conscience" for having "never been particularly responsive to contemporary composers, in general, and to contemporary composers who live in Los Angeles, in particular."[114] He felt the festival bordered on "tokenism," and criticized the "dingy ivory-tower environs of Royce Hall, UCLA." His tone changed when describing the Sunday concert:

> A bleaker aspect of the Schoenberg aesthetic came to the fore in the heart-wrenching "Survivor from Warsaw," which enlists *Sprechgesang* soloist who recounts the tortures of a Nazi death-camp as a prelude to the nearly optimistic eruption of a Hebrew prayer, as intoned by male chorus. Cantor William Sharlin paid more attention to the implied pitches and rhythms of the vocal line than many narrators do in this fragile opus, and intensified its poignance as a result.[115]

Donna Perlmutter of the *Los Angeles Herald Examiner* was more descriptive. She clarified that the Philharmonic was temporarily ousted from its home, the Dorothy Chandler Pavilion, which was being used by the New York City Opera. "Everyone knows that UCLA's gray, unattractive hall wouldn't ordinarily entice subscribers accustomed to the luxe Music Center even with its outstanding acoustics."[116] Of William she wrote, "[he] gave a positively riveting account of the ghetto victim's background, he was better equipped than most to imbue the Sprechstimme with fine detail; the result was a thing of chilling profundity."

William returned to the Schoenberg opus in July of 1987, joining the Los Angeles Philharmonic Institute Orchestra at the Hollywood Bowl under Peter Rubardt, a student fellow. The impressionable young conductor was much more receptive to William's suggestions. However, the *Los Angeles Times* was less kind. Reviewer John Henken did not pull punches: "Institute fellow Peter Rubardt led a glum, toothless account of 'A Survivor from Warsaw,' by Schoenberg. Cantor William Sharlin reduced the narration to clichéd melodrama, and the men of the Pacific Chorale rendered the concluding '*Sh'ma Yisroel*' as a lusty shout."[117] At an ACC conference a little while later, William gave a demonstration on how to perform the narration.[118]

In 1992 William narrated the debut of the organ reduction of Schoenberg's *Kol Nidre* (Op. 39, 1938), a complex reimagining of the Yom Kippur text originally written for speaker, chorus, and orchestra.[119] Among other creative elements, Schoenberg incorporated the creation myth into the *Kol Nidre* text and infused the modernist score with musical "phrases that a number of [traditional] versions had in common and put them into a reasonable order."[120] The organ version premiered during a concert retrospective on Jewish composers from Vienna who escaped the Nazis and settled in Los Angeles.[121] *The Los Angeles Times* noted favorably: "The performance, clearly a labor of love for all concerned, enlisted the services of Cantor William Sharlin, speaking the Yom Kippur-related text with simple dignity; Nick Strimple's Southern California Choral Society, singing with both touching sweetness and climactic heft, and Mark Robson, skillfully projecting [Leonard] Stein's orchestra-into-keyboard conjuration."[122]

On another occasion, William joined Jacqui for a radio performance of Robert Schumann's four-hand work, *Bilder aus Osten*, Op. 66. The couple played the six impromptus on a public radio program hosted by pianist-composer Leonid Hambro (KPFK, January 31, 1984). William had not played piano on the radio since his Manhattan School of Music days, when he performed his own pieces on WKXR, which had an avant-garde bent. Although Jacqui played the lead (treble) and William played the supporting line (bass), he insisted that she control the pedals—a task ordinary given to the bass player. The awkward positioning led to some staggered entrances and uneven executions. Still, the broadcast fulfilled its purpose of promoting a mini-marathon piano concert at Verdi Restaurant, an elegant Los Angeles eatery with an auditorium. The three-hour concert, featuring fourteen pianists and two harpsichordists, was part of Jacqui's campaign to publicize and provide venues for the city's many talented keyboard artists.

4. Leo Baeck Temple, Los Angeles

Father Sharlin

Isaac Sharlin silently admired William's involvement in the cantorate. He knew that LBT was far removed from the world of Orthodoxy. However, as he aged, he slowly eased his strict rule of the family. All of his children were adults, and time and circumstances mellowed his convictions. It is possible as well that he never forgave himself for the agonizing way things transpired with his eldest son Edward. William wrote of his father's feelings in an undated essay:

> When my Orthodox father first heard I had entered the Reform movement professionally as a *hazzan*, his response was silence. It became clear to me that he could be neither critical nor supportive of my decision. He controlled his troubled heart at my move into a virtually foreign religion—what he saw as the epitome of *chukat hagoy*—the manner of the Gentiles. He repressed any expression he might have felt.
>
> He concealed his displeasure because I was a devoted son with whom a rift would surely disrupt his need for peace within the home. Peace was to be preserved at almost any cost—barring intermarriage.
>
> Nevertheless, I was very comfortable joining him in *his* environment during my yearly visits to New York. I would sometimes spend an entire Shabbat with him—going to *shul*, sharing Shabbat meals and, of course, a nap and a stroll. He even showed a touch of pride, albeit in a guarded way, when he introduced me to his acquaintances. My professional vocation was never mentioned; he would just say, "Meet my son from Los Angeles."
>
> It was meaningful enough for him to simply show me as a son at home in his world. After all, I could take on *davening* in his *shul* and I could put on a good show with "small talk"—Yiddish conversation.
>
> There were occasions when I would arrive at his apartment when Shabbat was already in progress. Though I knew he would rather have it otherwise, he would avoid any negative comment, especially since he knew that I would be discreet in parking my car at a very safe distance to avoid embarrassment.[123]

Isaac passed away in 1978 at the age of 88. He spent the final stage of his life in Sherman Oaks, California, not far from William's home. William sensed that his father came to admire that his son had moved into a different (non–Orthodox) world. He still sometimes said, "You could have at least been a Conservative cantor," but it was no longer painful for him. Isaac occasionally visited William at LBT, though he would not enter the sanctuary, where men and women sat together and *kippot* were optional. He never heard his son lead a service. "By that time," William stated in his memoir, "my name was becoming more prominent in the Jewish world. My compositions were being performed at synagogues across the country. Sometimes my father would even attend concerts featuring my work, but would not applaud with the rest of the audience. He never openly praised me, though I know that, behind the scenes, he would talk with pride about me to his friends."[124]

This less than optimal father-son relationship had a positive impact on William's own parenting. He resolved to be anything but an overbearing or uncompromising father. Reminiscences from his daughters Ilana and Lisa are peppered with fondness for his devotion, playfulness, acceptance, generosity, leniency, and ability to make LBT feel like an extension of their home. Despite his busy schedule, he made sure that his daughters were shown unwavering affection and support—a departure from other fathers in his generation. What family time lacked in quantity, it made up for in quality. Ilana writes: "On top of his regular hours at the Temple and the College, his days and nights were filled with choir rehearsals, weddings, *b'nei mitzvahs*, board meetings, funerals, baby namings, visits to the sick and the bereaved and other vital activities."[125] Even so, he never missed an opportunity to praise Jacqui's cooking, drive the girls to school, sing a goodnight song, splurge on a family vacation, or buy the girls what they desired (so long as he was not required to go shopping). This is not to say that home life was always idyllic. William's loaded work schedule and

Isaac Sharlin, 1960s.

4. Leo Baeck Temple, Los Angeles

Halloween, 1968. From left: Jacqui, Lisa, William, Ilana.

occasional bouts with depression put obvious strains on Jacqui. But, for the most part, they managed to shield their daughters from any darkness.

This life was a stark contrast to his own upbringing. His childhood was one of cramped apartments, humble means, and dogmatic stringency. The home he and Jacqui created was just the opposite. Not only were they blessed with many more opportunities, but they also extended a sense of freedom to their daughters. This was most strongly felt when William blessed the marriage of Ilana and Brent, a non–Jewish native of South Africa. "He could see how happy I was," Ilana recalls, "and that this was a relationship of love and respect, and couldn't deny that it was meant to be."[126] His only proviso was that their children be raised in a Jewish home. Their two daughters, Kira and Simona, attend a Jewish day school in Cape Town, where the family resides.

5

Department of Sacred Music, Los Angeles

Jewish higher education came to Los Angeles in 1947 with the establishment of the University of Judaism (now American Jewish University). Rabbi Mordecai Kaplan, the school's "spiritual founder," intended the school to reflect the diversity of Judaic expression in the United States.[1] That aim was only partially fulfilled, as the school had official ties to the Conservative movement. The University of Judaism functioned as the West Coast branch of the Jewish Theological Seminary (JTS), and much of its professional leadership was drawn from JTS graduates.[2] This denominational alliance caused tensions between Conservative and Reform rabbis in Los Angeles, the latter being fearful of Conservative dominance in Jewish higher education, and teacher training in particular.

There was a scarcity of competent religious school teachers in Reform synagogues. Only about 40 percent of teachers had a year or less of adult Jewish education.[3] One rabbi complained, "there is not a single [Reform] religious-school here in Los Angeles with a faculty of teachers worthy to be found teaching in a religious institution. They are *'am ha-artzim'* [ignoramuses] in the truest meaning of the term."[4] Among the perturbed was Rabbi Edgar Magnin, whose influential rabbinate at Wilshire Boulevard Temple (B'nai B'rith until 1933) began in 1915 and spanned an astonishing sixty-nine years. Magnin had long

5. Department of Sacred Music, Los Angeles

advocated for a Los Angeles–based nondenominational school of higher learning. As he put it: "Hebrew is the same; Jewish history is the same; the Talmud is the same. The only difference is whether you want this ritual or that ritual."[5]

Magnin's focus shifted with the founding of the University of Judaism. In an effort to both raise education standards and prevent Conservative hegemony, Magnin teamed with his associate rabbi Alfred Wolf, who also headed the Southern California Council of UAHC. Seeking to train Reform Sunday school teachers and other interested adults, they recruited a handful of Reform rabbis and started the College of Jewish Studies in 1947—the same year as the University of Judaism—with classes held at Wilshire Boulevard Temple. (The University of Judaism originally held its classes at Sinai Temple.) The College of Jewish Studies advertised "popular courses in subjects of Jewish interest and Religious School training as a service to its affiliated congregations and the Jewish community of Southern California."[6]

Support for the fledgling institution was hard to come by. Nelson Glueck, then the newly minted HUC president, initially withheld his blessing. Magnin did, however, manage to solicit the aid of Maurice Eisendrath, the national head of UAHC. In 1948 Cincinnati expressed interest in using the College of Jewish Studies as the "spear-head and recruitment program" for prospective HUC rabbinic students.[7] Glueck made a personal visit to Los Angeles to grant the use of the HUC name, so long as the college found its own financial support. Funding came from local backers and the UAHC.

The dearth of national support limited the school's growth, and its future seemed modest if not bleak. That changed with the arrival of Rabbi Isaiah Zeldin. Zeldin took over Wolf's position as head of the region's UAHC in 1953, and was made dean of the College of Jewish Studies. Much like William, Rabbi Zeldin was born and raised in an Orthodox home in New York City and did not openly rebel against his father's Orthodoxy. He was drawn to the Reform movement as an adult because of its emphasis on the individual and personal choice, as opposed to the ultra-collectivity of the Orthodox system. He graduated from HUC Cincinnati in 1944. His early rabbinate included pulpits in the New York area and a five-year assistant deanship at HUC New York. Throughout his long career, he blended academic rigor, impressive oratory skills, and an entrepreneurial knack.

Within a year of Zeldin's arrival in Los Angeles, enrollment at the college doubled. In 1954 he informed Jack Skirball that a "Rabbinical Department can be accomplished on the West Coast if it is wanted by the Board of the College." Skirball convinced Glueck and the Board of Governors to authorize the plan, along with an initial grant of $10,000 from the HUC budget.[8] Zeldin introduced pre-rabbinic courses and a program for the training of cantors.

Max Helfman was recruited to direct the cantorial program. A recent arrival to Los Angeles, Helfman was a Polish-born composer-conductor who earned notoriety as music director of the Brandeis youth camps. In 1951 Shlomo Bardin, founding director of the Brandeis Camp Institute, closed the camps in Pennsylvania and North Carolina to focus on a new 3,200-acre camp in Santa Susana, California, approximately forty miles from Los Angeles. Helfman, who was dividing his time between the sites, made Los Angeles his permanent residence. Zeldin took notice of Helfman's success as the camp's charismatic music director, and utilized his talents to lay the foundation for a cantorial program.

Zeldin brought in William to help actualize the goal of a "full Department of Sacred Music." In a letter to the young cantor dated May 24, 1954, Zeldin wrote: "We have the beginnings of a good School of Sacred Music. It already has an excellent reputation and a fine student body. The only draw-back is that to date we have been offering only four hours of instruction." He planned to expand instruction to six hours per week, for which William would be paid $3,500 annually—a figure similar to what LBT offered. Zeldin noted William's interest in working with Helfman, and assured him, "My family and I love living in California and think that you will too."[9] Rabbi Zeldin's familiarity with William's abilities was not secondhand. Zeldin taught at HUC New York during William's student days. William excelled in the four courses he had with him: History of Jewish Liturgy (fall '49), History of Jewish Liturgy (spring '50), Liturgical Hebrew (spring '50), and Ancient Jewish History and Liter-

5. Department of Sacred Music, Los Angeles

ature (fall '50). Given William's affinity for those subjects, Zeldin was undoubtedly fond of him from the start.

At first, William taught a Tuesday night class for lay synagogue leaders on music pedagogy for the kindergarten classroom. That was new territory for him. He was not yet fully acquainted with the details of synagogue life, nor the idiosyncrasies of early childhood education. He prepared diligently for each lesson, staying one step ahead of his students and recycling children's songs he used at the Wisconsin camp.

In 1957 Helfman was hired as fulltime dean of the School of Fine Arts at the University of Judaism. He left the HUC affiliate, as well as his positions at the Brandeis Camp and Sinai Temple. William became chairman and adjunct professor of the cantorial curriculum, which gradually developed into the Department of Sacred Music (DSM). He remained with the school for forty years, teaching all areas of synagogue music to cantorial students. He also taught liturgy courses for rabbinic and education students, supervised student-led chapel services, and gave occasional master classes at the HUC campuses in New York and Jerusalem.[10] He briefly offered a one-year program for temple organists and choir directors, which introduced the mostly non–Jewish musicians to the basics of biblical cantillation and *nusach* (modal chant).

Max Helfman died of a heart attack in 1963 at the young age of 62. His failing health and premature death prevented him and William from deepening collegial ties. Still, Helfman lent invaluable support. As William recalled many years later, he faced opposition from established synagogue composers during the early part of his career. "I was considered a newcomer, often in a derogatory sense.... I remember being shrugged off as an arranger—not being respected as a full-fledged composer." Helfman's encouragement helped William overcome his disenchantment: "We had a meaningful, though not terribly close, relationship, and his interest in my work meant much to me."[11]

A crucial next step in the school's maturation was the procurement of accreditation—a prerequisite for offering credit for courses. This necessitated the procurement of a permanent location. Rabbi Magnin rejected the first plan, which would have classrooms at Wilshire Boulevard Temple legally recognized as college property. The second plan was to purchase an abandoned building in the Hollywood Hills that formerly housed Jewish asthmatic girls. Zeldin transferred the pre-rabbinic program there in 1956, along with graduate courses developed by Professor Samuel Cohon, who had retired to Los Angeles from Cincinnati. Classes for educators and laypeople remained at Wilshire Boulevard Temple. Music classes were initially offered in the Hollywood Hills, but next-door neighbors complained about the noise.[12]

Glueck again visited the Los Angeles school in 1957. He met with an accreditation team and was favorably impressed with the operations. Nevertheless, he strongly opposed Zeldin's ambitious proposal to expand the school into undergraduate education. Glueck did not want to compete with Jewish academies of general education, such as Brandeis University. UAHC also grew resentful of the tremendous time and energy Zeldin was putting into the school. Thus, despite garnering a five-fold increase in enrollment in just four years, Zeldin was forced to resign when his contract ended in 1958. He was undeterred. Within a decade he started his own synagogue, Stephen S. Wise Temple, named for the popular and influential rabbi and Zionist leader. By the end of the 1970s, Stephen S. Wise Temple and the University of Judaism were occupying adjacent sites atop Mulholland Drive.

Rabbi Alfred Gottschalk succeeded Zeldin as dean of HUC Los Angeles in 1959. During his tenure, Gottschalk earned a Ph.D. from the University of Southern California (1965). He used his university connections to negotiate a curricular relationship between USC and HUC, and in 1970 ground was broken for a new HUC campus next to USC.[13]

A Department of One

William developed a three-year cantors training program covering the essentials of *nusach*, *hazzanut*, cantillation, liturgy, and peripheral areas. The cycle of courses adhered more or less to the core requirements of the New York campus. Shabbat, Festival, and High Holiday *nusach* and repertoire constituted the basis, with units on historical subjects inserted throughout. The lecture topics are a catalog of William's research interests, including "The Psalms," "Temple Music," "Parallels Between Church

5. Department of Sacred Music, Los Angeles

and Synagogue," "Rossi, De Modena, and the Italian Renaissance," "State of Synagogue Music: East and West, 1700–1850," "Emancipation—Reform—Central Europe: Nineteenth Century," "Israeli Folk Music," and "Hazzan—Precentor."[14] For most of the program's duration, classes met mid-week in the afternoon in LBT's social hall. Tea and cookies were usually provided.[15]

The cantorial program had two central aims: filling knowledge and competency gaps for synagogue soloists, and preparing soloists for entrance examinations to the American Conference of Cantors (ACC). Part of the impetus was a shortage of HUC graduates to fill cantorial positions—especially part-time pulpits at synagogues that could not afford "full-fledged" cantors. Many of the students in the program were already working in synagogues. Some came with strong musical backgrounds but lacked mastery of synagogue song, while others had strong Judaic backgrounds but little vocal or musical training (similar to the situation at SSM in New York).[16]

From the outset there was an agreement with SSM that the Los Angeles program would not culminate in a paper degree. The idea was that students would go through William's courses and then transfer to SSM, which few actually did.[17] Most students were married and/or had other careers, making the prospect of moving to New York unrealistic. (Things were further complicated in 1986 when SSM began requiring students to take their first year in Jerusalem.) To solidify the distinction between the programs—as well as the institutional inferiority of the West Coast campus—William was only granted a department, as opposed to a school. Remarkably, too, it remained a department of one for his entire forty-year tenure. He was the lone instructor.

HUC's uneasiness about a West Coast cantorial program translated to a hands-off approach. William had full control of the curriculum and set his own assessment guidelines, which were minimal at best. Because the program did not include a recognized diploma, it did not require rigid structures to ensure student accountability. Students essentially entered and left the courses of their own accord, some staying for a brief time and others continuing past the three-year cycle. Tuition was also kept low thanks to generous subsidies from the Los Angeles HUC.[18]

Cantor William Sharlin

The program's external looseness should not be confused with laxity. William's high expectations and the pressure of performing for peers were enough to keep most pupils on task. William held students to the same high standards to which he held himself. He was seemingly unable to pay public compliments, even when warranted.[19] His approval came in subtleties, like a raised eyebrow or a rhetorical question, "Now doesn't that feel good? You can feel the difference, can't you?"[20] His own search for perfection made it difficult for him to see beauty in the efforts of others. But he was quick to point out flaws.

Opinions vary as to the root cause of this attitude. A minority saw it as a product of egotism, or a way of demarcating master from disciple. That opinion generally came from those who needed praise to offset their own insecurities. Most others appreciated it as a reminder to keep pushing forward. As William often said, complacency has no place in the sacred craft.[21]

Jacqui Sharlin offered a more intimate view. William did not possess a natural singing voice. Whatever he extracted from the instrument was the product of painstaking labor, sometimes bordering on the obsessive. His personal experience taught him that, without persistent work and a drive for perfection, the voice could never achieve its potential. William tended to project his own vocal deficiencies onto his students, even when they did not exhibit the same shortcomings or were blessed with finer voices. If they were not working as hard as he needed to, they were doing it wrong.[22]

One consequence was a propensity to keep students longer than he should have. Jacqui explained: "There comes a point when the student gets as much as he or she can from the teacher and vice versa. Good teachers know when they're not getting through, and when it's time to positively urge a change." But William "always felt he could make it better."[23]

In his defense, he felt duty-bound to get the best from his pupils, no matter how long it took. In line with Jacqui's observation, he connected this pedagogical agenda to his own search for perfection:

> Some of my students over the years have been very stubborn. They thought they already knew what they needed to know about singing and the cantorial

5. Department of Sacred Music, Los Angeles

world. They were, in a sense, complacent singers, making do with what they had, and were perhaps frightened of the possibility of singing with a totally abandoned voice. This attitude allows for vocal flaws, whatever they may be, to become part of the persona. My main job as a vocal teacher is to help free the singer from his or her self-constructed impediments. The tongue cannot be allowed to interfere with consonants and vowels, the jaw must be loose, the eyebrows must be raised, etc. And, the more one moves upward, the more one lets go. The voice becomes liberated.

In this way, the voice is among the most difficult instruments to teach or learn. The violinist can always buy a better violin, but the singer's instrument is his or her voice—an instrument bogged down by the tensions and complexities of everyday life. It is a living instrument. Sure, there are a select few who are born with natural voices; without taking lessons they sing quite beautifully. This happens once in a while. However, I for one was not born with a great voice; I had to work hard to set it free. Trusting the process, I grew over many years into a cantor.[24]

An example will elucidate the dynamics of the course. Joel Stern began studying with William in the 1980s.[25] Unlike most who entered the program, Joel was not seeking to advance his career in the cantorate. He wished primarily to expand his musical knowledge and gratify his love for synagogue song. He had fulltime employment as a technical writer, and a part-time position as cantor at Temple B'nai Emet in Montebello, a community just east of downtown Los Angeles. The Montebello Jewish community was well past its glory days of the 1940s, when it absorbed a sizable Jewish population that had migrated out of Boyle Heights. In the 1980s, the synagogue's High Holy Day services were still attracting hundreds of multigenerational families, but attendance at weekday and Shabbat services was much smaller, and there were just three or four *b'nei mitzvah* students per year.

Joel first came to admire William through his music. In 1978 he attended a Sunday afternoon concert at Lincoln Center sponsored by the ACC. The pieces William supplied for the program stood out to Joel as exquisite and moving compositions.

Joel came to the pulpit without any formal vocal or cantorial training. An English major at Columbia University, he spent his sophomore year at Yeshiva University to gain knowledge of traditional Jewish texts and practices. After college he studied on a kibbutz in Israel and, returning to New York, earned an M.A. in Jewish literature from the Jewish

Theological Seminary. His Jewish musical exposure came from regular synagogue attendance, six years in the Zamir Chorale in New York, and several years with the Kol Echad Chorale in Los Angeles, founded by Sharlin protégée Cantor Alan Weiner.

When Joel first came to William, he was told bluntly, "You're not ready." He recovered from the sting of rejection and worked privately with Cantor Weiner. He reapplied and was accepted the following year. During his three years of study, the cohort averaged eight students. Joel's observant background gave him an advantage over some of his classmates when it came to Hebrew and *nusach*. However, he was a "blank slate" in terms of vocal technique and other musical areas. The gap was amplified by the presence of conservatory-trained singers in the class. After completing the three-year cycle, for which he received the Saul Silverman Award in music,[26] Stern continued to meet with William privately at his office at Leo Baeck Temple.

Joel found William to be a supportive mentor. Once the cold exterior was cracked, a warm person was waiting to help his students along. From Joel's perspective, William's reticence to give compliments was part of a larger aim of ensuring that cantors stay focused on a "religious intention." The cantor's role is not to be the centerpiece, but a vessel of worship. Flattering words can distract from that ideal. It is also true that, because Joel was not a singer by background, the absence of gushing praise did not bother him as much as it did some of his classmates. He was attuned to William's approach: he offered praise only when he felt it was truly earned.

Another positive experience was that of Mark Saltzman, an opera singer and cantor emeritus of Kol Ami in West Hollywood.[27] Mark spent the early part of his life in Barstow, California, a small city fifty-five miles north of San Bernardino. During that formative period, Barstow's now-defunct synagogue was well connected with HUC in Los Angeles. The institution supplied a steady stream of rabbinic interns, some of whom stayed at Mark's family's home. As a teenager, his musical abilities earned him a role as the synagogue's "default cantor."

Mark moved to Los Angeles at the end of the 1970s after graduating from the music program at the University of California, Irvine. He spent

5. Department of Sacred Music, Los Angeles

a few years working with Cantor Aviva Rosenbloom, the pioneer woman cantor of Temple Israel of Hollywood and a student of William's. Aviva encouraged Mark to pursue formal studies at DSM. He joined a cohort of about a dozen students, and completed the class in two and a half years. He recalls William's keenness in giving students the full picture of synagogue music, "from the very beginning, to that moment—to what he was writing that day." This required sight singing a wide range of material, from chants to art songs to choral works. Weak readers did not escape William's notice. He bore down on them and drilled their individual parts. Mark saw this as "meeting people at their level," although he admits, "William could be harsh.... You could tell when he was not happy. He was sometimes tyrannical but never egotistical. He just wanted you to have it all."

Mark and William forged a lasting bond. Mark made frequent visits to William's home studio in the lower section of the house. William all but lived in that studio, surrounded by shelves over-stacked with music books. Activities centered around a well-worn and rarely in tune upright Yamaha piano. In the studio, William was even more music-obsessed than he was elsewhere. Mark sometimes entered the house through the top section to check in with Jacqui before going downstairs. William invariably became impatient and called out, "That's enough! Time to come down!" This all-business attitude could be difficult for Mark, who preferred his teacher's playful side. He discovered that William loosened up when he was in the garden outside of the studio. He tried to draw him there as often as he could.

Mark began working on compositions with William in the mid–1990s. Mark, who considers himself a tunesmith with popular leanings, used William as a sounding board, particularly when setting Hebraic texts. That did not prevent William from meddling. If he thought a piece was lacking in contrapuntal movement or harmonic density, he would add "Sharlinisms" to fill in the space: fugal patterns, canonic lines, expanded chords, etc. Whereas William could be less concerned with melody, Mark was not always harmonically focused. The combination of interests yielded some stimulating material, including a *niggun* (wordless song) Mark wrote and William arranged, which is a High Holy Day staple at Kol Ami.

Cantor William Sharlin

Contrast this with the experience of Cantor Perryne Anker, a Juilliard-trained singer who is now associate dean of the cantorial school of the Academy for Jewish Religion, California.[28] Perryne's involvement with synagogue music began at age fifteen, when she joined the choir of B'nai Jeshurun in her native Cleveland. She was mentored by the congregation's famed cantor, Saul Meisels, and at eighteen was accepted into the Juilliard opera program. She was a soloist at Rabbi Mordecai Kaplan's Society for Advancement of Judaism, and sang with prominent Jewish composers and cantors, including Sholom Secunda and Richard Tucker, before moving to Los Angeles in the early 1960s.[29] She joined the newly formed Stephen S. Wise Temple in 1964 as a choir member, soloist, and classroom music teacher.

In the early 1970s, the temple's senior cantor and rabbi, Richard Silverman and Isaiah Zeldin, asked her to become the assistant cantor. This was before women were officially allowed in the cantorate. She was advised to enroll in the HUC program. Always one to "do things the right way," she followed the advice.

Perryne recalls being intimidated by William. He reminded her of Sergius Kagen, an imposing Russian pianist, composer, and voice teacher who instructed her at Juilliard. Like William, Kagen spotted every vocal impurity and had little patience for *narishkayt* (trivialities). She dreaded sessions with Kagen, and came to dread William's classes as well. Although William presumably thought highly of her voice, he rarely paused to express his appreciation. He focused instead on her Hebrew pronunciation, which was less than flawless at the time. The absence of overt encouragement was such a hindrance that, on a few occasions, she concocted excuses not to come to class.

In later years Perryne came to love and respect William as an artist and friend. She went back for special coaching when she took senior positions at Temple Beth Sholom in Santa Monica (in 1978) and later at the Temple of the Arts. Even so, she never quite transcended her fear of him. She went on to become a successful cantor and highly regarded vocal coach, mentoring generations of cantors and singers in the Los Angeles area. Her warm and supportive style clashes sharply with William's, and serves to emphasize their fundamental incompatibility.

5. Department of Sacred Music, Los Angeles

Songwriter Debbie Friedman was another of William's students who did not resonate with his approach. She enrolled in the course for just one year (c. 1984).[30] She was already an established star of the American Jewish music scene, with five albums of original songs to her credit (beginning with *Sing Unto God* in 1972) and a successful concert career.[31] Her folk-rock songs, first conceived for the Jewish summer camp, were being integrated into Reform synagogues, spawning numerous admirers and imitators, as well as vehement detractors (especially within the cantorial establishment).[32]

Precisely what brought her to HUC is not clear.[33] She had no intention of becoming a cantor, and her music was popular despite—or perhaps because of—its departure from longstanding synagogue customs. One speculation is that Friedman entered the class at the urging of her mother.[34] Whatever the case, William embraced the opportunity to instill her with the rudiments of synagogue song.

Like many of his colleagues, William had mixed feelings about Friedman's popularity. On one hand, he admired her natural gifts, spiritual conviction, and ability to connect with contemporary Jews. On the other hand, he was troubled by what he saw as a lack of depth in her music. Her trend-setting songs undoubtedly struck a significant chord, but they left something to be desired from a Judaic standpoint. Realizing that liturgical folk-rock was not going away, William felt it wise to educate its central figure. Perhaps she could be inspired to ground her work in synagogue modes or cantillation motifs, thereby exposing her audiences to old customs through new modalities. William was all for innovation, as long as it acknowledged the past.[35]

The experiment fell short. Friedman was at a disadvantage in the classroom. Although she was a natural musician, she could not read notated music. A major part of the curriculum involved learning from songbooks and musical transcriptions; but she was strictly an auditory learner. She would either stay after class to record William singing, or pay other students to make recordings. Because of her reading deficiency, she did not absorb the material quickly and fell behind her classmates. She grew visibly resentful.[36]

Hard feelings were exacerbated by William's reserved personality.

Cantor William Sharlin

Friedman's stature as a popular performer made her accustomed to adoration. His meticulous approach did not allow for the star treatment she evidently expected. Perhaps to his own detriment, his standards did not waver. Friedman left HUC feeling bitter and disinclined to introduce synagogal flavors into her songwriting. It was a squandered opportunity.

    William's students forged a strong and lasting bond. Part of it was the intensity of the learning experience. The high standards gave them a shared sense of accomplishment and professionalism. Part of it was the example William set for them. His emphasis on cantor as "giver" and not "performer" imbued the group with a distinct collective persona. William also remained an active presence in their lives. He was available to answer questions, help with music, give vocal coaching, and offer career advice. There was the charm and profundity of his go-to aphorisms: "A verse or song should never be repeated more than once, unless it has a purpose"; "What is lai? Lai, lai, lai? Such an awful sounding syllable. But la la la.... Ahhh!"[37] And there was a sense that, like William, they were pioneers. As Californians, they were outsiders in a profession dominated by an Eastern establishment—a fact reinforced by their status as associate members of the New York–based ACC.[38] But this was not all bad. Being in the West, they were freer to experiment with their congregations and explore unpaved musical and liturgical roads. As Cantor Alan Weiner explains, "We were driven by authenticity, not by outside forces."[39]

    With each gathering of the ACC, the group was reminded of its place as the "other" in the Reform movement. Most Reform cantors trained at HUC in New York and were granted automatic membership in the organization. Annual conferences were usually held on the East Coast and were monopolized by concerns of that region. Cantors in Western states were ignored. Alan recalls one year in the 1980s when ACC broke with tradition and held the yearly gathering in Snowmass, Colorado. As he chatted with fellow Sharlinites on the hotel deck, the conversation turned to feelings of exclusion and the convenience of having the conference closer to home. They devised a plan to establish a Western region of ACC. They would hold their own meetings and address issues specific to area cantors. A proposal was brought to ACC

5. Department of Sacred Music, Los Angeles

president Cantor Richard Botton. He approved, and other regions followed suit.[40]

Women in the Cantorate

William's program was among the first to accept female students. His motives were not primarily feminist, despite his politically liberal orientation. Rather, he was cognizant of the changing times and Reform Judaism's growing egalitarian emphasis. He saw women in the cantorate as an inevitable outgrowth of that ethos, and determined that they would have to be "as good as the men."[41] They needed access to the same training and the same rigorous professional development.

Whether or not it was his intention, by opening DSM to women William became a trailblazer. Jewish legal consensus had long restricted women from leading public prayers. This is a tangled topic much larger than can be explored here. Without getting bogged down in *halakhic* (legal) minutia, it should be noted that the textual basis for this rule comes from an exhortative statement of Rabbi Sh'muel, a third-century Babylonian sage (c. 220 C.E.). Sh'muel searched for a biblical hook upon which to hang his view that a woman's voice is seductive. He found it in a verse from Song of Songs, in which a young man pleads to his beloved: "Let me hear your voice for your voice is sweet" (2:14). Using an interpretive method common in Talmudic discourse, Sh'muel changed the letters in the word *arev* ("sweet") to read *erva* ("indecent"—i.e., sexually stimulating), thus transforming a romantic and glorifying verse into a dire warning: "A woman's voice is indecent."[42]

Interestingly, this obscure remark was not presented as a law and was not further elucidated in the Talmud. Later authorities nevertheless grabbed hold of it, presumably because it resonated with misogynistic sentiments pervasive in their own times. Some took the extreme position that a man should never listen to a woman sing, while others suggested that a woman's voice should not be heard during prayer. From these varied discussions evolved the principle of *kol isha* ("the voice of a woman"), which at minimum bans women from religious singing.

Cantor William Sharlin

The norm carried into Reform congregations in spite of the movement's abolishment of myriad other "outdated" Jewish regulations. This is largely because the ruling was, as one cantor observes, mostly a cover "to hide what is really the bottom line, which is sexism, and not even so much sexism but self-protection. The people who might not be as qualified as they should be are afraid that a woman might take their job away from them."[43] This kept the cantorate in male hands until women's liberation in the 1970s began influencing liberal synagogues.

William offered his view on the subject in a provocatively titled article, "Why Can't a Woman Chant Like a Man?"[44] He emphasized that *halakha* does not emerge from a vacuum, but accomplishes one of two social aims: the continuance of a practice or the justification for a change in that practice. The first position is generally taken by Orthodox communities, hence the perpetuation of *kol isha* even in the modern-progressive age. The second is more characteristic of the Conservative movement. As the name suggests, the movement approaches change conservatively, adapting Jewish legal discussions to social forces and arriving at careful decisions. In the article, William predicted the eventual acceptance of women cantors in the Conservative movement—a decision that came twelve years after the Reform movement (1975 and 1987, respectively).

The article notes underlying financial motivations for opening the cantorate to women: the decreasing interest of male candidates, women's exploration of new professions, and the willingness of women (especially mothers) to accept part-time positions. These trends have steadily increased in the decades since the article was published.

William was most interested in musical conditions that made Reform communities comparatively open to women's voices. Because Reform congregants were not, by and large, raised or immersed in what William called "the old cantorial culture," there was less shock when women sang the songs of the movement, which essentially consisted of classical and popular-folk. Women soloists in Reform synagogues during the 1970s and 80s were comfortable singing that music, which does not discriminate between male and female voices in the same way as Eastern European *hazzanut*—a genre prominent in Conservative circles.

This led to William's central consideration: the literal implications

5. Department of Sacred Music, Los Angeles

of the question posed in the article, "Why can't a woman chant like a man?" He compared this to questioning the integrity of Bach's keyboard music played on a modern piano:

> *Hazzanut*, that vital musical heritage of our people, did, after all, develop its uniqueness out of the vocal distinctiveness and character of the male singer—the tenor no less. With a Bach prelude and fugue, one might argue that its musical substance is of such pure abstractness, that it loses nothing of its essence when played on a modern keyboard (many even say Bach would have eagerly accepted a well-tempered Steinway grand). But with *hazzanut* the simple transference from male to female voice is a difficult matter. The very heart of *hazzanut*—the indescribable earthiness, texture, taste, and pathos in need of a wide range of color and primitive-like ornamentation, deeply linked with the spontaneity of a male-*davening* congregation, chanted in a language that was almost exclusively reserved for men—should naturally and necessarily be bound up with the male voice.[45]

Instead of taking the simplistic view that a woman's physiology prevented her from chanting like a man, William proposed that a woman should not be expected to imitate the male instrument. Moreover, being a cantor does not require anyone—male or female—to replicate the sound of a different time, context, or vocal type. What is important is sincerity of expression and genuine engagement in the "worship entity." "Ultimately," he concluded, "it is the person that touches the congregant, not the baritone, contralto, tenor, or soprano; and when that happens, he or she will be genuinely identified as a *hazzan*."[46]

That being said, William did not individualize the coursework for women students. Core competencies were expected from all, including fluency in Eastern European modal patterns developed by and for the male (tenor) voice. Several women entered the program, including Perryne Anker and Aviva Rosenbloom, the first women to occupy cantorial positions in Los Angeles in the 1970s (at Stephen S. Wise Temple and Temple Israel of Hollywood, respectively). Other accomplished students included Patti Linsky, cantor emerita of Temple Ahavat Torah in Northridge, California, and Janece Erman Cohen, who continued her studies at SSM. William's daughter, Lisa, also went through the program.

Mention should be made of Dora Krakower, believed to be William's first female cantorial student. Krakower's story, detailed in her published memoir, begins at the Cantors Collegium of the University of Judaism.[47]

Cantor William Sharlin

The program began in the mid–1960s as a Conservative-leaning equivalent to William's curriculum at HUC. Krakower was the only female student in her cohort and did not receive universal acceptance. She was permitted to study, but was told that she could not hold a pulpit. In spite of the restrictive caveat, the Academic Council presented her with the Benjamin Platt Award in 1967 for her work in the collegium. "It had never occurred to me to become a cantor," she explains. "I was primarily intrigued with the study of the chant. But I was alert to any possibility of performance even if I had to initiate it."[48]

That possibility came in 1970. Rabbi Harry Essrig of University Synagogue, a Reform congregation in West Los Angeles, was preparing an experimental Shabbat service that "welcome[ed] women to serve as equal participants in the preservation of the Jewish faith."[49] Essrig invited Krakower to serve as cantor for the groundbreaking service. Needing to brush up on the fundamentals, she made an inquiry to the Los Angeles HUC. She met with William in the fall of 1970, just after the High Holidays. "Cantor Sharlin wanted to know my age," she recollects. "I wouldn't reply. In no way would I take the risk of permitting myself to be prejudged because of my chronological age. He did not pursue the matter. 'I suppose what matters the most is how you relate to a congregation.' He heard me sing and never again questioned my age."[50]

Krakower studied with William in preparation for the University Synagogue service, held on November 21, 1970. A write-up in the *Los Angeles Times* noted: "Rabbi Harry Essrig and Cantor Barry Hyams took back seats to women last week when Dora Krakower chanted services as [University Synagogue] and Sisterhood officers delivered sermonettes." It was heralded as a "breakthrough" and a "first in Southland Reform Jewry."[51]

Krakower was afterward invited into HUC's DSM. Her entrance was again conditional: she would not be able to study biblical cantillation. It was thought that giving the ritual to women would be so controversial as to imperil their entrance into the cantorate. Krakower protested: "If I am to be in the program, it has got to be all or nothing." William hesitated for a moment. "O.K. You're in."[52]

Krakower excelled in her studies, earning the Saul Silverman Award.

5. Department of Sacred Music, Los Angeles

The *B'nai B'rith Messenger* of July 16, 1971, quoted William, who cited her "great passion for cantorial music and deep sensitivity for its style" and her "dedication, musical ability and scholarship."[53] The award was not an act of favoritism or an attempt to draw attention to the program. While cynics may have viewed the honor as a ploy to publicize women's competency as pulpit leaders, such a scheme would have clashed with William's character. Publicity was of little interest to him, and unwarranted accolades were against his nature.

Some time later, William asked Krakower to sub for him at LBT while he was away at summer camp. She jumped at the opportunity. It was the first time she chanted publicly from the Torah. She recounts: "The comments of my work were very complimentary, but I was acutely aware of a reserve, a latent attitude of hostility towards a woman cantor. I became discouraged. 'I don't feel that I belong,' I told Cantor Sharlin. But he replied, 'Stay with it, Dora.'"[54]

Like most of William's students, male and female, Krakower came to the program with prior experience in Jewish sacred singing. She had been singing music of Jewish content since the late 1940s. Cantor Anker was already employed at Stephen S. Wise Temple. Stories like these appear in the biographies of almost all of William's students. His curriculum catered to their unique needs as active singers in Jewish contexts.

This stands in interesting contrast to Barbara Ostfeld-Horowitz, the first woman to earn a cantorial degree from SSM in New York. Horowitz was inspired by Sally Priesand, HUC's first female rabbinical student, who was in line for graduation in 1972. SSM lowered the requirements in its eagerness to guide a woman to cantorial investiture. Horowitz describes the situation: "I was seventeen. I had never gone to Hebrew school…. As far as my Judaic background, it was a child's Judaic background…. They put a Hebrew prayer book in front of me and I said, 'I'm sorry, gentlemen, I can't read.' And they were astonished. Why they accepted me, I can't tell you."[55]

William would have told someone of Horowitz's background to reapply when she was ready. He would have cringed at the political considerations that drove SSM's decision. He had no resistance to women entering the profession, and "saw the writing on the wall."[56] But his high expectations were applicable to all.

Horowitz nevertheless persevered, becoming the first officially invested woman cantor at her graduation in 1975. In recent years, SSM has seen its cantorial enrollees shift to a female majority. The Conservative movement's Jewish Theological Seminary, which began investing women cantors in 1987, boasts similar statistics, as do the transdenominational seminaries, such as the Academy for Jewish Religion, California. These figures confirm a study published in 1981, showing upward trends in female enrollment at Jewish and Protestant theological schools.[57]

A Serious (but Not So Serious) Man

William's demeanor changed as he became more established in the field. By the 1980s he was noticeably less tolerant when others fell short of his expectations. He was temperamental with colleagues and moody around the house. He consumed himself in various projects, often at the expense of family and friends. He would lose track of the audience during a lecture because he was so absorbed in what he was saying. He had little interest in socializing or material things, sometimes to the aggravation of those closest to him.

These personality developments came with a name change. Up to that point, he had been known as "Bill"—a hypocorism connoting intimacy and informality. It was a name well suited for a guitar-playing song leader; but it conflicted with William's self-image as a serious cantor, scholar, and composer.

When he first announced the change to "William," many assumed it was a joke.[58] He enjoyed the discussion it stimulated, and took pleasure in correcting those who slipped up and called him "Bill." Even Jacqui struggled with the change, finding it easier to call him by his Yiddish name Velvel. But it was hardly a trivial matter. Sheldon Merel remarks: "Bill was always Bill, but as he matured and became the chairman at HUC and respected in his community, he saw himself more seriously.

5. Department of Sacred Music, Los Angeles

The shift was physical, too. Bill was too familiar. The change occurred within him, too. He began pulling away."[59]

Evidence of the change appears as early as 1984.[60] "Bill" with a mustache became "William" with a beard.[61] Some saw it as a cover for self-doubt and insecurity.[62] Others viewed it as a response to the injustice of never being promoted above adjunct professor.[63] William spoke of the lack of respect shown to him, especially by the Eastern establishment.[64]

This does not mean that William lived in a perpetual state of solemnity. As he told his daughters, "It's okay to take yourself seriously, but not too seriously."[65] His sense of humor often peaked through his compositions. There are overt examples, like the choral setting of *Hinei Ma Tov* (after a Hasidic Festival melody), which has a sixteen-measure optional ending that sets the Hebrew to the iconic opening bars of Beethoven's Fifth Symphony. The winter holiday song, "*Ch...*," sets "White Christmas" and *Ma'oz Tzur* as counter melodies (the title refers to the simultaneity of *C*hristmas and *C*hanukah). A canon setting of *Sim Shalom* bears the subtitle "Play a Round for Peace."[66] A more subtle play is heard in the recurring motif of a flatted sixth, fifth, and root in several of his pieces. This "inside joke" was his musical cryptogram, following in the footsteps of Bach and Shostakovich (though without direct reference to an alphabet).[67]

In the interpersonal realm, too, there are stories of endearment. For instance, William used to play with Hebrew words and philological speculations. These "brain games" were shared with Rabbi Bill Cutter, an HUC colleague who lived close to the Sharlins.[68] When Bill Cutter began teaching Hebrew literature at HUC Los Angeles in 1965, he

Press photograph, 1990s.

Cantor William Sharlin

was eager to meet Leonard Beerman—the social-activist rabbi with a national reputation. LBT's associate rabbi, Sanford Ragins, pulled him aside and said: "We have a cantor who's more important than the rabbis." Bill set up a lunch with William. Descriptions of the deeply knowledgeable cantor with an Orthodox background intimidated him; he was afraid to eat the wrong thing. Tensions eased when William ordered a bacon, lettuce, and tomato sandwich.

The two connected over a shared interest in music and the Hebrew language. William embraced Bill, eighteen years his junior, as his protégé and Shabbat walking companion. As they strolled the neighborhood together, they exchanged bad jokes in between creative insights on musical and linguistic matters. Bill was mesmerized by William's dexterity with Hebrew, Yiddish, and English.

William also retained close and jocular ties with his old friend Joseph Glaser. Following his ordination in 1956, Joseph took a rabbinic position at Temple Beth Torah in Ventura, California. That put him in close proximity to the HUC campus, where he served as registrar and instructor for the duration of his Ventura employment (1956–1959). After that, he was made director of the Northern California/Pacific Northwest Region of UAHC (1959–1971). In that capacity, he also directed the Saratoga Camp, where William spent many summers as music leader. For two decades, then, William and Joseph were geographically connected: from Cincinnati to Los Angeles to Saratoga. (After 1971 Joseph served as executive vice president of the Central Conference of American Rabbis in New York, a position he held until his death in 1994.)

William and Joseph's friendship is memorialized in a series of letters. In one letter Joseph wrote: "Forgive me, I cannot get used to 'William.' You are my oldest and dearest friend in this rabbinic chapter of my life and at this point, I am not going to make myself in any way uncomfortable by trying to get used to a name that really doesn't mean very much to me. So there!" (February 3, 1994). A little over two months later, Joseph sent William another letter congratulating him on his upcoming honorary doctorate of humane letters, conferred by HUC in June of 1994.

> Our close personal friendship aside, I cannot think of anyone more worthy of honors such as this than you. Indeed, I can go so far as to say that you are the

5. Department of Sacred Music, Los Angeles

one that brings honor to the degree and to the institution more than it to you.

You are a superb, and unique, combination of strength, gentleness, artistry, scholarship, spiritual power and practical wisdom. You are independent, yet utterly loyal. You are a hard working, completely reliable fulfiller of the mundane goals and purposes which are the essential fabric of life and you have a grand vision that will always be before you. You are the music in so many of our lives.

William wrote back to Joseph after joining him for the June ceremony. Joseph was battling lung cancer (he died three months later), and William's emotions were not concealed:

> Your invitation to join with you June 1st brought me the deepest fulfillment—a high moment in my life and the life of the Glaser-Sharlin bond. The heart and eloquence of tribute to you moved me to tears. The summit of it all and perhaps the sum of it all was the experience of hearing you express so beautifully the essence of mind and spirit of your being—as a Jew and as a human.... I cannot recall the service very clearly Joseph, because, I believe I was so caught up in the stream of prayer and healing—it was as if I had entered a cloud but everything purified. So may it be for you brother Joseph.... To stand side by side with you in prayer completed the circle of past and present.

Scholarship and Composition

William's position at HUC gave him a platform to disseminate his thoughts on synagogue music. He became a noted authority, sought-after lecturer, and occasional contributor to popular and academic periodicals. The demands of work prevented him from being a prolific scholar. Most of his essays are small in scope.[69] Nonetheless, the originality and quality of writing place him in the august line of HUC music professors Abraham Z. Idelsohn and Eric Werner. In contrast to these men, whose work is weighed down with technical jargon, William was a public scholar: his arguments were sophisticated and thought provoking, but never beyond the grasp of the interested layperson. Although he was capable of detailed comparative and formal analyses, he wrote as a philosopher and critic. He addressed topics that concerned him as a practitioner: *davenning* and congregational singing; particularism and universalism; privacy and performance; insider and outsider musicians;

listening music and group song; diversity and mainstream; secular and sacred; past and future; rabbi and cantor.

An example is his most popular essay, "When the *Chazzan* 'Turned Around,'" published in the *Central Conference of American Rabbis Journal* (1962).[70] Like his music, the essay is compact (under 750 words) yet demonstrates penetrating insight and careful construction. It proposes that of all the worship changes that accompanied the rise of the Reform movement in the nineteenth century, the one that most affected the "*inner* character of worship" was the turning of the cantor (*chazzan*) to face the congregation. For centuries, it was customary for the cantor to face the ark. It was a paradoxical space from which he led the assembly, yet isolated himself in his "innermost thoughts" and the "power of solitude." With back turned to the people, the cantor achieved a state of spiritual abandon that gave rise to the "primitive and expressive characteristics of *Chazzanuth*."[71] The spontaneity was infectious: the congregation, in turn, experienced a quality of freedom.

Fast forward to the modern Reform synagogue. Cantors face the congregation and only rarely turn toward the ark. Privacy is replaced with self-consciousness, and inward expression with outward performance. As William put it: "Instead of praying alone as part of the Assembly they now lead in prayer, an experience that is as static as it is mechanical." Congregants respond to the cantor's self-awareness with insecurity of their own; they are stifled by a dependency on the pulpit. Recognizing the impossibility of returning to an older mode of worship, William suggested that the cantor "reconsider 'turning around' but not in a physical sense. Perhaps the challenge is to find seclusion and true prayer by turning around without moving at all."[72]

"When the *Chazzan* 'Turned Around'" continues to resonate in the cantorial community. William gave offprint copies to his students.[73] It is a go-to essay in cantorial courses,[74] and appears in syllabi of international universities.[75] It is addressed in academic articles,[76] and is frequently discussed among rabbis and cantors.[77]

Much of William's scholarship bears the imprint of Eric Werner. This does not mean William was merely an expositor of his mentor's ideas. Rather, their thoughts converged on important matters. A point

5. Department of Sacred Music, Los Angeles

of intersection involves their reviews of significant books on scriptural cantillation: Solomon Rosowsky's technical treatise, *The Cantillation of the Bible: The Five Books of Moses* (1957), and Abraham W. Binder's practical guidebook, *Biblical Chant* (1959).[78] Published roughly a year apart (April 1959 and June 1960 respectively), the reviews not only demonstrate their mutual interest, but also reveal their shared scholarly temperament.

Eric tackled Rosowsky's lengthy tome. Considered the cantor-scholar's "magnum opus,"[79] it scientifically elucidates the musical and grammatical aspects of biblical cantillation, sparing no ink in the process. Although commending the author (then a professor at JTS's Cantors Institute) for his "enormous enthusiasm, his great patience, his fresh and boldly original approach [and] his loving care over the grammatical and musical minutiae,"[80] most of the review highlights earlier sources that Rosowsky either ignored or failed to acknowledge: "Rosowsky ... bypasses all these efforts [of musical notation] in almost complete silence; I do not know whether it should be construed as a sign of disapproval or as lack of knowledge."[81]

William mirrored this approach in his review of Binder's *Biblical Chant*. The book includes musical illustrations for the six systems of scriptural chant in Ashkenazi communities.[82] While William applauded the author's success in "organiz[ing] the system of biblical accents (*te'amim*) and their various musical realizations into a systematic and practical order," he, too, dwelled on the book's omissions:

> [W]hen Dr. Binder discusses the events leading up to the writing of his book, the reader might possibly assume that the author is the first to notate cantillation. He fails to mention the numerous publications which have appeared during the past 100 years—including the great pioneering work of Idelsohn—all of which contain detailed notation of many systems. While they do not have the practical organization of Dr. Binder's work, they nevertheless exist.[83]

The similarities between these reviews are obvious. Eric gave William an inscribed copy of his review, but it is unclear if this was before or after his own review was published. If obtained before, we can presume that Eric's review informed William's observations. If received after, perhaps Eric was excited to show convergences between them.

Cantor William Sharlin

William was then in the early stage of his career, so either scenario is possible. Of the two, Eric's review is more thorough and authoritatively written—partly because Rosowsky's book is more sophisticated and partly because of the magnitude, breadth, and maturity of Eric's scholarship. But William's is bolder. Binder was his professor at HUC, and they both taught cantillation to Reform students.[84] Added to that, the review appeared in the main scholarly periodical of the Reform movement, the *Central Conference of American Rabbis Journal*. Chutzpah was another trait William and Eric had in common: they had the audacity of the uncompromising seeker of truth, no matter whose feathers were ruffled along the way.

William also composed pieces for HUC students. As with his service music, these pieces served practical purposes and filled particular voids. Largely because of this approach, most of William's music is unpublished, undated, and without clues of context. Even his published compositions and arrangements—a small portion of his oeuvre—were often written years before they came into print.[85] A rare exception is his setting of *Ahavah Rabah* ("With Abounding Love"), a prayer of gratitude for the gift of Torah and the ability to put its teachings into practice. Although the sheet music is undated, it is a stand-alone melody with a discernable backstory.

William was a master of composition and the Hebrew language. The two streams flowed together in his works. Very rarely do his melodies move in a simplistic direction, and never are they rigid frameworks into which words are merely placed. His approach was logogenic, or word-born: words form the basis for musical contours and patterns. His interpretation of texts would sometimes result in wide interval leaps, syncopated phrases, non-diatonic pitches (esp. chromaticism and whole tones), and other dramatizing techniques. For many cantors, his music demands more practice than it is worth, given how averse most congregations are to "sophisticated" sounds and "listening" music.[86]

Ahavah Rabah is one instance where William exerted his musical sensibilities in an accessible manner. He never embraced the Ashkenazi folk-like melody commonly sung in morning services, which has little to do with the text—both in terms of mood (a love song in gloomy minor)

5. Department of Sacred Music, Los Angeles

and language (awkward placement of syllables and repetition of words to fit the tune). "Like many songs used for the Jewish liturgy," William frowned, "it is simply a melodic shell into which the holy text is stuffed."[87] His own setting grew from a liturgy class for rabbinic students, where they discussed the importance of text in worship music. He distributed the sheet music, and invited the students into the melody.

The music is not instantly assimilated. Subtle changes abound in the soft melodic line, which is broken into four verses alternating between the keys of F and Ab major. The phrases are syncopated to accommodate the syllabic distribution and shift between three and two measures, thus departing from the ubiquitous four-bar phrasing of Western music. This allows for surprising turns, both within a verse and as one verse moves into the next. Unusual chord progressions are present throughout, with roughly half of the markings indicating compound or "slash" chords.[88] With a few exceptions, there are two chords for each four-beat measure, creating intricate colorations. For instance, for the first two verses: (m.1) F, Gm/F, (m.2) Bb/F, Bbm/F, (m.3) Fsus, (m.4) F, Gm/F, (m.5) Bb/F, Bbm/F, (m.6) F; (m.1) Ab, Bbm/A6, (m.2) Ab7, Dbm/Ab, (m.3) Fm, Bb9/F, (m.4) Db, Bb, (m.5) Db7, Fsus.

William described presenting the piece to his students:

> When I introduced the new melody I knew the students would not take to it right away—I had to be patient. Added to that, most of them did not jump for joy when they first heard it; they were so used to the old tune. But I introduced it with my heart and soul, and they eventually accepted the melody as their own. In fact, when this group of rabbis graduated from the school, they presented me a beautiful manuscript of the *Ahavah Rabah* music I had composed. I still occasionally hear this melody sung at rabbinic conventions. The piece made an impact.[89]

As noted, *Ahavah Rabah* is illustrative of William's text-first compositional process. The chief inspirations for his word-centered approach were Ernest Bloch and biblical chant. William was near obsessed with Bloch's *Sacred Service*. He sang the full service with choir and orchestra on several occasions,[90] and incorporated sections into the LBT repertoire. The music is through-composed and motif-heavy—both of which allow room for the text to direct the flow of the melody. William was especially taken by Bloch's comment on the *Sacred Service*: "I know [the liturgy's] significance word by word.... But what is more important, I have absorbed it to the point that it has become mine and as if it were the very expression of my soul."[91] These words could have come from William himself.

Cantillation, which likewise captivated William, is an even more word-centric musical system. Melodic motives are subordinate to and directed by the syntax and punctuation of the verses. Its movements and melismata are "word-born" rather than independently produced. William used to listen to chanted passages and anticipate the next trope marking by ear. He internalized the logic of the linguistic-musical system, and knew where the chant was headed without reference to the printed accents. He also applied trope markings to liturgical texts of non-biblical origin, such as *Se'u She'arim Rosheichem* ("O Gates, Lift Up Your Heads"), which he set to Torah cantillation for Shabbat mornings.[92] He was overjoyed to receive a copy of Joshua Jacobson's 2002 book, *Chanting the Hebrew Bible: The Complete Guide to the Art of Cantillation*—a mathematical tome of nearly 1,000 pages covering the history and technical points of this musical grammar.[93] William wanted the most he could get on a subject, and *Chanting the Hebrew Bible* offered rare satiation (unlike Binder's ultra-practical guidebook).

Intimacy with language was the foundation of all of William's music. It was the sacred platform upon which he laid his "musical building blocks." He elucidated a handful of pieces during a concert-lecture for the 1989 UAHC Biennial Conference. His description of *Eilu D'varim* is particularly relevant. The didactic text of mishnaic origin customarily comes in the beginning of the morning service. It lists "obligations without measure, whose reward, too, is without measure."[94] For the setting, he envisioned two yeshiva students studying the text together. Two voices interact in an improvisation-like dialogue, clashing with dissonances, interrupting with soaring phrases, and eventually coming to musical resolution. Each voice performs the text in a free and naturalistic style, mimicking the patterns of a heated conversation. All the while, the organ plays a simple and disciplined supporting line. In William's conception, the steady accompaniment represents the fixed text, while the spontaneous-like voices portray the energizing force giving life to the words.

5. Department of Sacred Music, Los Angeles

Attention is also owed to the Kol Echad Chorale, directed by Cantor Alan Weiner. The ensemble was established in 1975, while Alan studied at DSM.[95] A Cal Arts graduate and conductor, Alan imagined taking over the Roger Wagner Chorale when its famed music director retired. He mentioned this to his friend as they applied Asiatic makeup for Puccini's *Turandot*. They were part of an expanded chorus that joined the New York City Opera for a Los Angeles run. Alan's friend said, "Don't do that, start a Jewish choir." And so he did.[96]

Alan wanted to bring the best Jewish concert music to Southern California audiences. The mostly volunteer Kol Echad Chorale sang for roughly two decades. At times, it comprised over thirty singers and a chamber orchestra contracted by Alan's wife, cellist Amy Simon-Weiner. The chorale performed at Jewish and non–Jewish venues,[97] debuted works,[98] made radio and television appearances,[99] and received write-ups in major newspapers.[100] It was touted as the "premier Jewish choral group in the West" and concertized throughout the year.[101]

Kol Echad was an important platform for William's music. From the beginning, Alan programmed William's pieces alongside music by composers past and present, such as David Nowakowsky, Marc Lavry, Darius Milhaud, Ernest Bloch, Leonard Bernstein, and Aminadav Aloni. Alan sometimes contributed his own compositions.[102]

One concert deserves special mention. It was the final event of the 1990–91 season of the Friends of Jewish Music, an umbrella organization Alan set up to showcase musical acts beyond the chorale. The other concerts that year included "Jewish-American Sound" pioneers SAFAM!, Elizabeth Swados's antic and anachronistic *Esther: A Vaudeville Megillah*, and Morton Gold (composer) and Harold Lerner's (librettist) oratorio, *Haggadah: The Search for Freedom*, featuring Cantor Sheldon Merel. The program of William's music, aptly called "Tradition and Modernity," offered "diverse compositions reflecting the tradition of the past and the musical world of modernity."[103] Solo parts were given to bass-baritone Cantor Boris Kazansky of Rodeph Shalom, Philadelphia, and mezzo-soprano Cantor Laura Croen, who assumed the LBT pulpit after William's retirement in 1988.

"Tradition and Modernity" featured stunning orchestrations for most of the twenty-one selections. William entrusted Alan with converting keyboard accompaniments into parts for a sixteen-piece chamber orchestra.[104] For the remaining keyboard parts, William and Shirl Lee Pitesky rotated duties with Kol Echad accompanist Ty Woodward. The result was a re-imagining of some of William's more familiar compositions and arrangements. The delicate distribution of the music to multiple instruments helped bring out the intricacies of William's ideas, and highlighted the careful design of each piece. Of course, William was not wholly satisfied with the outcome. Although he considered it a high point of his career, Alan remembers, "Even the night of the performance he was giving me notes—little things that were very important to him."[105]

There was a downside to William's perfectionism. Unlike most professional composers, he did not turn out pieces for the sake of remuneration. He made very little from his published works, and most of his music never reached a publishing house. This was not due to a lack of interest in his music.[106] But, as a meddling perfectionist, he was not as prolific as he could have been, and much of his oeuvre consists of miniatures averaging two minutes apiece. Jacqui explained:

> Something that he wrote—it could have been a phrase, or not even a full phrase—but something bothered him about it, which you or I would be unaware of, he would return to it again and again and again. When I see how other people turn compositions out—particularly professionals—they all learn that you've got to let it go and move on to the next thing. But William felt his pieces had to get better and better.[107]

6
Saratoga, California

Shortly after taking the pulpit and beginning his professorship, William was engaged as song leader at the NFTY Camp for Living Judaism in Saratoga, California, about an hour's drive from San Francisco. Formerly the estate of Kathleen Norris, a popular early twentieth-century author, the campsite sprawled over 208 acres, much of which was unusable canyon land. The Camp Saratoga Committee bought the property for $150,000 with a down payment gift of $25,000 from Ben Swig, the philanthropic owner of San Francisco's Fairmont Hotel. The site was later renamed Camp Swig.

The Camp for Living Judaism opened in 1953 with Rabbi Wolli Kaelter as founding director. Wolli was born in Danzig, Prussia (now Gdansk, Poland), on February 12, 1914. The son of a rabbi, he expressed an early desire to follow in the footsteps of his father, who died when he was just eleven. In 1935 Wolli was one of five students from the Berlin Rabbinical Seminary rescued from Nazi oppression and brought to study in the United States. He was ordained at HUC Cincinnati in 1940, and served congregations in Pennsylvania, Illinois, and Arkansas before joining the staff of UAHC.

When Wolli settled in Saratoga with his wife and two children, the camp had little to recommend it. The opening session was "over-subscribed" with 120 campers: "[T]he dishes had not yet arrived, we had no functioning toilets, and we were short of bedding."[1] Yet, the camp survived until 2008, transforming thousands of boys and girls into Jewish enthusiasts.

Cantor William Sharlin

Wolli resigned as camp director after just three summers. He explained the decision in his autobiography (with a hint of self-pity): "[W]hen the third summer rolled around, I was still tired from the second. It was an unbelievably demanding job. Everything rested upon me, from the functioning of the toilets to the programming, despite the fact that other rabbis were there and assumed responsibilities."[2] The camp continued Wolli's mission, which mirrored that of the Oconomowoc location: social justice (which he called "prophetic Judaism") and a vitalizing immersive experience in Jewish identity.

Another major player at Saratoga was Samuel Kaminker, an inspiring teacher and youth leader "who exerted a lasting influence on all those who came in contact with him."[3] Samuel was born in Naroditch, Ukraine. As a young boy he moved to Chicago, where his rabbi-father assumed the pulpit of a Hasidic congregation. Samuel was drawn to the Zionist youth movement, and in 1931 joined the newly formed Chicago chapter of Hashomer Hatzair (a secular Socialist-Zionist youth organization). That experience inspired a lifetime of involvement in the Jewish camping movement.

During World War II, Samuel served as a recruiter and director of Jewish youth volunteers for Victory Gardens, which planted vegetable, fruit, and herb gardens in public parks and private residences to ease pressure on the national food supply. He was then appointed director of Camp Avodah and supervisor of youth activities for the Chicago Board of Jewish Education. He moved to California in 1948 and held positions with B'nai B'rith Youth Organizations, the Los Angeles Bureau of Jewish Education (BJE), and the Union Hebrew High School, which he helped establish.

Samuel was also director of education, youth, and camping activities for the Western States Region of UAHC. In that capacity he was instrumental in developing Camp Saratoga. In 1954 he spearheaded the camp's Solel Unit, which aimed to stimulate campers' interest in Hebrew as a living language. Joining him were Irving Sores of the Los Angeles BJE, and Wolli's wife Sarah, an experienced Hebrew teacher.[4] Samuel remained active in the camp until his untimely death in 1964. A eulogy published in the journal *Jewish Education* described him as "a warm and vibrant personality, with an indefatigable capacity for resourceful work, constantly in search of something new, something different."[5]

Creating Summer Camp Music

William was hired as camp song leader in 1955, the year Wolli resigned. He spent summers there through the 1970s, and made regular appearances thereafter. It was a way of life for the Sharlin family. William took time off from LBT each summer. Jacqui, who had friends in nearby Los Gatos, came along.[6] Their daughters were "staff brats" until they were old enough to be campers. Lisa stayed on as a camp song leader, and contributed a popular setting of *Yom Zeh L'Yisrael*.[7]

Prior to William's arrival, counselors assigned to other duties led informal song sessions. He was hired to "take singing to the next level."[8] Campers sang after meals, during services, and at other designated times. William created an inviting balance between American folk and protest songs and Hebrew songs pulled from the liturgy and the young State of Israel. He kept the goal of memorization from the Oconomowoc camp: "[S]ongs were written on large pieces of butcher paper and posted around the *chadar ochel* [dining hall] during the week, and they would be taken down for Shabbat, by which time the campers had memorized the songs."[9]

Much of the music William brought to Saratoga came from his Oconomowoc repertoire, including folk songs from the Weavers, Woody Guthrie, and the Kingston Trio, songs of Israeli *chalutzim* (pioneers), like "Zum Gali Gali," "Ufaratzta," and "Tzena Tzena" (also popularized by the Weavers), an occasional Yiddish melody, selections from the 1940s Jewish Agency songbook, and hymns adapted from the Reform *Union Songster* (1960).[10]

As time passed, he began incorporating music of Neo-Hasidic musician and spiritual leader, Shlomo Carlebach. Shlomo was a guest at the camp during summer session. He made a strong and lasting impression on William.[11] They shared a maverick streak and a mission of outreach through music.

Cantor William Sharlin

Shlomo was born in Berlin in 1925 into a line of Orthodox rabbis. The family moved to Baden, Austria in 1930, escaped the Nazis to Lithuania in 1938, and arrived in Brooklyn in 1939. Shlomo became immersed in Hasidic worship, and began writing simple settings of short Hebrew phrases drawn from the liturgy. The tunes captured the musical essence and ecstatic flavor of Hasidic *niggunim* (wordless or nearly wordless songs), but incorporated guitar strumming and a countercultural aesthetic.

Although he received *smicha* as a rabbi, Shlomo left the pulpit and avoided the title. He found his place among young people estranged from their Jewish heritage. He frequented cafés and college campuses throughout the 1950s, singing his simple, infectious melodies, and spreading a message of love, peace, and spiritual connection. He eventually broke from the Lubavitcher movement, which frowned upon his use of simplified liturgical texts and his co-ed gatherings of young Jews of all persuasions (called *Kumzitz*; Yiddish for "come, sit").

In 1959 Shlomo produced the first of some twenty-five albums (many unauthorized recordings were also distributed during and after his lifetime). These albums represent a small fraction of his melodies, which are estimated at nearly one thousand—with quite a bit of repetition and recycling of musical ideas. He remained a tremendously popular and influential performer until his death in 1994.[12]

William's acceptance of Shlomo's music provides a window into his thinking on synagogue song. William had a deep interest in classical Hasidic music (mid–1700s to the early 1900s), but saw a corruption of style and motivation in later imitative practices. The Neo-Hasidic phenomenon, which Shlomo headed, contributed to a culture of simplistic sing-alongs in liberal American synagogues. For William, Shlomo embodied something of the irretrievable past. He was imbued with an authentic spirit, stemming from his background and singular personality. In William's assessment, the conditions that gave rise to Hasidism in Eastern Europe could not (and should not) be reproduced on American soil. Attempting to retrieve the emotions of that time and place would be at best unrealistically nostalgic, and at worst damagingly misleading. Shlomo was an exception, not the rule.

William addressed the issue at an international conference in 1975.[13]

6. Saratoga, California

He criticized the eagerness with which congregations seize upon Neo-Hasidic songs. "At the heart of this change," he said, "is a sliding into secularity."[14] In his analysis, the bulk of Neo-Hasidic music does not, as some contend, infuse sanctity into communities consumed by secularity, but rather feeds into that environment by borrowing from secular idioms and appealing to ordinary musical needs: entertainment, feeling good, lively rhythms, effortless involvement. "There are some tunes that approach the genuineness of the folk as well as the classical Hasidic quality," he acknowledged. "[Yet there] are others that attempt to achieve this end but result in a sad mixture of the contrived and the pop. And finally there are those tunes which are wholly permeated with the pop, totally commercial in character."[15] He cautioned: "A [classical] *niggun* was never rushed! Space in time was understood as a prerequisite for entrance into the energy of the tune."[16] Furthermore, the use of the songs to cultivate a frame of mind contrasts with the original function of adding to a pre-existing state. For the Hasidim, the *niggun* was an add-on to devotion; for modern worshipers, it is a stand-in for true devotion. He reiterated this point in another lecture some twenty years later: "In the past the role of the music was not to stimulate the intensity, but to take an existing spiritual condition and to elevate it into a higher and higher realm, a deeper and deeper realm."[17]

There are no re-settings of Shlomo's tunes in William's catalog, which includes numerous arrangements of synagogue standards. The sole reference to Shlomo appears in William's *Ahavah Rabah*. The piece ends with a segue to the unaltered singing of Shlomo's *Vehaeir Eineinu*, a song that premiered at the first annual Hasidic Song Festival in Israel in 1969.[18] It is a typical Neo-Hasidic (read: pop) song: two contrasting eight-bar sections, the second in a higher register; logical melodic sequence; three-chord harmony (I, IV, V); and a short text taken from a larger prayer (Ps. 121:1–2).[19] The fact that William left it alone indicates his respect for the simple yet effective melody.

This was not the case for other Neo-Hasidic songs. For instance, William was not satisfied with Nurit Hirsch's popular setting of *Oseh Shalom*, which also debuted at the 1969 Hasidic Song Festival. Already in the early 1970s, William felt the song's exuberant reception waning (although it is still widely sung). His "salvaging" arrangements include a setting for four-part choir, keyboard, and horns, and a version for three voices (high, medium, and low) and keyboard.[20]

The heady topic of musical appropriateness was reserved for heady crowds. William was careful to meet the campers at their level. Camp was not the place for in-depth "insider" discussions, as much as they occupied William's private thoughts. His role was to inspire by example, and to translate philosophical concerns into accessible experiences.

He recalled one session with particular fondness. A delegation of Jewish organizational leaders from San Francisco visited the camp. Most impressive to them was the lively Shabbat service put on by the students and counselors, with William at the helm. The lessons of the week became the focal point of the highly musical service. The presentation convinced the visitors that they were witnessing a new generation of active, joyous, and committed American Jews.

Another memorable routine occurred during "Upside Down Day" each session. There would be breakfast for dinner, evening activities in the daytime, and so forth. William would drive his small Volkswagen into the dining hall, hop out, and begin singing.

During the 1960s, William also served as dean of NFTY's Song and Dance Leaders' Institute, held at the newly opened Kutz Camp in Warwick, New York. There were usually about eight students in attendance. Among them were Jeff Klepper and Dan Freelander, who would become pioneers of the Jewish folk-rock sound. According to Wally Schachet-Briskin, an expert on Reform camping and LBT's cantor from 1996 to 2009, "Song leading and dance leading students would learn a fair amount of each other's repertoire, then spent most of the day improving their own craft by learning new material, technique and practicum. Student volunteers could help lead the dining hall song sessions."[21]

The Saratoga camp also brought William into contact with Rabbi Iser L. Freund, a San Jose–based rabbi who served as a chaplain at San Quentin State Prison. Freund was impressed by the enthusiasm William sparked in the young people, and felt he could get "better musical participation by the congregation [of Jewish inmates] as a result of the Cantor's fine instruction." William visited San Quentin one Shabbat morning.

6. Saratoga, California

He led a standard morning service followed by a sing-along. "[T]he men were delighted when he doffed clerical garb, rolled up his sleeves and took his guitar in hand.... The audience sang with the Cantor, many had never enjoyed this type of song before but found themselves singing lustily. The Los Angeles man captivated them with the melodies."[22]

A handful of William's musical settings became NFTY camp standards, including *Ashreinu/Sh'ma* and *Lo Yareyu*.[23] Both pieces originated in a completely different context: the inauguration service of HUC president Alfred Gottschalk (Cincinnati, 1972).[24] In that formal ceremony, the songs were fully orchestrated with horns and a multi-part male choir. However, both had rhythmic and harmonic support from a steel-string guitar, rather than a keyboard instrument. This eased their adaptation to the informal camp setting. *Ashreinu/Sh'ma* combines William's setting of *Ashreinu* with a *Sh'ma* melody by Max Helfman, a fellow camp music director-professor-composer. It begins with guitar and a single vocal line, and develops into a round with horns providing coloration. Similarly, *Lo Yareyu* (from Isa. 11:9), which builds on a melody by Ezra Gabbai, begins with guitar and a rhythmic vocal pattern, and fills out with vigorous horns and punctuated vocal parts. These pieces transitioned naturally into the youth camp, where they were simplified to invite participation. The guitar bridged two ostensibly incompatible environments.

A Musical Rabbi

William and Rabbi Wolli Kaelter had little opportunity to interact at Camp Saratoga, but the two remained linked. Wolli served as rabbi of Temple Israel in Long Beach, California from 1955 to 1979, and thereafter as rabbi laureate until his death in 2008 at age ninety-three. He also taught for thirty years at HUC in Los Angeles. William and Wolli connected over music at the school.

Wolli was a trained cellist, and served as rabbi and (*de facto*) cantor for most of his time at Temple Israel. He considered himself "a true [vocal] amateur, in love with music." He was supported by a quartet of "moonlighting professionals" positioned next to the organist in a small choir loft.[25] His tenure as chairman of the Central Conference of American Rabbis' Committee on Synagogue Music greatly expanded the temple's repertoire, and gave him access to Eric Werner, composer Abraham W. Binder, and other luminaries.

Wolli represented something of an ideal for William, who regretted the disproportionate influence of the rabbi's musical tastes on the worship service. Wolli possessed a refined musical sense. A retrospective in the Long Beach *Press-Telegram* described him as a classical music aficionado who considered J. S. Bach to be the "last great composer."[26] It is hard to imagine anyone, let alone a classical music fan, identifying an eighteenth-century composer as the "last great." Nevertheless, his love for the German master was the stuff of local legend, and something he shared with William. Wolli was a visible supporter of the Long Beach Bach Festival (est. 1974), and was often the first to rise from his seat to offer a standing ovation.[27]

William was commissioned to write the *Shabbat Suite* (a.k.a. *Sabbath Suite*) for mixed choir and woodwind quintet to commemorate Wolli and Sarah Kaelter's eighteenth (*chai*) year at Temple Israel. It was an important milestone in Wolli's career, as his beloved father served for eighteen years as a rabbi in Danzig before his death. "An Evening of Music for Sarah and Wolli" was held at Millikan High School in Long Beach on September 16, 1973.[28] The celebration was free and open to the public. Even so, the organizing committee decided to give it a personal focus. Instead of bowing to the tastes of the time, they programmed music that was meaningful to Sarah and Wolli. Along with William's multi-movement choral work were pieces by Schumann, Schubert, Mahler, and Ravel.

William was characteristically unhappy with the premiere of the *Shabbat Suite*. He was slightly more pleased with a later performance by a madrigal group at the University of California, Los Angeles. Recordings were made at both venues but have since been lost. The *Suite* had its New York Premiere on November 10, 1974, during a concert of the International Jewish Music Library at Lincoln Center's Alice Tully Hall. Performers included the Cantica Hebraica Chorus and Chamber Orchestra and a variety of guest cantors.[29] The concert comprised twenty-two

6. Saratoga, California

pieces by prominent Jewish composers, including Eliezer Gerovitsch, Darius Milhaud, Jacob Rapaport, Frederick Picket, Julius Chajes, Lazar Weiner, Max Helfman, Yechezkiel Braun, and Louis Lewandowski. *New York Times* music critic Robert Sherman called the *Shabbat Suite* "a gracious setting."[30]

As is often the case in synagogue music, small portions of the work were later extracted and reset for use as stand-alone liturgical pieces. Most notable is *Shalom Aleychem*, which began as an expansive thirteen-page Renaissance-style setting with keyboard accompaniment and marked "*moderato e misterioso*," and became a brisk two-page a-cappella piece marked "with spirit" and running just over a minute. The latter version is William's most widely performed composition, and was the opening selection of the historic 2010 concert of the American Conference of Cantors at the Basilica of Santa Maria degli Angeli e dei Martiri in Rome.[31]

William's disappointment at the Temple Israel performance had no lasting effect. The following year, the temple observed its Golden Jubilee (fiftieth anniversary). The evening featured a lecture on the Holocaust by Elie Wiesel, and a performance of Ernest Bloch's monumental *Sacred Service (Avodath Hakodesh)* by the Long Beach Camerata Singers. William sang the cantor part. He also offered an original *Mi Shebeirach* for Wolli.[32] William's memoir records the esteem he had for his rabbinic friend and colleague:

> [T]hrough rabbis like Wolli Kaelter, music of substance—both old and new— is able to enter the synagogue. Even more than the cantor, the rabbi has a unique and important responsibility to create the musical culture of his or her synagogue. If the rabbi is sophisticated, the music will be sophisticated; but when the rabbi lacks knowledge or is insecure in the area of music, the congregation—and indeed the cantor—will likely be drawn into simplistic, unchallenging, and oftentimes spiritually empty settings of the liturgy. This is why the musical life of the rabbi is so crucial—not necessarily the rabbi as musician, but as someone who appreciates music of substance.[33]

The Guitar

William's involvement in Reform Jewish camping led to one of the major innovations in twenty-century synagogue song: guitar strumming on the *bimah*. Initially, the informal music scene at NFTY camps was an isolated youth activity. Campers embraced the lack of distinctions between dining hall and worship, and reveled in the participatory atmosphere. This was a dramatic departure from conventional Reform Judaism, which favored the "proper" sounds of choirs, organs, and hymnals. However, beginning in the 1960s and 70s a slow and steady stream of camp and camp-inspired songs began to flow into liberal American synagogues—a phenomenon that was less a revolution than a sociological inevitability.

When the youth returned home after their summer sessions, they were no longer content to sing the songs of their parents. Instead, they wished to replicate the camp experience inside the synagogue walls. Many congregations complied, seeing it as a way to increase youth involvement in Jewish life. As these young men and women began having families of their own and attending synagogue as adults, they continued to look for services that included their musical tastes. As a result, the sonic complexion of most Reform, Conservative, and other liberal synagogues is dotted with melodies reminiscent of the campfire, complete with guitar accompaniment.

William has been credited with introducing the guitar into the synagogue—a once-radical innovation that is now a staple of liberal Judaism.[34] He first played the instrument at confirmation ceremonies and religious school/family services when LBT was still on San Vicente Boulevard (1954–1963). When the congregation moved to Sepulveda Boulevard, he gradually expanded its use to regular services. At the time, the organ was the mainstay instrument of the Reform synagogue, as it had been since the nineteenth century. William respected that history, and often used guitar and organ together.[35]

The shock of strumming in a sanctified space should not be underestimated. William recalled with amusement: "A colleague, in response to a recommendation that he attend services at Bill Sharlin's synagogue, said, 'You won't catch me going into that guitar-playing cantor's place! He's just a camp-song leader.'"[36] That sentiment was, at first, fairly common. For many, the guitar was a profanation: an intrusion of popular sounds in an environment meant to rise above the ordinary.

Guitar playing was too much for some to bear. William sympathized

6. Saratoga, California

with their concerns. He never intended the instrument to supplant the organ, dilute the service, or facilitate superficial connections. In William's hands, the guitar was a purely functional device: it provided harmonic and rhythmic support, but never overshadowed the singing. He was known to walk among congregants, putting his "golden feet" to work, strumming his guitar, and building up group cohesion. He made himself one with the collective and led from within. Like Shlomo Carlebach, he used the instrument to deepen spiritual involvement, not to create a diversion. Most important, he played it in carefully selected spots, creating a service that artfully blended diverse modalities and musical styles. There were, however, occasions when he felt the guitar was inappropriate, such as the High Holy Days.

William did not expect synagogue guitar playing to catch on the way it did. The instrument was an extension of his persona, and a tool to enact his philosophy of communal togetherness. It was the musical complement to his favorite gesture: facing the congregation with outstretched arms.[37] "When I led congregational singing," he said, "I was truly involved. I wanted my heart to reach out to the congregants."[38] Had he known he was starting a trend, he might have been more hesitant. On more than one occasion, he voiced frustration over the quality of guitar-driven synagogue services: "[T]here are some service leaders—cantors and rabbis—who hide behind the guitar. They play around with the instrument, plucking out fancy passages, without realizing they are in a sacred setting. What is it that they wish to communicate to the congregation—how to play the guitar? What does that have to do with prayer?"[39] At times, trivial guitar playing and the void it sought to fill made him long for the past: "Spirituality did not have to be worked at. Cantors did not have to pick up the guitar to warm up the congregation. The people brought their own spiritual instruments."[40]

Giving the guitar a limited and unobtrusive role was central to William's musical agenda. This is clearly articulated in a 1967 letter to a congregant fearful that the guitar would replace the organ. His description of the organ's inconspicuousness speaks both to his desire to continue its usage—thereby blending heritage and innovation—and an underlying concern that the guitar could become a distraction.

Cantor William Sharlin

> The organ is here to stay. It is the most practical—the cheapest, in the long run, but more important it is the most unobtrusive form of accompaniment the pulpit desires. After all, unobtrusiveness was the major theme for the "reforming" rabbi. De-personalization or de-dramatization motivated the shape of things to come. Removing the person is part of it all. Is it not true that the organ is the instrument whose performer we focus least upon when we listen? The gap between the organist at the console and the sound produced is very large. Even the word console suggests a computer-like instrument "producing" sounds with a man at the controls pressing buttons and levers off to the side somewhere. The organ console is always off to the side or above or behind, out of the way. Of course one need not mention its natural, impersonal, less controversial tone. It will never gush or even soar—it will never speak tenderly or even with anger. Most important is the fact that it is totally dependable—the tone will always be there without fail. It cannot, God forbid, crack, falter even slightly in pitch, run out of breath—abrupt changes in the weather mean nothing—it is emotionally so stable. In short, being the least human of the instruments it is the most controllable. And this is what they wanted.[41]

Another problem with guitar-led services is the tendency to pull from overly simplistic songs. Music of substance is abandoned for music of expediency. According to William, this phenomenon has two causes: a belief that inclusive participation trumps all other objectives, and the song leader's lack of proficiency on the instrument. Basic melodies with basic chord progressions satisfy both concerns. William distanced himself from that mindset. In his assessment, instant participation could only inspire instant (read: superficial) involvement. Moreover, strumming simple chords to hide ineptitude on guitar is just as lamentable as plucking fancy lines to hide ineptitude in prayer. If the guitar is to be used, respect must be given to the instrument and to the congregation.

A case in point is William's setting of *Aleinu* and *Vene'emar*, which was written as a lead sheet with chord symbols (suitable for guitar), but travels in unusual and challenging directions. The thirty-four-bar through-composed piece travels through sixty chord changes. The opening twelve measures offer a series of evocative colorations: Fm–C–C7–Fm–B♭m–C–D♭7–Fm–B♭m–E♭7–D♭–B♭m–C–Fm–D♭m–A♭–Cm–C.[42] This contrasts with the simple I–IV–V–I pattern of the more familiar waltz setting (attributed to Sigmund Sabel and Salomon Sulzer). William's *Aleinu* is conducive to congregational singing, but it is not

6. Saratoga, California

absorbed upon first exposure. Learning it takes attentiveness and patient repetition. As he remarked to an assembly of cantors and rabbis: "These things are accessible to almost any congregation. The only requirement is that you have to attend services regularly."[43] *Aleinu* is attainable enough to invite participation, yet sophisticated enough to stimulate continued interest.[44] Incidentally, Temple Israel of Long Beach is among the synagogues that regularly sing the setting—a custom started under Rabbi Wolli Kaelter.

The liturgical use of guitar is a defining component of William's legacy. Rabbi Bill Cutter recalls: "Cantor Sharlin took people's natural inclination to sing and play and brought that into prayer. He used his guitar at Leo Baeck Temple and at HUC-JIR to get people to sing, and to introduce complex musical ideas. He challenged all clichés about prayer."[45] Cantor Patti Linsky, one of William's devoted students, remembers: "Cantor Sharlin opened our souls to the beauty and majesty of traditional chant, the glory of our sacred music, the vulnerability and sensitivity of transcending the profane and elevating one's soul. He played an out of tune guitar, wrote children's songs, blessed us with complicated choral music and sang oh, so beautifully."[46] According to Shirl Lee Pitesky, a self-described "Baroque woman," the music he wrote for guitar was "never pop or rock—it was dignified. Pop music is garbage, as far as I'm concerned, and William didn't do that."[47] A historical survey cites his impact: "The guitar strumming of cantor William Sharlin set the tradition-breaking tone of Reform."[48]

Epilogue

The last quarter century of William's life can be characterized as a productive retirement. It was a prolonged period that witnessed a number of achievements and milestones. This is not to say that he was perpetually relevant in his field. Particularly in the final decade, when his public appearances were few and dementia began to take its toll, there was the looming specter of obsolescence. Yet he continued to coach a few students at his home, make corrections to his music, compose short pieces, and work on his own voice. Despite the impediments of advanced age, his mission remained the same and his standards never wavered. "As far as I'm concerned," he preached in his late eighties, "there is never an end to learning.... I am constantly being driven to the next step. I often ask myself, 'Where do I go from here?' As a singer, I've never stopped pursuing the possibilities of moving further ahead."[1]

William used the phrase "Trust the process" when he detected frustration or a slight improvement in a student, or felt that the student was trying too hard. He had little interest in culminations or conclusions. Process was his philosophy and his way of life. His own maturation as an artist and human being was gradual. He lived a sheltered existence longer than most. His career path was not swift or straightforward. He entered the cantorate at the nudging of others, and was slow to get married. Compositional notoriety came to him in mid-life, and he never rushed to turn out a piece. His life was one of constant refining and perpetual searching. The steady employment he enjoyed might have encouraged

Epilogue

stagnancy or self-satisfaction; but comfortable boxes held no attraction for him. He extended himself in as many directions as he could: service leading, composing, researching, writing, teaching, lecturing, producing, and conducting.

When William retired from LBT at age sixty-eight, he still had much to give. In a retirement announcement letter dated January 1988, he stressed: "it is precisely because I am still in good health (give or take a few joints that have a mind of their own) that I wish to enter into, and enjoy, a change of life-experience with freedom to choose in both work and play."[2] At his retirement weekend on October 7–8, there was a heavy sense that he was irreplaceable. As cantor emeritus, he would no longer be the vigorous presence he had been for the better part of four decades. One presenter elucidated what would be hardest to let go: the way he welcomed Shabbat with his guitar, sang with the children in the nursery school, encouraged campers to add more silly verses to "Hey Lawdy Dawdy," taught Hebrew to bar and bat mitzvah students, added quiet wisdom to board meetings, and introduced musical settings that enabled congregants to appreciate old texts in new ways.[3]

Rabbi Richard N. Levy, a lecturer in rabbinics at HUC Los Angeles and later director of the campus's rabbinic program (1999–2009), offered his perspective as a colleague and admirer:

> You taught me the difference between *davening* and singing, between listening to a *chazzan*'s prayer and singing along. You taught me that listening is also praying, and while there are times for congregational singing, there are also times for congregational listening. A *chazzan* like you is not a showman; he is, she is, the essence of a *sheliach tzibbur*: the person the congregation has chosen as its emissary to focus its prayers and gather them into a song that can make its way from the depths of the heart, into the hearts of heaven. You don't talk much about God, William—but your song, abides in the heights.... Had Leo Baeck Temple been filled with *daveners* from the *shtetl*, the music you sang and wrote would have been very different—and I know there are times when you wish it could have been. But your own aesthetic, your own social conscience, permitted you to find in this place a vehicle to turn your *chazzanish* soul to Jewish art music, and to create an oeuvre where the *shtetl* recognized their kinship, and where plaint and poetry, that time and this place, could be one.[4]

William continued as chairman of the HUC Department of Sacred Music for another six years. Upon his retirement in 1994, he was made

Epilogue

adjunct professor emeritus, received an honorary doctorate of humane letters, and stayed active in the ACC as honorary vice-president. HUC Los Angeles established an award in his name: The Cantor William Sharlin Award for Excellence in Liturgy. An outpouring of gratitude and congratulatory letters followed. Alexander M. Schindler, then present of UAHC, wrote: "Beyond the giving of your talents, you have always been there for colleagues and students to approach when they were in need of counsel or advice. The degree of Doctor of Humane Letters truly fits the wonderful mensch that you are."[5] William did not think much of honorary degrees, but he felt his was legitimately earned.

William could now pursue ventures he had set aside. One was a recording project with the Milken Archive of Jewish Music, the leading disseminator of audio recordings of liturgical and concert music representing "the vast body of music that pertains to the American Jewish experience."[6] William was interviewed by artistic director Neil Levin, and plans to record several of his works were apparently under way. However, for reasons unknown, the project never came to fruition. This was a lingering source of disappointment for William and Jacqui. The Milken Archive has since completed its recording program and is in the process of producing and distributing previously unreleased material.

The goal of producing a compact disc eventually materialized, albeit on a grassroots level. Framed as the "culmination of William Sharlin's life as an artist and as a Jew," the album was made possible with a grant from the Endowment Fund of LBT. Titled *In Pursuit of the Sacred: The Music of Cantor William Sharlin*,[7] the high-quality CD includes twenty-two selections from published and un-published scores.[8] The pieces are quintessential Sharlin. Each is short and tightly constructed. Taken together, they present a tapestry of Renaissance techniques, twentieth-century modalities, Eastern European folk song and chant, contrapuntal devices, intricate layering, inventive harmonies, and surprising colorations from an unobtrusive keyboard. The liner notes aptly describe the effect: "Accessible, yet sophisticated, its intricacies leave more to be discovered upon each new hearing."

The album was recorded in the sanctuaries of the Parish of Saint Matthews, Pacific Palisades (February 5 and 6, June 19 and 20, and

Epilogue

August 12, 2000) and Temple Israel of Hollywood (October 16 and November 13, 2000). Choral arrangements were sung by Zephyr: Voices Unbound, a Los Angeles–based self-conducted cooperative of thirteen high-caliber singers.[9] Soloists included Robert Lewis, longtime principle bass at LBT, Diane Thomas, a veteran soprano soloist at LBT, William's daughter Cantor Lisa Sharlin Klein, and Cantor Wally Schachet-Briskin, who was then cantor of LBT. Instrumental parts were divided between flutists Terri Dixson and Angela Weigand, violinist Peter Kent, and keyboardists Deborah Daugherty-Alonzo, Stephen Grimm, and Delores Stevens.

A highlight of the album is William's own voice, heard on four songs—twice as cantor solo (*Esa Enai* and *Yom Zeh L'Yisrael II*), once in duet-dialogue with his daughter Lisa (*Eilu D'varim*), and once alternating solos with Lisa (*Va-ani T'filati*). Predictably, William was not wholly satisfied with the end product. His compulsion to nitpick was directed at all aspects: choral tempos, dynamics, soloists' interpretations, his own singing, etc. Nonetheless, careful execution is audible on every track, and William's eighty-year-old voice is remarkably smooth and expressive.

Wally Schachet-Briskin recalls William struggling to tame his perfectionism during the sessions, as more rehearsals and additional takes would have meant higher costs.[10] William's session notes have been lost, but they were no doubt copious. Still, whatever issues he had were likely small. He was grateful for the opportunity and appreciated the overall quality. With considerable irony, two selections from the album were recently included in a digital compilation released by the Milken Archive.[11]

Shortly after the recording, William received his final commission. It came from a longtime friend and colleague, Cantor Jay Frailich of University Synagogue, Los Angeles. Frailich, a recent retiree, commissioned over thirty major liturgical works and dozens of single pieces during his forty years at the synagogue. He asked William to write a song of healing.[12] The choice fell upon three Hebrew texts: Numbers 12:13, *R'fa-eiynu* (from the weekday *Amidah*), and *Mi Shebeirach* (a traditional healing prayer, which William adapted and expanded). The blend of

Epilogue

sources yielded *Eil Na R'fa Na* for cantor, SATB choir, and keyboard.[13] The piece includes seventeen meter changes in just seventy-seven measures, creating a sense of pulse-less-ness suitable for a meditation on healing.[14] Harmonic dissonances and frequent accidentals reinforce the ethereal effect.

William wrote his last composition in 2006.[15] Entitled *Higid Lecha Adam*, it sets of a verse from the Book of Micah: "It has been told to you, O man, what is good, and what the Lord requires of you: Only to do justice, and to love goodness, and to walk humbly with your God" (Mic. 6:8). This ethical summation has a distinctly didactic quality, presenting the fundamental qualities of an upstanding life. Rabbi Samlai viewed the passage as a compendium of all the *mitzvot* (commandments): "Six hundred and thirteen precepts were communicated to Moses.... Micah came and reduced them to three."[16] The decree is simple yet difficult to enact: justice, goodness, and humility are ideals that everyone can support, but few accomplish without great effort and occasional stumbling.

William's setting for solo voice plays upon tensions between simplicity and complexity. No words are repeated, no rests appear in the vocal line or piano accompaniment, and the entire piece spans just sixteen measures: eight for the Hebrew text and eight for the English translation. (The English section is a direct musical repetition of the Hebrew, making the compositional content just eight measures.) The miniature structure is filled with nuance, illustrating the deceptive concision of Micah's phrase. The piano part is a study in dense coloration and motivic expansion. The right hand begins with an ominous figure, which sets the intervallic tendencies of the piece: $C-B-A^\flat-G-C-F$. *Higid l'cha adam* ("It has been told to you, O man") is then sung to $C-D^\flat-F-G-C-A^\flat$. William's penchant for chromatic movement comes to the fore with *ma Adonai* ("what God"), $E-F-G-A^\flat-B^\flat-B$, and appears again in the voice and piano. The mood briefly turns tender with a light melisma for *ahavat chesed* ("love goodness"), and moves to a stepwise eighth-note descent for *v'hatznei'a lechet* ("and walk humbly").

These features are indicative of a late Sharlin composition. The vocal line is demanding. It seems, at times, more concerned with achieving a harmonic end than accommodating the vocal instrument. The accompaniment is rife with accidentals, shifting moods, dense harmonies, tiny steps, and giant leaps. The piano is more prominent than it is in his earlier works, though the doubling of the vocal line in the right hand mitigates that impression.

Yet, while the performance demands are typical of William's later writing, the piece remains fundamentally Sharlinesque. For one thing, it uses a text not often set to music. We can speculate about his attraction to the verse: William was eighty-six at the time, and Micah's words exude the wisdom of advanced age. The brief setting displays his attention to minute detail. It took months to complete, and the final draft contains numerous post-print changes. Such re-editing was not uncommon, though it was probably exaggerated due to the onset of dementia. Most important, while *Higid L'cha Adam* incorporates atonality, chromaticism, and unexpected twists, it remains engaging and affecting. It approaches the text as a meditation or study, interpreting in gentle tones Micah's solemn decree. As with most of William's pieces, the music serves the text, changing subtly to accentuate each of the three virtues, and imbuing the words with an added degree of purpose and profundity.

Several retrospective projects were undertaken during William's final years. A comprehensive CD-ROM of his compositions was distributed in June of 2007.[17] Compiled by Lisa Sharlin Klein and her husband, *Cantor William Sharlin: A Library of Original Scores* contains an alphabetized catalog and accompanying sheet music for over 170 published and unpublished pieces. It encompasses nearly all of his output, including variant arrangements and orchestrations. The disc was distributed to members of the American Conference of Cantors.

He also made two important contributions to literature on Jewish music. The first was a collection of essays written during the course of his career, *Jewish Sacred Music and Jewish Identity: Continuity and Fragmentation* (2008).[18] I had the pleasure of assembling the essays with my co-editor, Brad Stetson. Themes of the book include the cantor's role in contemporary Jewish life, the ever-changing sources of synagogue song, and the blurry line between sacred and secular in Jewish music.

Epilogue

Around the time I put that book together, Jacqui Sharlin requested that I record William's oral history. The idea was spurred on by his declining memory. Pieced together from a series of interviews conducted in the late spring of 2007, it was published as "Trust the Process: My Life in Sacred Song" (2009).[19] Although it cannot be considered comprehensive—both because of its modest size and the disjointedness of the recollections—the memoir is the best we have of "William on William." Alongside autobiographical vignettes are his insights on singing, explanations of his compositional process, thoughts on the state of the cantorate, and a host of philosophical ruminations.

William passed away on Tuesday, November 5, 2012, at age ninety-two. It was a quick and peaceful passing after an aggravating decline into the darkness of dementia. Details of his condition would serve no purpose here. It will suffice to include these words, which Lisa wrote in a eulogy for her father:

> If I may ever so briefly enter the wretched territory of what was robbed of dad, and of us, in these last 10 years or more—I want to say very publicly that it was always mom who settled him, cared for him and ferociously guarded his dignity with grace and compassion. In his final few months, it became only mom's arrival in a room that could bring a great smile to dad's face and calmness to his soul.[20]

The funeral was held on the morning of November 9 at LBT, followed by interment at Mount Sinai Memorial Parks and Mortuaries in the Hollywood Hills. Lisa coordinated the service and invited Cantor Mark Saltzman to officiate. "I was honored to get the call," Mark explains. "I asked who else would be doing it with me. Generally speaking, when a colleague of note passes, it's a major production with several leaders, a cantorial choir, etc. My heart dropped when Lisa said it would just be me. I knew what the community would think."[21] Jacqui and Lisa requested choral music. However, they were not interested in the usual pick-up cantorial choir. Mark enlisted his four favorite singers from the Los Angeles Master Chorale—a tribute to the quality of the quartet William had by his side for decades.

The service began with a performance of "Simple Gifts," a song of great lyrical and musical meaning for William. He was not interested in

Epilogue

material things. He was a minimalist when it came to opulent delights. He derived pleasure from crossword puzzles, nightly Beefeater Gin with crackers and nuts before dinner, sunflower seeds that he kept stashed in his car, watching sports on television, and his morning grapefruit. Ilana Sharlin mused about "Simple Gifts" in her father's eulogy, one of many given that day: "I think that my father's greatest gift was to make the complex simple yet infinitely more beautiful, filling our lives with love and joy, while especially for me, giving us a sense of peace and security that we are indeed on the right path. And when we are in the place just right, 'twill be in the valley of love and delight."[22] Cellist John Walz began with the unaccompanied melody of "Simple Gifts," the piano added an accompaniment written by William, and Mark sang in canon with the cello.

The quartet sang two pieces: William's *Shalom Aleychem* and an a cappella setting of *Shiviti* by nineteenth-century master Louis Lewandowski. The latter selection was a nod to William's love of early Reform music and his belief that, in order to move forward artistically, one must be cognizant of what has come before. Mark sang William's setting of *Yesh Kochavim*, a fitting text from Hannah Senesh: "There are stars whose radiance is visible on earth only when they cease to exist. There are people, the brilliance of whose memory continues to light the world, though they are no longer with us. These lights which shine in the dark of night—they light the way for humanity." He also improvised a chant for the memorial prayer, *El Maleh Rachamim*, following William's example.[23] Walz closed the service with an unaccompanied suite by Bach.

There were roughly 300 people in attendance, including an assortment of cantors and rabbis. Among the many speakers were William's daughters and Rabbis Leonard Beerman and Bill Cutter.[24] Some were upset that HUC, as an institution, was not involved in an official way. But the simple and personal farewell was precisely what the Sharlin family needed.[25]

When asked in his twilight years how he wished to be remembered, William replied, "As a composer."[26] He was, of course, many things: a teacher, a mentor, a scholar, a cantor, a pianist, a conductor, a song leader, a public speaker, a pioneer, a son, a brother, a husband, a father, a friend. But at core he was a composer, with all the intensity, creativity, moodiness,

Epilogue

William Sharlin, 1962.

exuberance, precision, imagination, and inwardness the word implies. Specifically, he was a *Jewish* composer, which he understood not as a monolithic construct, but as something deeply personal:

Fundamentally, I am a Jew. Even when I compose a piece for the synagogue—something intimately linked with a Jewish text—I do not ask myself, "How can I make this sound Jewish?" On the contrary, I simply immerse myself in the text, draw upon my musical knowledge, and emerge with something saturated with my internal experience as a Jew. As much as I rely on my secular training as a musician, my Jewishness remains a central part of my musical personality. My intimacy with synagogue music and the larger musical world are merged as one.[27]

Appendix: The Writings of Cantor William Sharlin— An Annotated Bibliography

Cantor William Sharlin is best known as a composer, cantor, and teacher of cantors; but he also had a philosophical side. He wrote a number of insightful and challenging essays over the course of some fifty years. I had the great honor of collecting and co-editing (with Brad Stetson) many of his essays for *Jewish Sacred Music and Jewish Identity: Continuity and Fragmentation* (St. Paul, MN: Paragon House, 2008). That book is listed below as *JSMJI*.

This annotated bibliography includes fifty-two entries, eighteen of which remain unpublished. Viewed as a whole, they touch upon ten philosophical tensions: (1) Active and Passive Assimilation; (2) Davening and Congregational Singing; (3) Privacy and Performance; (4) Insiders and Outsiders; (5) Listening and Singing; (6) Diversity and Mainstream; (7) Secular and Sacred; (8) Cantor and Rabbi; (9) Static and Dynamic (text and music); and (10) Past and Present.

1. "Active and Passive Assimilation." *JSMJI*. 59–62.
   Discusses the "heterogeneous accumulation" of musical styles in the American synagogue. Builds on a theory first proposed by Eric Werner (after Hermann Cohen), which claims that synagogues guided by a mainstream— "a reasonably steady body of music"—tend to absorb outside elements without compromising the musical character of a service (active assimilation). In

Appendix

contrast, many modern synagogues surrender to outside musical influences and incorporate them as they are, due to an absence of a stabilizing mainstream (passive assimilation). Departs from Werner in proposing that passive assimilation can achieve an active quality when the foreign elements are "assimilated experimentally—by the sheer energy of a living worship entity" (e.g., Hasidic *niggunim*).

2. "The American Synagogue in Search of Its Musical Idiom." *Shalshelet: The Chain* 2:2 (1976): 6–8. [Abridged version reprinted in *JSMJI*. 92–93.]

Contrasts musical instability in contemporary worship with the "stable entity" of the past, and proposes that synagogue music achieves a defined character ("tradition" or "custom") only when worshipers are comfortable with the concept of worship itself. Cites three primary and sometimes conflicting needs driving the current search for meaningful prayer-music: (1) the needs of today's congregations; (2) the needs of individual functionaries (cantor, composer, choir director); and (3) the need to preserve a sense of continuity with the musical culture of the past.

3. "The Artist and the Sacred." *Unpublished*, n.d.

Contends that artists are rarely drawn to the usual aspects of religious life: regulated rituals, group affiliation, and formalistic prayers. Posits that utterly artistic people—those who exist in an almost perpetual state of inward reflection and inspired invention—live the ideals that religion strives to impart through texts and structured practices. The artist is intimately familiar with transformation and elevation, making religion's attempt to manufacture these qualities superfluous or even disruptive.

4. "Ashkenazi Tradition." *JSMJI*. 64–66.

Discusses biases and obstacles composers bring to settings of liturgical prayers, including varied levels of familiarity with Jewish worship, the Hebrew language, and the heritage of synagogue music. Also addresses the built-in limitations of older chant formulas, known as *nusach ha-tefillah*, which can obscure textual meanings through the imposition of specific chant patterns on blocks of prayers—a practice that often ignores the multiple moods and themes that are present in the prayers.

5. "An Autobiographical Sketch." *JSMJI*. 35–38.

Offers brief reflections on Sharlin's life and work, including his Orthodox upbringing in New York and Palestine, the loss of his mother at age sixteen, his education at yeshivot, Manhattan School of Music, and Hebrew Union College, his gradual embrace of universalism, and insights about the cantorate, composition, teaching, and singing.

Appendix

6. "The Born Believer." *JSMJI*. 75.

Looks nostalgically at the faith and rituals of Orthodox Jews, who are "almost literally born in a state of belief" and "live in the context of three thousand years." The subtext is Sharlin's own movement away from the simple faith of his father and the fixed system of practice that supported it.

7. "Cantor as Link." *Unpublished*, n.d.

Portrays the Reform cantorate as an embodiment of stability in a landscape permeated with doubt. Cantors are held up as a model of faith, tradition, and commitment for those who are alienated from the Jewish past. Their singing forges a more tangible and immediate link to Jewish heritage than the largely intellectual work of the rabbi.

8. "Chasidism." *Unpublished*, n.d.

Frames the rabbi-centric model of Hasidism as a necessary strategy. Because the movement represented a radical break from the academic rabbinism of the time, it required an intellectual-spiritual leader to take center stage. This forced the cantor into a secondary (and sometimes invisible) role in liturgical worship. A similar phenomenon occurred when Reform Judaism developed in Central Europe. The charismatic "thought leader" took control of the synagogue service, forcing the cantor into a diminished status, and in some cases out of a job.

9. "'The Commandment'—Discipline and the Artist." *Unpublished*, n.d.

Connects the discipline required of the observant Jew to that of the creative artist. Both are in pursuit of the "sacred": an essence and awareness transcending the ordinary. Maintaining Jewish continuity requires "performing it, searching it for new meanings, preserving it." Likewise, the artist is both rooted in and expands upon the heritage of his/her art.

10. "Comments Made to the Cantor." *Unpublished*, n.d.

Quotes contradictory remarks overheard after Friday evening services, illustrating a diversity of opinions in liberal Judaism regarding the nature and sentiments of the prayer service. Locates the source of conflicting reactions to a lack of unity within the Jewish community and the complicating forces of modernity and individualism.

11. "Composers of Synagogue Music." *JSMJI*. 51–53.

Attributes the increase of divergent musical styles in the synagogue to a general breakdown of the inner need for prayer, and the perception that music can stimulate a resurgence of spiritual-religious connection. In contrast to the *hazzanim* of Eastern Europe and their congregations, who were "insiders" intimately involved in the liturgical-musical experience, many composers and

Appendix

congregants today are "outsiders" (or "partial outsiders"), who grope for an emotional entryway into worship.

12. "Congregational Singing Past and Present: Continuity and Fragmentation." *Central Conference of American Rabbis Journal* (Spring 1994): 31–41. [Reprinted in *JSMJI*. 19–32.]

Compares the *davening* atmosphere of pre–Enlightenment Central European synagogues with the choral and eventually congregational singing that would come to define the Reform aesthetic. Gives attention to the dialogical quality of *hazzan* and *daveners*, and its erosion in the cantor (or song leader)/singing congregation model of the present Reform movement. Despite a somewhat critical tone, it cautions that musical changes occur for legitimate and complex sociological reasons, and that different musical forms address different needs.

13. "A Conversation with Cantor William Sharlin," with Jonathan L. Friedmann. *JSMJI*. 39–48.

Touches on a range of subjects, including the challenge of American secularism to the preservation of Jewish identity, the (misguided) use of music to compensate for a lack of inward devotion, the need to balance the old with the new in synagogue compositions, and the insufficiency of "just" singing in the synagogue (i.e., superficial engagement in congregational song).

14. "Davening and Congregational Song." In *Emotions in Jewish Music: Personal and Scholarly Reflections*, ed. Jonathan L. Friedmann. Lanham, MD: University Press of America, 2012. 45–53. [Originally delivered at the Pacific Area Reform Rabbis Convention, Los Angeles, January 1973.]

Examines *nusach ha-tefillah* as an organic outgrowth of a socio-religious experience situated in a particular time and place. Argues that it is both difficult and somewhat artificial to reinstitute *nusach* in modern liberal synagogues, where the link to the past is broken and external congregational song is favored over the discipline required of modal chant.

15. "Environment of the Sacred." *Unpublished*, 2000.

Seeks to reframe song leading as an integrated part of the sacred experience, rather than an activity with its own function. Twelve questions are considered: (1) Does the cantor's (or rabbi's) personal experience drive congregational singing? (2) Does instrumental accompaniment support or detract from the experience? (3) What is the role of hand clapping? (4) Do congregations engage in mindless repetition of simple and well-known melodies? (5) Do congregations effectively utilize responsive singing? (6) What roles do tempo and dynamics play? (7) Do congregations corrupt the experience by over-borrowing from secular or "ordinary" sources? (8) Do congregations

Appendix

avoid melodies that require longer exposure to learn? (9) Does the use of hand gestures invite participation? (10) Is transliteration a deterrent to internalization? (11) Does the split pulpit (cantor-rabbi) present the danger of fragmentation? (12) What can synagogues learn from the camp phenomenon?

16. "The Experience of Listening in Worship." *Unpublished*, n.d.

Paper delivered to cantors and rabbis explaining the difficulties of stimulating prayerful listening when clergy partners themselves struggle to navigate the uneven format of song and spoken word. Without unity on the pulpit, congregants will not be at one with the experience. Congregational singing becomes the sole point of entry (superficial though it often is), and active listening becomes a relic of an older time.

17. "From Sinai." *JSMJI*. 57.

Meditation on the traditional idea of the reception and transmission of Torah, and how each generation—and each individual—is responsible for continuing the line of transmission. It concludes: "And so may we learn that what we teach does not come from us but *through* us."

18. "Future Models of Worship." In *Toward New Models of Future Worship; Papers Delivered at the Centennial Biennial Assembly of the Union of American Hebrew Congregations, November 12, 1973*. New York: Central Conference of American Rabbis, 1974. 9–11 [Response to paper, "New Models of Worship," by Rabbi Herbert Bronstein, North Shore Congregation Israel, Glencoe, Illinois. Reprinted in *JSMJI*. 88–90.]

Cautions against making predictions for the future of Reform ritual, as such predictions can impede the natural course of development. Articulates a view of authenticity as "the *by-product* of a long development of discovering, digesting, performing, and assimilating, and not a fixed, idealized beginning." This "building process" requires an expanded foundation in the Hebrew language, as well as patience with melodies that are not immediately accessible.

19. "Gates of Prayer." *Central Conference of American Rabbis 1976 Year Book* (1976): 123–126. [Reprinted in *JSMJI*. 97–102.]

Presents reactions to the publication of the Reform prayer book, *Gates of Prayer* (1975). Proposes that the revised prayer book was created "artificially" to provide solutions to perceived problems of worship, and posits that for any *siddur* to reach its highest potential, it must be integrated through an "unconscious inner process." Otherwise, it will remain an externalized support system for an uncertain and fragile identity. The process of creating new prayer books, like *Gates of Prayer*, is further complicated by the involvement of rabbinic personalities, who infuse services with their own ideologies and

Appendix

proclivities, thereby giving it a clearer stamp of individuality than the more-or-less folk-developed traditional *siddur*.

20. "High Holiday Music." *Unpublished*, n.d.

Discusses two broad sources of synagogue music: the "content" school and the "spiritual Judaism" school (or "prophetic humanistic" school). The content school expresses its need for withdrawal and isolation (nationalism or chauvinism), while the spiritual Judaism school favors universalism, progress, and a generalized ethical message. Reform High Holiday music is drawn from these two schools, typified by so-called "*Mi-Sinai* tunes" on one hand, and compositions from Ernest Bloch and Sharlin himself on the other.

21. "In Search of Relevance." *JSMJI*. 81–83.

Argues that when the sacred and secular aspects of life are in reasonable balance, healthy dialogue occurs between the music of the synagogue and that of the outside world. However, when the secular—the desire to "preserve an ethnic link"—overshadows the sacred—a deep motivation to "connect with the divine"—communities turn to all sorts of musical idioms in order to preserve the otherwise remote language of the synagogue service.

22. "Israel's Influence on American Liberal Synagogue Music." In *Gates of Understanding*, edited by Lawrence A. Hoffman. New York: Central Conference of American Rabbis, 1977. 122–128. [Paper delivered at the International Conference on Jewish Music, New York, November 1975. Reprinted in *JSMJI*. 66–73.]

Examines the eagerness with which American congregations have embraced music originating from the Hasidic Song Festivals and other Israeli secular and quasi-secular contexts. Assesses the phenomenon as a consequence of two factors: a surge of pride in the aftermath of the Six-Day War, and the general secularization of the American "worship entity." Notes: "The secular always contributes to the sacred, but when the sacred diminishes, the secular is not only allowed to retain its own character, but also participates in the further weakening of spiritual energies."

23. "Israeli Music at 37: Those Were the Days." *The Jewish Newspaper*, April 27, 1985, 6.

Looks nostalgically at the idealistic songs of the *chalutzim* and critiques the comparative superficiality of contemporary musical fads in the state of Israel. Suggests that the inspired songs of the earlier period will survive as historical-cultural symbols, while the pop songs will "fade away as fast as they give immediate satisfaction."

24. "Jewish Identity." *JSMJI*. 51.

Reflects on the often-fragile link between the individual Jew and his/her

Appendix

Jewish identity. Cites multiple possible sources of connection, including familial, a sense of common struggle, and romantic ties to biblical narratives. Alludes to the dilemma of "surface Jews": those who want to remain Jews, but are unsure how to foster deep connections.

25. "L'dor V'dor: From Generation to Generation." *JSMJI.* 87–88.

Recounts when Sharlin told his Orthodox father that he had entered the Reform movement. His father kept his disappointment to himself in an effort to keep peace in an already strained relationship.

26. "Listening to the Pulpit." In *Koleinu B'Yachad: Our Voices as One, Envisioning Jewish Music for the 21st Century*, edited by John H. Planer and Howard M. Stahl. New York: American Conference of Cantors/Guild of Temple Musicians, 1999. 24–25. [Reprinted in *JSMJI.* 53–55.]

Advocates for the spiritual value of listening to artistic music in the synagogue, juxtaposing it with the "externalized" activity of congregational song. Identifies the root causes of the decline of active listening as a distancing from the words and rituals of the service, and the fragmentation of the pulpit, which has the cantor and rabbi vying for pieces of the service and leaves the congregation passively awaiting instructions. The more unified the atmosphere of the service, the more listening is an integral part of worship.

27. "Mozart Mounts the *Bimah*—What a Mass!" *The Jewish Newspaper*, March 14, 1985, 6.

Depicts a fictional conversation between two bewildered synagoguegoers. They are dismayed to learn that some of their favorite synagogue melodies were borrowed from outside sources and reset to Hebrew prayers (contrafaction). Three lessons are drawn: (1) It is sometimes best not to know the origins of cherished synagogue songs; (2) The passage of time obscures musical origins; (3) Text and context determine a song's identity.

28. "Myth." *Unpublished*, n.d.

Contends that, while biblical and liturgical texts may not be historically or scientifically "true," they help make sense of reality and point to greater lessons. Compares worship to mythic theater: "Ritual is also a myth. We are expected to act out a role—to read and listen to words and ideas that someone else has written—to pray those words as if they were our own, even when some of it or much of it is rationally problematic."

29. "Nothing and Everything." *Unpublished*, n.d.

Explains that synagogue music has always been influenced by music of surrounding cultures. While there is probably nothing *exclusively* Jewish in the music of the Jews, any type of music can potentially be used for Jewish

Appendix

ends. Cites three reasons for this historical openness: (1) No controlling or standardizing institution ("the Church had the priest; the synagogue had the layman and *hazzan*"); (2) The synagogue was a holistic cultural experience, blending together the secular and sacred; (3) There was a need for a dynamic force (music) to counterbalance the static liturgy.

30. "On Nusach." *Unpublished*, n.d.

Argues that *nusach ha-tefillah* tends to direct the text for which it is used, rather than the reverse. Two reasons are given: (1) Formulaic patterns are imposed on blocks of text containing varied sentiments and ideas; (2) The distinct musical qualities (color, mood, texture) seem to have evolved from conditions outside of the literal content of the liturgical passages. *Nusach* can thus be thought of as having a life and purpose of its own.

31. "On Turning Around; Or, Can You Achieve Privacy in Public?" *Leo Baeck Temple College Bulletin* 1:2 (Winter 1967): 3. [Reprinted as "Can You Achieve Privacy in Public?" *JSMJI*. 90–91.]

Asks whether the Reform cantor, who is expected to face the congregation and "perform" sacred songs, can achieve the same level of inwardness and spontaneity as the "old model" cantor, who faced the ark and turned his back toward the congregation. Explains that *hazzanut* (originally an improvisatory art) emerged organically from a state of aloneness that a front-facing cantor cannot easily replicate, if at all. [Note: This essay reworks ideas in Sharlin's more well-known essay, "When the *Chazzan* Turned Around."]

32. "Problems of Jewish Music." *Unpublished*, n.d.

Explains that the Diaspora experience does not allow for a pure culture to develop. Perpetual wandering and adaptation does not afford the same degree of nationalistic culture as exists among land-centered ethnic groups. This is described as a blessing and a curse, allowing for freedom/creativity yet inducing insecurity/angst. Uniqueness in Jewish music is not found in the music itself, but in elements such as the Hebrew language, specific functions that the music serves, and the manner of performance (e.g., stylistic/idiomatic signifiers in klezmer and *hazzanut*).

33. "The Purim Theme in Jewish Music." *The Jewish Newspaper*, February 28, 1985, 7. [Reprinted as "Midrash and Music in the Scroll of Esther," *Koleinu: A Publication of the American Conference of Cantors* 5:4 (March 1997): 2–3.]

Discusses the interpretive role of musical departures in the cantillation of Esther. Rabbinic literature contains imaginative readings of Esther, much of which seeks out God's presence where it is not explicitly found in the text. Several of these *midrashic* passages are recalled through associative melodies during the public chanting of Esther on Purim.

Appendix

34. "Remembering Leonard Bernstein." *Unpublished*, 1990.

Acknowledges the tendency among Jews to locate a "Jewish something" in the lives and careers of prominent celebrities of Jewish birth. Bernstein is an easier case than many, as a number of his works deal with Jewish themes or subjects, bear titles connected to Jewish life, and utilize the Hebrew language. Cites the *Jeremiah Symphony* as the "one exception" in which Bernstein went beyond language and theme to utilize elements of Haftarah cantillation and other folk-liturgical motifs, albeit "disguised in a typical Bernsteinian rhythmically agitated way."

35. "Renewing the Old and Sanctifying the New." In *20th Century Synagogue Music: Essential Readings*, edited by Jonathan L. Friedmann. Los Angeles: Isaac Nathan, 2010. 173–177.

Offers a critique of the conventional attitude that musical change can counteract disengagement with the Jewish prayer service. If treated carelessly, the pluralistic tapestry can create further distancing and fragmentation. Recommends looking to the past as a potential source of reinvigoration, citing Rav Kook's famous phrase: "The old must be renewed and the new must be sanctified."

36. "Review of *Biblical Chant* by A. W. Binder." *Central Conference of American Rabbis Journal* (June 1960): 65–66.

Reviews Abraham W. Binder's handbook of musical illustrations for the six systems of scriptural chant in Ashkenazi communities. Applauds the author's success in organizing the systems of chant in a logical and practical order, but criticizes his failure to acknowledge older publications on the topic from which much of his material is derived.

37. "The Role of the Cantor." *Unpublished*, 1965.

Compares the role of the Reform cantor as pulpit "officiant" with the "old synagogue" cantor, whose being was interwoven with the congregation. The physical and mental separation between cantor and worshipers in Reform services is compounded by the involvement of formal choirs, which struggle to simulate the organic folk essence of "old synagogue" song. Expresses hope that the revival of the Hebrew language and decline of choir-dominated services will create space for the restoration of unity between pulpit and congregation.

38. "The Search." *Unpublished*, n.d.

Observes that the search for relevance in worship can lead to a musical open-door policy, inviting all that is current and disregarding all that is "outdated." While exploring the full spectrum of musical possibilities is a modern-

Appendix

day reality, doing so can create an environment in which the internalizing process of exposure over time cannot take root.

39. "The Search for Answers." *Unpublished*, 1972.

Discusses the experiential separation between cantor and congregation, cantor and rabbi, and individual and liturgy. Frames this disjointedness as a carry-over from the Classical Reform period, where emphasis on decorum, pulpit presentation, and a "leader-follower" ethos turned the congregation into a passive audience. The search for new modes of participation will fall short if cohesion between pulpit and pews is not first achieved.

40. "The 'Secular' Side of the Jew." *JSMJI*. 77–79.

Discusses the slow pace of musical change in congregations that intensely engage in prayer, versus the rapid change where religious motivations are weakened. Jewish religious life exhibits a constant tension between preservation and innovation. Those communities that are secure in their devotional obligations and Jewish way of life tend to maintain a musical mainstream that keeps the tension in balance.

41. "The Seeking of God and Knowledge of God's Existence." *JSMJI*. 75–77.

Surveys divergent approaches to Jewish theology and prayer, from simple piety to ethnic identification to nostalgia. Offers more questions than answers to the complex issue of an individual's motivation to pray.

42. "The State of Music in the Reform Temple." *Unpublished*, n.d.

Relates the heterogeneous nature of Reform service music to the diversity of the congregations: "We now have congregations that are introverted, extroverted, sophisticated, lowbrow, large, small, rich, poor." Notes that most service music composed during the first half of the twentieth century is either outdated (e.g., *The Union Hymnal*) or devised for "cathedral" temples with substantial budgets and a full complement of music director, organist, choristers, and (sometimes) cantor.

43. "The Static and Dynamic in Synagogue Song." *JSMJI*. 57–59.

Outlines the constant interaction of two forces in synagogue song: static words of the prayer book, and the dynamic musical "play on words." The stability and continuity of the liturgical script owes to the vitalizing power of its musical presentation. Without the animating musical settings, the words themselves would need to be changed.

44. "Text and Context." *Unpublished*, n.d.

Explores the question of what makes synagogue music sound "Jewish." Identifies the Hebrew language, "ethnic" colorations (e.g., *hazzanut*), and the location of exposure (e.g., Jewish services) as the determining factors.

Appendix

45. "Training for a Future in Doubt." *JSMJI*. 102–105.

Discusses diverse issues in cantorial education, including the insufficiency of the curriculum to address challenges faced on the job, the false impressions that can come from student pulpits, and the tendency to set the educational bar according to the literacy of the general community ("The less knowledgeable the layman, the less knowledgeable the professional must be").

46. "Trust the Process: My Life in Sacred Song," transcribed and edited by Jonathan L. Friedmann. In *Perspectives on Jewish Music: Secular and Sacred*, edited by Jonathan L. Friedmann. Lanham, MD: Lexington, 2009. 97–136.

Memoir of Sharlin's experiences growing up in an Orthodox family in New York and pre-state Israel, his embrace of universal music and liberal Judaism, and his eventual rise to prominence as one of his generation's most well-regarded composers and teachers of synagogue song. Gives insights into the nature of the cantorate and changes in American synagogue music over the twentieth century.

47. "The Union Prayer Book." *Unpublished*, n.d.

Examines the Reform *Union Prayer Book* (1940) as both a departure from the Orthodox *siddur*—especially in terms of its brevity and free translations—and a preservation of the older prayer book's form and theology.

48. "The Unmovable Anchor." *JSMJI*. 62–63.

Examines the interplay between the fixed texts ("anchors") of Torah and liturgy and the creative treatments of music and *midrash*. The freedom of interpretation accelerates depending on the relative stability or instability of the mainstream. Although engagement with new musical styles is characteristic of contemporary synagogues, the article also cites historical examples, such as early modern rabbinic concerns about cantors appropriating operatic material for the synagogue.

49. "What Kind of Music Is Conducive to Worship?" *JSMJI*. 83–85.

Shifts the focus from musical style, *per se*, to questions of motivation. When a musical setting is felt to be out of sync with worship, it can be an issue of "essence": a palpable extra-musical quality that is detected in the presentation, but hard to pinpoint or quantify. Music is not conducive to prayer when it submits the sacred to more secular needs: "It is our very loss of touch with the sacred, the transcendent, the essence that has opened the doors for the secular, the ordinary, the anything."

50. "When Religious Music Turns 'Cultural.'" *The Jewish Newspaper*, April 11, 1985, 7. [Reprinted as "Sacred Music as 'Culture.'" *JSMJI*. 79–81.]

Maps the transition of *hazzanut* and choral compositions from the synagogue, where they addressed immediate experiential needs, to the more

Appendix

remote and antiseptic concert stage. When the passion and pathos of prayer give way to communal-ethnic concerns, simple and non-threatening tunes become the norm, and the higher art of synagogue music is relegated to the cultural sphere.

51. "When the *Chazzan* Turned Around." *Central Conference of American Rabbis Journal* (January 1962): 43–44. [Reprinted in *20th Century Synagogue Music: Essential Readings*, edited by Jonathan L. Friedmann. Los Angeles: Isaac Nathan, 2010. 92–94.]

Proposes that the phenomenon that most affected the inner character of worship during the early Reform movement was the turning of the cantor to face the congregation. When the cantor had his back to the *daveners*, he achieved a state of spiritual abandon in which the "primitive and expressive characteristics of *Chazzanuth*" were born. But when the cantor turned to face the congregation, privacy was replaced with self-consciousness and inward expression with outward performance. Recommends that the cantor "reconsider 'turning around' but not in a physical sense. Perhaps the challenge is to find seclusion and true prayer by turning around without moving at all."

52. "Why Can't a Woman Chant Like a Man?" *The Jewish Newspaper*, n.d. [Reprinted in *JSMJI*. 93–97.]

Foreshadows the eventual acceptance of women cantors in the Conservative movement, which occurred in 1987. Notes underlying financial motivations for opening the cantorate to women—namely, the decreasing interest and availability of male candidates, the desire among women to explore new professions, and the willingness of women (especially mothers) to accept part-time positions. Explains that because Reform congregants were not immersed in the "old cantorial culture," there was less shock when women began singing the music of the movement, which was essentially a mixture of classical and popular-folk. The aesthetic did not discriminate between male and female voices in the same way as Eastern European *hazzanut*—a genre prominent in Conservative circles.

Chapter Notes

Chapter 1

1. William Sharlin, "Trust the Process: My Life in Sacred Song," in *Perspectives on Jewish Sacred Music*, ed. Jonathan L. Friedmann (Lanham, MD: Lexington, 2009), 99.
2. According to the 1940 United States Federal Census, Isaac Sharlin had a third-grade education.
3. *Ibid.*
4. William Sharlin, interviewed by author, Los Angeles, CA, February 18, 2006. Published as Jonathan L. Friedmann, "A Conversation with Cantor William Sharlin," in *Jewish Sacred Music and Jewish Identity: Continuity and Fragmentation*, ed. Jonathan L. Friedmann and Brad Stetson (St. Paul, MN: Paragon House, 2008), 45.
5. Sharlin, "Trust the Process," 103.
6. *Ibid.*, 98.
7. *Ibid.*, 99.
8. *Ibid.*, 100–101.
9. *Ibid.*, 101. Presumably, these were American-style doughnuts, not the jelly doughnuts (*sufganiyot*) of North African origin, which are an Israeli Hanukkah staple.
10. *Ibid.*, 101.
11. *Ibid.*, 101–102.
12. William's spring 1937 transcript from the Mizrachi Teachers Seminary includes thirteen courses completed during his first two years there: Tanach; Mishna; Talmud; Hebrew; Jewish History; Psychology; Algebra; Geometry; Ancient History; World Geography; Biology; Physics; Physical Training.
13. 1940 United States Federal Census.
14. Janet D. Schenck, *Adventure in Music: A Reminiscence; Manhattan School of Music, 1918–1960* (New York: Manhattan School of Music, 1961), 7–67.
15. Sharlin, "Trust the Process," 103.
16. For a fuller picture of the Manhattan School of Music in the 1940s, see Janet D. Schenck, *Adventure in Music*, 48–66.
17. *Ibid.*, 49.
18. William's Transcript of Record from MSM shows that he completed a full schedule of courses in 1942–43. It states that he "Withdraw to enter Armed Services" in 1945–46. The document leaves out the academic years of 1943–44 and 1944–45, implying Army service in those years as well. Another source lists his leave of absence as 1942–1945: Kerry M. Olitzky, Lance J. Sussman and Malcom H. Stern, ed., *Reform Judaism in America: A Biographical Dictionary and Sourcebook* (Westport, CT: Greenwood, 1993), 189–190. Those years are repeated in the *Encyclopedia Judaica* entry on William Sharlin (2007 ed., vol. 18, 414), which cites *Reform Judaism in America*. The likely source for these dates is Janece Erman Cohen, "The Life and Music of Cantor William Sharlin" (M.S.M. thesis,

Notes. Chapter 2

Hebrew Union College–Jewish Institute of Religion, New York, 1990).

19. Ilana Sharlin, "Eulogy for Dad" (presented at the Funeral of William Sharlin, Leo Baeck Temple, Los Angeles, November 9, 2012).

20. Jacqui Sharlin, interview by author, Los Angeles, CA, July 5, 2014.

21. Sharlin, "Trust the Process," 104.

22. *Ibid.*

23. *Ibid.*, 105.

24. Jacqui Sharlin, interview.

25. The dual graduation date of 1949 is contradicted in William's transcript from Hebrew Union College, which indicates that he earned his B.M. in 1942 and M.M. in 1949. Other documents confirm the conferring of both degrees in 1949, including his Manhattan School of Music transcript and a self-prepared biographical statement dated July 1961.

26. F. A. Gore Ouseley, "Canon," *Grove's Dictionary of Music and Musicians, Vol. 1*, ed. H. C. Colles (New York: Macmillan, 1939), 548.

27. *Shalom Aleychem*, unpublished/undated sheet music.

28. Sharlin's *Shalom Aleychem* exists in three settings, the first of which was composed for a concert honoring Rabbi Wolli Kaelter's eighteenth year at Temple Israel of Long Beach, CA (1973). It consists of thirteen pages with keyboard accompaniment. The other two are brisk two-page a-cappella renditions, one for SATB and the other for two voices. The latter two are available through Transcontinental Music Publications. Recent high-profile performances include the American Choral Directors' Association Shabbat Service at Anshe Emet in Chicago on March 11, 2011, part of the ACDA's 2011 National Conference.

29. Sharlin, "The Musical World of Cantor William Sharlin."

30. *Yom Zeh L'Yisrael II* and *Esa Einai* can be heard on *In Pursuit of the Sacred: The Music of William Sharlin*, Leo Baeck Temple, 2001, compact disc.

31. The HUC cantorial school was renamed The Debbie Friedman School of Sacred Music on January 27, 2011, following the death of Reform Jewish singer-songwriter and HUC professor Debbie Friedman (1953–2011) earlier that month. The naming came with a substantial endowment.

32. Sharlin, "Trust the Process," 104.

33. There were three female "special students" in William's class, including Johanna Spector, who would become a prominent Jewish musicologist and faculty member at the Jewish Theological Seminary. Another esteemed female student was Judith Kaplan Eisenstein, who entered SSM in 1959 at age 50, received her Ph.D. (1966), and taught at HUC (1966 to 1979) and the Reconstructionist Rabbinical College in Philadelphia (1978 to 1981).

Chapter 2

1. The Society of American Cantors was succeeded by The Cantors' Association in 1908.

2. Substantially revised editions of the *Union Hymnal* were published in 1914 and 1932. A fourth volume, the *Union Songster: Songs and Prayers for Jewish Youth*, was published in 1960. Each volume was published under the Central Conference of American Rabbis.

3. I. Moses, "The Cantor as a Religious Functionary," *Annual Report of the Society of American Cantors* (1904). See also "Society of American Cantors," in *American Jewish Yearbook*, ed. Cyrus Adler and Henrietta Szold (Philadelphia: Jewish Publication Society, 1904), 275–276.

4. Bruce Ruben, "A History of the School of Sacred Music at Fifty: The Franzblau Years" (paper presented at the Fiftieth Anniversary of the School of Sacred Music, Hebrew Union College-Jewish Institute of Religion, Cincinnati, OH, 1999).

5. Mark Slobin, *Chosen Voices: The Story of the American Cantorate* (Urbana: University of Illinois Press, 1989), 64.

Notes. Chapter 2

6. Judah M. Cohen, *The Making of a Reform Jewish Cantor: Musical Authority, Cultural Investment* (Bloomington: Indiana University Press, 2009), 35–36.

7. Ruben, "A History of the School of Sacred Music at Fifty."

8. The trans-denominational leadership of the Society for the Advancement of Jewish Liturgical Music included Sephardic rabbi David Cardozo (president), Conservative rabbi Israel Goldfarb, Conservative cantor David Putterman, Reform rabbis James Heller and Bernard Bamberger, Orthodox cantor Pinchas Jassinowski, musicologists Eric Werner, Joseph Yasser, and Curt Sachs, and composers Jacob Weinberg, Max Helfman, Isadore Freed, and Abraham W. Binder.

9. Ruben, "A History of the School of Sacred Music at Fifty."

10. Cohen, *The Making of a Reform Jewish Cantor*, 37.

11. See W. Belskin-Ginsburg, "The Cantors Assembly: Its Creation and Growth," *Proceedings of the Cantors Assembly* (1972): 13–19.

12. Neil Levin, "Music at JTS," in *Tradition Renewed: A History of the Jewish Theological Seminary*, vol. 1, ed. Jack Wertheimer (New York: Jewish Theological Seminary, 1997), 748.

13. See Benji-Ellen Schiller, "The Hymnal as an Index of Musical Change in Reform Synagogues," in *Sacred Sound and Social Change: Liturgical Music in Jewish and Christian Experience*, ed. Lawrence A. Hoffman and Janet R. Watson (Notre Dame: Notre Dame University Press, 1992), 187–212.

14. These arguments were supported by an exploratory survey of North American Reform congregations, conducted by Abraham Franzblau. From 275 responses, Franzblau concluded that less than twenty-five percent of American congregations employed a cantor, seventeen percent of the other congregations were interested in hiring a cantor, and more than sixty percent of cantors had responsibilities outside of ritual leadership, "most of them educational." Cohen, *The Making of a Reform Jewish Cantor*, 37.

15. The SSM cantorial program was changed to a four-year program in 1953–54, culminating with a B.S.M. and Cantor's Diploma. In 1954–55 an M.S.M. option was added for students who wished to continue their studies for a full year. In 1955 the school dropped the education component, and in 1958 the B.S.M. was expanded to a five-year program, which included more cross registration with rabbinic students. The first female student was enrolled in 1970. Beginning in 1983, graduating students were awarded an M.S.M. with Investiture, which was changed to Ordination in 2010. The change in terminology followed that of the Academy for Jewish Religion in New York and Los Angeles, trans-denominational seminaries (related in name only) that had been ordaining cantorial graduates for several years.

16. Gershon Ephros was the only cantor on the original faculty.

17. Ruben, "A History of the School of Sacred Music at Fifty."

18. *Ibid.*

19. Paul M. Steinberg, "School of Sacred Music of The Hebrew Union College–Jewish Institute of Religion," in *The Cantorial Art*, ed. Irene Heskes (New York: National Jewish Music Council, 1966), 81.

20. Cohen, *The Making of a Reform Jewish Cantor*, 39.

21. Saul Goldzweig, Press Release, October 17, 1948 (American Jewish Archives). Twelve of the sixteen first-year recruits lived in the New York metropolitan area: Robert Blumstein, Henry Cordy, Kurt Silberman, Richard Fulton, Harry Sebran, Wolf Hecker, Henry Herman, Pinkus Papiercyzk, Irving Robinson, Joseph Portnoy, Leo Mirkovic, and David Olsen. The others were Louis Gordon and Gerhard Gluck, both of Massachusetts, Israel Tabatsky of Pennsylvania, and George Wald of Connecticut.

22. The three women were Minnie

Notes. Chapter 2

Cohen, Janet Goldberg, and Johanna Spector.

23. See Cohen, *The Making of a Reform Jewish Cantor*, 30, 34–35; and Geoffrey Goldberg, "Maier Levi of Esslingen, Germany: A Small-Town *Hazzan* in the Time of the Emancipation and his Cantorial Compendium" (Ph.D. diss., Hebrew University of Jerusalem, 2000).

24. Sheldon and Marcie Merel, interview by author, Encinitas, CA, August 10, 2014.

25. *Ibid.*

26. *Ibid.*

27. A representative article from the period is Eric Werner, "The True Source of Jewish Music," *Commentary* 7:4 (1949): 382–387.

28. Ruben, "A History of the School of Sacred Music at Fifty."

29. Kurt Silberman, cited *ibid.*

30. Merel, interview.

31. Wolli Kaelter, *From Danzig: An American Rabbi's Journey*, with Gordon Cohn (Malibu, CA: Pangloss, 1997), 54–55.

32. Merel, interview.

33. See Eric Werner, "Workshop: Practical Applications of Musical Research," (paper presented at the Convention of the American Conference of Cantors, 1958). Reprinted in Eric Werner, *From Generation to Generation: Studies on Jewish Musical Tradition* (New York: American Conference of Cantors, 1967), 135–148.

34. Ruben, "A History of the School of Sacred Music at Fifty."

35. Nelson Glueck, quoted in Steinberg, "School of Sacred Music," 81.

36. Eric Werner, message published in *Shalshelet: The Chain; Publication of the School of Sacred Music Alumni Association* 2:3 (Fall 1976): 16.

37. Sheldon Merel, "Memories of My Friend Cantor William (Bill) Sharlin," unpublished, November 26, 2012.

38. Biographical sketch adapted from Marcie Merel, liner notes to *Standing Ovation: Cantor Sheldon F. Merel, Tenor, Live in Concert*, Music Lab, 2000, compact disc.

39. Slobin, *Chosen Voices*, 94–111.

40. Merel, Interview.

41. *Ibid.*

42. Sharlin, "Trust the Process," 107.

43. Rabbi Leonard Thal shared the following at an event commemorating William's retirement from Leo Baeck Temple: "Last night, William's dear friend, Sheldon Merel, called [William] a 'cantor's cantor.' I can appreciate that statement just as I am persuaded that the highest compliment one rabbi can give to a colleague is to refer to him as a 'rabbi's rabbi.' Well, Cantor, in my eyes, you are a rabbi's rabbi! You have been my teacher, my mentor, my gentle critic" (speech presented at the Evening of Tribute to Cantor William Sharlin, New York, October 8, 1988).

44. Sharlin, "Trust the Process," 107.

45. *Ahavat Olam* was widely distributed but never published. It is included in Lisa Sharlin Klein, comp., *Cantor William Sharlin: A Library of Original Scores*, Pacific Southwest Region of the American Conference of Cantors, 2007, CD-ROM.

46. "Hadassah Menorah Marks 5th Birthday," *New York Post Home News*, April 1, 1951.

47. S. Merel, "Memories of My Friend Cantor William (Bill) Sharlin."

48. Sharlin, "Trust the Process," 106.

49. Merel, interview.

50. M. Merel, liner notes to *Standing Ovation*.

51. Eric Werner, Preface to Adolph Katchko, *Services for Sabbath Eve and Morning and Three Festivals* (New York: Hebrew Union School of Education and Sacred Music, 1952).

52. *Ibid.*

53. William used spiral-bound photocopies of the volumes for his own classes at HUC Los Angeles.

54. Sharlin, "Trust the Process," 107. The three volumes were apparently unavailable for public purchase until 1986.

55. Volume 1: Shabbat and Festivals; Volume 2: Weekday; Volume 3: High Holidays.

56. Eric Werner, "A Statement of Prin-

Notes. Chapter 3

ciple from the 1952 Preface," in Adolph Katchko, *A Thesaurus of Cantorial Liturgy* (all volumes) (New York: HUC School of Sacred Music, 1986).

57. "Acknowledgments" in Katchko, *Cantorial Curriculum Material*.

58. Chemjo Vinaver, "Out-of-Print Classics of Cantorial Liturgy," *Commentary*, January 1, 1957, 556.

59. Eric Werner, "Preface to the Out-of-Print Classics Reissue by the Hebrew Union School of Sacred Music" (various volumes) (New York: Sacred Music Press, 1953).

Chapter 3

1. William completed an intermediate reading course in German (2 parts), July 6 to August 13, 1948. He also completed courses at New York University in English Literature, and Medieval and Modern European History in the summer of 1947. Interestingly, his NYU record has his birthdate as December 15, 1919, while his actual birthdate is January 7, 1920. The enlistment record from World War II also shows his birth in 1919. Another mainstream source mistakenly has his birth year as 1918: Nick Strimple, *Choral Music in the Twentieth Century* (New York: Hal Leonard, 2005), 273.

2. His Ph.D. program is listed as Hebraic and cognate studies in his graduate record of 1951–1952. His record from 1954 shows Jewish Music as his major subject (under Eric Werner), Modern Hebrew Literature as his first minor subject (under Elias L. Epstein), and Jewish liturgy as his second minor subject (under Samuel L. Cohon).

3. During his academic career at HUC in New York and Cincinnati, William took eight courses taught by Eric Werner: Introduction to Jewish Music (1949); Workshop (1949); Workshop (1950); Score Reading (1950); Music 2 (1952); Liturgy 4 (1953); Music Seminar (1953); Music 6 (1953). Eric was also William's dissertation advisor.

4. Eric Werner, "De quibusdam relationibus inter accentus Masoretarum et neumas liquescentes." ["On Certain Relationships between Masoretic Accents and Liquescent Neumes."] (Ph.D. dissertation, University of Strasbourg, 1928).

5. Eric Werner's articles comparing church and synagogue chant include: "Preliminary Notes for a Comparative Study of Catholic and Jewish Musical Punctuation," *Hebrew Union College Annual* 15 (1940): 335–366; "The Lost Chords: Notes about Synagogue and Church Music," *Hebrew Union College Monthly* 29:2 (1942): 8; "The Influence of Jewish Music on the Gregorian Chant," *Proceedings of the Music Teachers National Association* 68 (1944): 241–247; "The Doxology in Synagogue and Church: A Liturgico-Musical Study," *Hebrew Union College Annual* 19 (1945–56): 275–351; "The Conflict Between Hellenism and Judaism in the Music of the Early Christian Church," *Hebrew Union College Annual* 20 (1947): 407–470; "Hebrew and Oriental Christian Metrical Hymns: A Comparison," *Hebrew Union College Annual* 23:2 (1950–51): 397–432; "The Common Ground in the Chant of Church and Synagogue," *Congresso Internazionale di Musica Sacra* (1952): 134–148; and "Die jüdischen Wurzeln der christlichen Kirchenmusik," in *Geschichte der katholischen Kirchenmusik, Vol. 1*, ed. Karl Gustav Fellerer (Kassel: Bärenreiter, 1972), 22–30.

6. See Peter Jeffrey, "*The Sacred Bridge, Volume 2*: A Review Essay," *Jewish Quarterly Review* 77:4 (1987): 293–298.

7. For a complete listing of Eric Werner's 217 publications, see Israel J. Katz, "Eric Werner (1901–1988): A Bibliography of His Collected Writings," *Musica Judaica* 10:1 (1987–88): 1–36.

8. Variations include "L'talmidi v'chaveri Ze'ev Sharlin, b'yedidut"—"To my friend and my fellow Ze'ev Sharlin, in friendship," which appears on the cover of an offprint of Eric Werner, "The Origin of the Eight Modes of Music," *Hebrew Union College Annual* 21 (1948): 211–255.

9. Judith K. Eisenstein, "The Professor

Notes. Chapter 3

in Room 202," *Shalshelet: The Chain* 2:2 (1976): 3–4. That issue of *Shalshelet*, a publication of the Cantorial Alumni Association (CAA) of SSM, was made in tribute to Eric Werner on the occasion of his seventy-fifth birthday. In addition to Eisenstein's essay, it includes a brief introduction by Paul M. Steinberg, then dean of SSM, Cantor Murray E. Simon, president of CAA, an article by Jack Gottlieb on the intersection of secular and sacred music in Werner's writings, a piece on *hazzanut* and art music by Werner himself, and a philosophical essay by William that bears the stamp of Werner's teachings, but does not mention him directly: William Sharlin, "The American Synagogue in Search of Its Musical Idiom," *Shalshelet: The Chain* 2:2 (1976): 6–8.

10. Eric Werner, "O, There Was a Magic-Kabalistic Song," *Sh'ma: A Journal of Jewish Responsibility* 11:210 (1981): 73–74.

11. Ibid., 73.

12. Ibid., 74.

13. William Sharlin, "Comments Made to the Cantor" (paper presented at Leo Baeck Temple, Los Angeles, CA, 1985.)

14. The camp was formally incorporated in the state of Wisconsin on May 22, 1952, as the Union Camp Institute of the Union for American Hebrew Congregations.

15. For a detailed look at this chapter in the Reform camping movement and William's involvement in it, see Judah M. Cohen, "Singing Out for Judaism: A History of Song Leaders and Song Leading at Olin-Sang-Ruby Union Institute," in *A Place of Their Own: The Rise of Reform Jewish Camping*, ed. Michael M. Lorge and Gary P. Zola (Tuscaloosa: University of Alabama Press, 2006), 173–208.

16. Cohen, "Singing Out for Judaism," 182.

17. Sharlin, "Trust the Process," 110.

18. See Ray M. Cook, *Sing for Fun* (New York: UAHC, 1955). This "experimental songbook," prepared at the request of the Commission on Jewish Education, contains "a collection of original songs for the primary grades of the Jewish religious school."

19. Cohen, "Singing Out for Judaism," 182.

20. J. Sharlin, interview.

21. Beatrice Landeck, ed., *"Git on Board": Collection of Folk Songs Arranged for Mixed Chorus and Solo Voice* (New York: Edward B. Marks, 1950).

22. William Sharlin, quoted in Ruben, "A History of the School of Sacred Music at Fifty."

23. *H.U.S.S.M. Bulletin* 1:1 (October 1952).

24. Merel, interview.

25. See Belskin-Ginsburg, "The Cantors Assembly," 13–19.

26. "History of the American Conference of Cantors," http://www.accantors.org/acc/node/24

27. Ruben, "A History of the School of Sacred Music at Fifty."

28. "History of the American Conference of Cantors."

29. Joseph Portnoy (1922–2008), an SSM graduate, was cantor of Temple Emanu-El in San Francisco from 1959 to 1986. George Weinflash (1924–2004), an SSM graduate, was cantor of Temple Beth El in Spring Valley, New York, from 1952 to 1985. Harold Orbach (1931–2014), an SSM graduate, was cantor of Temple Israel in Detroit (later West Bloomfield) from 1962 to 2002. Walter Davidson (1903–1989), a founding board member of SSM, was cantor of Temple Beth Emeth in the Flatbush section of Brooklyn from 1928 to 1978. Samuel Kelemer (1918–2008) was a cantor from age nine and served for some thirty years at Temple Beth Am in Los Angeles. In later years, William was made an Honorary Vice President of the organization.

30. *Special Songster of New Materials for Congregational and Solo Singing; prepared for The First Institute on Sacred Music of the American Conference of Certified Cantors, June 8–11, 1953, in New York City* (New York: Hebrew Union School of Sacred Music, 1953).

Notes. Chapter 3

31. There were isolated cases of women serving in cantorial positions prior to their official training and recognition. The earliest known example is Julie Rosewald, who served as "cantor soprano" at Temple Emanu-El in San Francisco from 1884 to 1893. For a detailed account, see Judith S. Pinnolis, "'Cantor Soprano' Julie Rosewald: The Musical Career of a Jewish American 'New Woman,'" *The American Jewish Archives Journal* 62:2 (2010): 1–53. Betty Robbins was the first woman appointed as a cantor in the twentieth century. She was hired by Temple Avodah in Oceanside, New York in 1955.

32. Sharlin, "Trust the Process," 109.

33. Although William only completed two chapters of his doctoral dissertation, he did produce a full chapter outline: (1) Background of Hasidism—a. Theologic, b. Sociologic, c. Political, d. Main geographic areas; (2) Scientific Approach to Musical Folklore—a. General anthropologic, b. Method of comparative musicology, c. Application of both methods to Hasidic music; (3) Function of Hasidic Music—a. Liturgic, b. Tzadik and his circle, c. Ritual and superstitious function; (4) Sources—a. Descriptive sources, b. Music written and oral; (5) Styles—a. Modes, b. Melodic mannerisms, c. Characteristic rhythms of metrical tunes; (6) The Nigun—a. History, b. Function; (7) Development of Hasidic Music—a. Leading generations of dynasties, b. The various influences, c. Era of parodies and travesties (8) Philosophy of Hasidic Music—a. Classical Hasidism, b. Chabad; (9) Typical Examples of the Various Trends with Full Analysis; (10) Impact of Hasidic Chant on East European Hazanuth; (11) Decline of Hasidic Music—a. Internal reasons, b. Musical reasons; (12) Conclusion.

34. Eisenstein, "the Professor in Room 202," 3.

35. Eric Werner, *A Voice Still Heard: The Sacred Songs of the Ashkenazic Jews* (University Park: Pennsylvania State University Press, 1976), 312, n. 35. These adjectives were originally from Chaim Harris, *Toldot ha-Neginah veha-Hazanut be-Yisrael* (New York: Bitzaron, 1950), 346. Werner quotes them in agreement.

36. Werner, *A Voice Still Heard*, 53.

37. Levin, interview with William Sharlin, Milken Archive of American Jewish Music, undated.

38. William's scholarly writings are collected in Jonathan L. Friedmann and Brad Stetson, ed., *Jewish Sacred Music and Jewish Identity: Continuity and Fragmentation* (St. Paul, MN: Paragon House, 2008).

39. Sharlin, "Trust the Process," 115. In his memoir, recorded in his late eighties, William conflated this memory with a recollection from decades earlier: "...I was asked to present some of [Eric's] compositions. I was well on my way vocally, and when I finished singing Werner's *Kedushah*, I stepped off the *bimah* and walked past two cantorial voice teachers who had known me in the past. I noticed a look of awe on their faces—they couldn't believe the improvement in my voice." Ibid.

40. Sharlin, "Trust the Process," 112.

41. "Sunday Morning Service," *The Temple Bulletin* 43:12, Dec. 23, 1956, 1.

42. Sharlin, "Trust the Process," 111.

43. Ibid.

44. *Birth of a Baby* received a nine-page story in *Life Magazine*, and prompted the opposition of religious groups who saw it as an intrusion on natural mysteries.

45. These include exhibitions at the HUC Los Angeles (Jack H. Skirball Campus), the Skirball Gallery at HUC Cincinnati campus, and the Skirball Museum and Archaeological Building on the Jerusalem campus.

46. In 1983 Jack and Audrey Skirball (later Skirball-Kenis) provided the initial funding to Uri D. Herscher for the development of a new cultural center in Los Angeles. Jack Skirball was also instrumental in locating a site for the project. It was named the Skirball Cultural Center in his honor.

47. Sharlin, "Trust the Process," 113.

48. The CCAR conference was held in Pike, New Hampshire from June 22 to 27,

Notes. Chapter 4

1954. Leonard Beerman recalled this first meeting in a Leo Baeck Temple tribute book, *A Life of Sacred Music: In Honor of Cantor William Sharlin* (Los Angeles: Leo Baeck Temple, 2000), 7, distributed at a concert of William's music at the Temple presented on the occasion of his eightieth birthday. In another source, William remembered his first meeting and informal audition with Leonard Beerman occurring in Cincinnati. Sharlin, "Trust the Process," 113.

49. Leonard Beerman, interview with Robert Corsini, Interfaith Communities United for Justice and Peace, Los Angeles, CA, September 2013.

50. Kurt Streeter, "At 93, Rabbi Leonard Beerman still stirs passions with pacifist views," *Los Angeles Times*, Nov. 26, 2014.

51. Through the years, Rabbi Leonard Beerman was involved in numerous organizations and special committees, including: Los Angeles Community Relations Conference; Committee for Sane Nuclear Policy; Committee to Abolish Capital Punishment; United National Association of Los Angeles; Commission on Justice and Peace; and Jewish Peace Fellowship. For a complete list, see "Beerman, Leonard," in *Reform Judaism in America*, 13.

52. Sharlin, "Trust the Process," 113.

53. Judith Gertler, interview with William Sharlin, "Leo Baeck Oral History Project: 1947–1963," Leo Baeck Temple, Los Angeles, CA, April 23, 1990.

Chapter 4

1. Leonard Beerman, letter to William Sharlin (Los Angeles, CA, June 11, 1954).

2. Leonard Beerman, letter to William Sharlin (Los Angeles, CA, May 25, 1954).

3. J. Sharlin, interview.

4. Streeter, "At 93, Rabbi Leonard Beerman still stirs passions with pacifist views."

5. Gertler, interview with William Sharlin.

6. *Ibid*. Two prominent congregations, one in Cleveland and one in San Francisco, invited him be their cantor. Leonard Beerman received similar invitations during his early years at LBT.

7. *Ibid*.

8. *Ibid*.

9. J. Sharlin, interview.

10. Alan Weiner, interview by author, Agoura Hills, CA, December 8, 2014.

11. The rented facilities included the Westside Jewish Center and a motel at Wilshire Blvd. and Beverly Glen, which ultimately became Sinai Temple. High Holiday services were held at the Academy Award Theater, then on Melrose Blvd., and confirmation services were held at Temple Isaiah on Pico Blvd.

12. Shirl Lee Pitesky, interview by author, Los Angeles, CA, September 6, 2014.

13. *Ibid*.

14. *Ibid*.

15. *Ibid*.

16. *Ibid*.

17. *Ibid*.

18. The string quartet consisted of members of the Myrow and Konviser families.

19. J. Sharlin, interview.

20. Gertler, interview with William Sharlin.

21. Sharlin, "Trust the Process," 115–116. Jacqui Sharlin recalls this taking place in Los Angeles.

22. J. Sharlin, interview.

23. Eugene Gash, *Memoir* (New York: Vantage, 1995), 66.

24. *Ibid*.

25. J. Sharlin, interview.

26. *Ibid*.

27. See Jonathan L. Friedmann, "Cantor Reuben Rinder, Frederick Jacobi and Temple Emanu-El of San Francisco: Commissioning the Sacred," *Western States Jewish History* 45:4 (2013): 321–332.

28. Ernest Bloch, *Avodath Hakodesh* (Sacred Service) [1933], and Darius Milhaud, *Service sacré pour le samedi matin* (Sacred Service for Sabbath Morning) [1947].

29. Gash, *Memoir*, 66.

30. J. Sharlin, interview.

Notes. Chapter 4

31. The remainder of the program included: Robert Schumann's *Sonata in G minor*, Op. 22; Maurice Ravel's *Jeux d'eau*, *Menuet* (from Le Tombeau de Couperin), and *Alborada del Gracioso*; Carlos Chavez's *Prelude No. 5* and *Prelude No. 8*; Ernst Toch's *Capriccetti*, Op. 36; and Louise Talma's *Sonata No. 1*.

32. J. Sharlin, interview.
33. *Ibid.*
34. *Ibid.*
35. *Ibid.*
36. *Ibid.*

37. "Historic-Cultural Monument Application for the Kallis House," Recommendation to the Cultural Heritage Commission, Los Angeles Department of City Planning (Recommendation Report CHC 2006-7810-HCM).

38. *Ibid.*

39. Kallis House, Los Angeles Conservancy. https://www.laconservancy.org/locations/kallis-house

40. J. Sharlin, interview.
41. Sharlin, "Trust the Process," 114.
42. Streeter, "At 93, Rabbi Leonard Beerman still stirs passions with pacifist views."
43. *Ibid.*

44. Leonard Beerman, "From Rabbi Beerman," *Leo Baeck Temple College Bulletin* 1:2 (winter 1967): 2.

45. See Abraham Maslow, *The Farther Reaches of Human Nature* (New York: Viking Press, 1971).

46. Sharlin, "Comments Made to the Cantor."
47. Bill Cutter, interview by author, Los Angeles, CA, September 15, 2014.
48. Sharlin, "Trust the Process," 114.
49. L. Sharlin, "William Sharlin."
50. William Sharlin, "Myth" (undated lecture presented at a Shabbat service at Leo Baeck Temple, Los Angeles).
51. Levin, interview with William Sharlin.
52. This remark was recorded in 1968 or 1969. Marc Lee Raphael, *The Synagogue in America: A Short Story* (New York: New York University Press, 2011), 173.

53. Leonard Beerman, tribute in *A Life of Sacred Music*, 7.
54. Sanford Ragins, tribute in *A Life of Sacred Music*, 5.

55. See William Sharlin, "Israeli Music at 37: Those Were the Days," *The Jewish Newspaper*, April 27, 1985, 6, and "Israel's Influence on American Liberal Synagogue Music," in *Gates of Understanding*, ed. Lawrence A. Hoffman (New York: Central Conference of American Rabbis, 1977), 122–128.

56. William kept several copies of the program from the 1963 concert, along with newspaper clippings highlighting the event. For example, "Tri-Culture Music Concert at Leo Baeck Wednesday Eve," *B'nai B'rith Messenger*, October 18, 1963, 32.

57. Eric Werner, *The Sacred Bridge: Liturgical Parallels in Synagogue and Early Church* (New York: Columbia University Press, 1959).

58. The HUC Cantors Ensemble consisted of Cantors Sidney Bloom, Samuel Brown, Maurice Glick, Felix Groveman, Max Roth, and Saul Silverman.

59. The choral pieces included: Synagogue—*Yigdal Elohim Chai* (Halevy), *Ashre Yoshve Vesecho* (Leonard), *Sh'ma* (Milhaud), *L'chu N'ran'no* (Schalit), *Adonoy Moloch* (Freed); Roman Catholic—*Credo, Missa de Breata Virgine* (Josquin), *Tantum Ergo* (Palestrina), *Gloria, Missa Dominicalis* (Viadana), *Sanctus Credo, Mass, Pacem in Terris* (Biggs); Greek Orthodox—*Tin Anastasin* (Desby), *Soma Christou* (Tikey Zes), *To Pnevma Su* (Desby), *Aineite* (Desby).

60. *Songbook for The American Conference of Cantors, Twelfth Annual Convention*, Sportsmen's Lodge, Los Angeles, CA, June 28–July 1, 1965. The booklet also includes pieces by Meir Ben Uri, Maurice Goldman, Charles Davidson, Max Wohlberg, Philip Moddel, and Jacob Weinberg.

61. Levin, interview with William Sharlin.
62. Pitesky, interview.

Notes. Chapter 4

63. *Ibid.*
64. *Ibid.*
65. Cutter, interview.
66. Lisa Sharlin Klein, "William Sharlin" (presented at the Funeral of William Sharlin, Leo Baeck Temple, Los Angeles, November 9, 2012).
67. J. Sharlin, interview.
68. S. L. Kopald, Jr., chairman of the HUC Board of Governors (1966–1972), was the only presenter not to have graduated from the school.
69. Robert Blinder, letter to William Sharlin (St. Louis, MO, February 25, 1972). Incidentally, several years earlier Eric Werner wrote a scathing essay criticizing Blinder's lack of musical knowledge and appreciation. Werner used Blinder's article on music and liturgy (*CCAR Journal*, April 1965) as an illustration of the "rabbi-centrism" of the Reform movement and its impoverished view of the role of music. Eric Werner, "What Function Has Synagogue Music Today?" *CCAR Journal* 13:4 (1966): 35–40. Perhaps some of Blinder's surprise at Sharlin's mental agility reflects the rabbi's broader view of music (and cantors) as inferior to words (and rabbis).
70. Joining Blinder in requesting copies of the service music were Rabbi Alexander M. Schindler of the Northwest Council of UAHC (Chestnut Hill, MA, February 25, 1972), Rabbi Leonard A. Schoolman of the New York offices of UAHC (New York, February 25, 1972), Rabbi Myron Silverman of The Suburban Temple (Cleveland, OH, February 25, 1972), Rabbi David Polish of Beth Emet the Free Synagogue (Evanston, IL, February 28, 1972), Rabbi B. Safran of Achduth Vesholom Congregation (Fort Wayne, IN, May 3, 1972), and Cantor Eli H. Cohn of Congregation B'nai Israel (Sacramento, CA, February 29, 1972).
71. Robert A. Alper, letter to William Sharlin (Cincinnati, OH, March 6, 1972).
72. Jack Skirball, letter to William Sharlin (Los Angeles, CA, February 29, 1972).
73. Joseph Glaser, letter to William Sharlin (New York, February 24, 1972).
74. Alfred Gottschalk, letter to William Sharlin (Jerusalem, March 6, 1972).
75. William Sharlin, *T'filat L'misrat Torah: A Service on the Receiving and Transmission of the Torah on the Occasion of the Inauguration of President Alfred Gottschalk, Hebrew Union College–Jewish Institute of Religion* (New York: CCAR, 1972).
76. The pieces on the record and song book are: Processional—*Pitchu Li* (melody for *Hodu Ladonay Ki Tov*: S. Hofman); *Ata Nigleyta—Ala Elohim*; *Mi Ya'ale*; *Moshe Kibel—Al Shlosha D'vareem* (melody for *Al Shlosha D'vareem*: D. Weinkranz); *Eylu D'vareem*; *Ashreynu—Sh'ma Yisrael* (melody for *Sh'ma Yisrael*: M. Helfman, uncredited); *Ve'ahavta* (melody: Torah cantillation); *Lo Yareynu* (melody: E. Gabbai); *L'cha Adonay*; *Hodo Al Eretz—Etz Chayim*; and *Oseh Shalom* (melody: N. Hirsch).
77. Sharlin, *T'filat L'misrat Torah*, 1.
78. Perryne Anker, telephone interview by author, June 5, 2014.
79. Gertler, interview with William Sharlin.
80. *Ibid.*
81. In private, William confessed that he would have liked more active involvement from Rabbi Leonard Beerman. Cutter, interview.
82. Gertler, interview with William Sharlin.
83. Sharlin, "Trust the Process," 118.
84. *Ibid.*
85. Linda Rabinowitch Thal, introduction to "The Musical World of Cantor William Sharlin" (paper presented at UAHC Western Region Biennial, Los Angeles, CA, 1989).
86. Pitesky, interview.
87. Sharlin, "Trust the Process," 117.
88. Cutter, interview.
89. L. Sharlin, "William Sharlin."
90. For example, Rose Engel, Judith Berman, and Lita Greenberg, *My Sabbath Prayer Book* (Los Angeles: self-published, 1977).
91. For a complete chart of the Sharlin Method for cantillation, see Helen Lene-

Notes. Chapter 4

man, "Teaching Trope: The Hows, Whys, and Whens," in *Bar/Bat Mitzvah Education: A Sourcebook*, ed. Helen Leneman (Denver, CO: A.R.E., 1993), 151–152.

92. *Ibid.*, 146.

93. William also had opportunities to sing Broadway favorites at LBT. For example, he was involved in "It's a Grand Night for Singing: Music from Broadway & Beyond," a concert also featuring Cantors Shula Kalir-Merton (Temple Beth El, Alisa Viejo), Mark Saltzman (Congregation Kol Ami, West Hollywood), Wally Schachet-Briskin (LBT), and Lisa Sharlin (Temple Beth David, Westminster), accompanist Paul Zuill, and the LBT Youth Choir, "Sing Thing." The June 6, 1999, concert included music from Gershwin, Porter, Sondheim, Bernstein, Rodgers & Hart, Webber, Simon and Forest & Wright.

94. Los Angeles Drama Critics Circle, 1969–1979 Awards. http://ladramacriticscircle.com/1969-1979-awards/

95. William's *Jewish Newspaper* columns include: "The Purim Theme in Jewish Music" (February 28, 1985); "Mozart Mounts the *Bimah*—What a Mass!" (March 14, 1985); "When Religious Music Turns 'Cultural'" (April 11, 1985); "Israeli Music at 37: Those Were the Days" (April 27, 1985); "Why Can't a Woman Chant Like a Man?" (date unknown).

96. William Sharlin, "Mozart Mounts the *Bimah*—What a Mass!"

97. The article includes this line: "I was told he has a Ph.D. in musicology. C: What's a person with a Ph.D. doing as a *chazen*? It doesn't sound right. R: Well, I was also told he had a traditional, Orthodox background. He *davened* three times a day until he was eighteen." *Ibid.* It is unclear whether William ever claimed he completed his Ph.D.

98. Werner, *A Voice Still Heard*, 218.

99. B. J. Davis, "Funny, It Didn't *Sound* Jewish," *Washington Jewish Week*, April 9, 1992, 38.

100. *Ibid.*

101. Werner, *A Voice Still Heard*, 295, n. 30.

102. See, for example, these articles by Werner: "Meyerbeer, Mendelssohn, Mahler: Ein Crescendo des Judentums," *B'nai B'rith Mittelungen für Österreich* 36 (1926): 188–122; "Gustav Mahlers Weg (Zu seinem Todestag am 18. Mai)," *Jüdische Rundschau* 39:40 (1934): 13; "Felix Mendelssohn—Gustav Mahler: Two Borderline Cases of German-Jewish Assimilation," *Yuval* 4 (1982): 240–64; "Gustav Mahlers Symphoniethemen: Eine typologische Untersuchung der ersten vier Symphonien," *Musicologica Austriaca* 7 (1987): 69–127; Unpublished manuscript: "An Outline of the Music of Mahler." Werner also wrote a lengthy tome, *Mendelssohn: A New Image of the Composer and His Age* (New York: Free Press, 1963).

103. For instance, Anshe Chesed Fairmont Temple of Cleveland, Ohio commissioned a setting of *V'shamru* (New York: Transcontinental, 1987).

104. Sarah J. Sager, letter to William Sharlin (Cleveland, Ohio, April 9, 1985). The choir for that weekend included the Fairmount Temple Choir, the Fairmount Temple Auxiliary Choir, and the Choral Arts Performing Society, under the direction of A. Edward Battaglia.

105. William Sharlin, "The Ever-Changing Musical Tradition of the Jewish People: Diversity Through the Ages" (program presented at Congregation Beth Am, Los Altos Hills, California, April 3–5, 1981).

106. "Cantor William Sharlin: Composer, Conductor, Soloist, Scholar-in-Residence" (Congregation B'nai Jehudah, Kansas City, MO, Mar. 7–9, 1986).

107. See the various essays anthologized in Friedmann and Stetson, ed., *Jewish Sacred Music and Jewish Identity*.

108. The Festival of Music Made in Los Angeles included: on November 28, Stravinsky's *Ebony Concerto* and *Variations (Aldous Huxley Memoriam)* and *Agnon*, and Brahms-Schoenberg's *Piano Quartet* in G minor, Op. 25 (orchestral version); on December 5, "music by Cage, Castelnuovo-Tedesco, Chihara, Dahl, Eisler, Foss,

Gershwin, Harris, Korngold, Kraft, Krenek, Levant, Michalsky, Schoenberg, Still, Stravinsky, Toch, Weiss and Others"; on December 13, Schoenberg's *Prelude to Genesis Suite*, *A Survivor from Warsaw*, and *Piano Concerto*, and Stravinsky's *Requiem Canticles* and *Symphony in Three Movements*.

109. Sharlin, "Trust the Process," 130.
110. *Ibid.*
111. *Ibid.*
112. J. Sharlin, interview.
113. Boston Symphony, *Beethoven—Symphony No. 9; Schoenberg—A Survivor from Warsaw*, RCA, 2000, compact disc.
114. Martin Bernheimer, "Tilson Thomas Closes 'Made in L.A.' Festival," *Los Angeles Times*, December 15, 1981.
115. *Ibid.*
116. Donna Perlmutter, "Heady Dose of Modern Masters," *Los Angeles Herald Examiner*, December 15, 1981.
117. John Henken, "Raccoons Join Institute Orchestra at Bowl," *Los Angeles Times*, July 28, 1987.
118. "American Conference of Cantors Demonstration: On the Performance of Schoenberg's *A Survivor from Warsaw*, op. 46, with William Sharlin," *Journal of the Arnold Schoenberg Institute* 14:1 (1991): 38.
119. Arnold Schoenberg, *Kol Nidre*, Op. 39, reduced for organ by Leonard Stein, registration by Mark Robson (Los Angeles: Belmont Music, 1997).
120. Arnold Schoenberg, Letter to Paul Dessau, November 22, 1941. Reprinted in Erwin Stein, ed., *Arnold Schoenberg Letters* (Berkeley: University of California Press, 1987), 213. For a history and analysis of Schoenberg's *Kol Nidre*, see John F. Guest, "Commissioning Émigré Composers in Los Angeles, 1938–1945: Rabbi Jacob Sonderling's Contributions to Jewish Musical History" (M.J.S.M. thesis, Academy for Jewish Religion California, Los Angeles, 2018), 69–87.
121. The concert, titled Lebewohl Wien (Farewell Vienna), was held at the Gindi Auditorium of the University of Judaism (now the American Jewish University) in Los Angeles, and was produced by Neal Brostoff, a pianist, lecturer, and founder of the local Jewish Music Foundation. Lebewohl Wien was part of a two-year serialized international conference-festival, "A Voice for Our Time," organized and directed by Neil W. Levin, artistic director of the Milken Archive of Jewish Music.
122. Herbert Glass, "Dance and Music Reviews: A Vienna-to-Los Angeles Concert at Gindi," *The Los Angeles Times*, May 30, 1992.
123. William Sharlin, "L'dor V'dor: From Generation to Generation," in *Jewish Sacred Music and Jewish Identity: Continuity and Fragmentation*, ed. Jonathan L. Friedmann and Brad Stetson (St. Paul, MN: Paragon House, 2008), 87–88.
124. Sharlin, "Trust the Process," 116.
125. Ilana Sharlin, "Eulogy for Dad" (presented at the funeral of William Sharlin, Leo Baeck Temple, Los Angeles, November 9, 2012).
126. *Ibid.*

Chapter 5

1. See Mordecai Kaplan, *Judaism as a Civilization: Toward a Reconstruction of American-Jewish Life* (New York: Macmillan, 1934).
2. In 1973 the University of Judaism (UJ) took its first steps toward independence from JTS. The UJ board of directors undertook plans to finance and build the new Bel Air campus. In 1995, the UJ opened the first American rabbinical school in the Western United States, the Ziegler School of Rabbinic Studies, which would become an official constituent of the Conservative movement, despite the school's nondenominational orientation. In March of 2007, UJ merged with the Brandeis-Bardin Institute to become American Jewish University.
3. Deborah Dash Moore, *To the Golden Cities: Pursuing the American Dream in*

Notes. Chapter 5

Miami and L.A. (Cambridge, MA: Harvard University Press, 1994), 135.

4. Rabbi Albert M. Lewis to Maurice Eisendrath, head of UAHC in New York. Quoted *ibid.*, 135.

5. Edgar Magnin, quoted *ibid.*

6. *Ibid.* Announcement of Courses for Adult Education and Religious School Training.

7. *Ibid.*, 136.

8. *Ibid.*, 137.

9. Isaiah Zeldin, letter to William Sharlin (Los Angeles, CA, May 25, 1954).

10. The HUC School of Sacred Music has offered a practicum, "The Music of William Sharlin." Cohen, *The making of a Reform Jewish Cantor*, 117.

11. Sharlin, "Trust the Process," 119.

12. Harry Newman, *Thirty-Four Years on the Bimah: Vignettes of My Life as a "Professional" Jew* (Bloomington, IN: Author House, 2007), 14.

13. Moore, *To the Golden Cities*, 305, n. 39.

14. Sharlin kept his undated lecture notes in a closet drawer in his home studio.

15. Joel Stern, interview by author, Los Angeles, CA, May 11, 2014.

16. *Ibid.*

17. Janece Erman Cohen, cantor of Congregation Or Chadash in Tuscan, AZ, is among the few students who went on to attend SSM in New York. She began her studies with William in Los Angeles, flying in weekly from Arizona. She later graduated from the New York program in 1990. Her master's thesis focused on William's life and music.

18. Stern, interview.

19. Anker, interview.

20. Mark Saltzman, interview by author, Pasadena, CA, October 20, 2014.

21. Stern, interview.

22. J. Sharlin, interview.

23. *Ibid.*

24. Sharlin, "Trust the Process," 129.

25. Stern, interview.

26. The Saul Silverman Award was established by Temple Israel of Hollywood, California, where Silverman was cantor.

27. Saltzman, interview.

28. Anker, interview.

29. Perryne Anker sang in the choir for Richard Tucker's two Jewish albums for Columbia Records, arranged and accompanied by Sholom Secunda: *Kol Nidre Service* (1959) and *Passover Seder Festival* (1962).

30. J. Sharlin, interview.

31. Debbie Friedman's first five albums are: *Sing Unto God* (1972); *Not by Might, Not by Power* (1974); *Ani Ma-amin* (1976); *If Not Now, When?* (1980); and *The Youth Shall See Visions* (1981). When Friedman died in 2011 at the age of fifty-nine, her albums totaled over twenty. Many of her songs are collected as songbooks and appear in various anthologies.

32. See Keith Kahn-Harris, "Jews United and Divided by Music: Contemporary Jewish Music in the UK and America," in *Religion and Popular Music in Europe: New Expressions of Sacred and Secular*, ed. Thomas Bossius, Andreas Häger, and Keith Kahn-Harris (London: I. B. Tauris, 2011), 71–91.

33. According to Jacqui Sharlin, Debbie Friedman's mother prodded her into taking the course. J. Sharlin, interview.

34. *Ibid.*

35. Stern, interview.

36. *Ibid.*

37. Sharlin Klein, "William Sharlin."

38. Full membership in the American Conference of Cantors was open to Department of Sacred Music graduates who served in a pulpit for five years and took qualifying examinations.

39. Weiner, interview.

40. *Ibid.*

41. Anker, interview.

42. BT *Berakhot* 24a.

43. Interviewee quoted in Mark Slobin, *Chosen Voices*, 122.

44. William Sharlin, "Why Can't a Man Chant Like a Woman?"

45. *Ibid.*

46. *Ibid.*

47. Dora B. Krakower, *Trusting the Song*

Notes. Chapter 5

That Sings Within: Pioneer Woman Cantor (Santa Monica, CA: Azure, 1994).

48. *Ibid.*, 84.
49. *Ibid.*, 88.
50. *Ibid.*, 88–89.
51. "Women Lead Jewish Services," *Los Angeles Times*, November 22, 1970.
52. Krakower, *Trusting the Song That Sings Within*, 89.
53. "Mrs. Krakower Earns Silverman Music Award," *B'nai B'rith Messenger*, July 16, 1971.
54. Krakower, *Trusting the Song That Sings Within*, 90.
55. Barbara Ostfeld-Horowitz, interview excerpted in Slobin, *Chosen Voices*, 123–124.
56. Anker, interview.
57. Ari L. Goldman, "As Call Comes, More Women Answer," *New York Times*, October 19, 1986.
58. Pitesky, interview.
59. Merel, interview.
60. Radio host Leonid Hambro joked about the change from Bill to William during his introduction to Jacqui and William's live performance of Robert Schumann's four-hand work, *Bilder aus Osten*, Op. 66 (KPFK, January 31, 1984).
61. Stern, interview.
62. Merel, interview.
63. Cutter, interview.
64. Sharlin, "Trust the Process," 132.
65. Sharlin Klein, "William Sharlin."
66. Weiner, interview.
67. This observation comes from Alan Weiner. According to Jack Gottlieb, the flatted sixth is a fitting "Jewish coloration": "That whole step, on the sixth step of the scale, makes all these [popular American songs] sound 'WASPy.' When the sixth (a.k.a. the submediant, but don't ask why) in a major key is flattened, the music takes on a beguiling quality, major in the bottom half—called tetrachord in theoretical terminology—and minor in the top half. But when the submediant ... [is] lowered a half-step, the gypsy emerges: half steps both below and above, which is to say, the fourth step is raised and the sixth step is flattened."

Jack Gottlieb, *Funny, It Doesn't Sound Jewish: How Yiddish Songs and Synagogue Melodies Influenced Tin Pan Alley, Broadway, and Hollywood* (New York: SUNY Press, 2004), 95.

68. Cutter, interview.
69. See Friedmann and Stetson, ed., *Jewish Sacred Music and Jewish Identity*.
70. William Sharlin, "Music of the Synagogue: When the *Chazzan* 'Turned Around,'" *CCAR Journal* (winter 1962): 43–44.
71. *Ibid.*, 43.
72. *Ibid.*, 44.
73. William also repackaged the essay for the LBT community, shifting the focus to the congregation's response to the cantor. "On Turning Around; Or, Can You Achieve Privacy in Public?," *Leo Baeck Temple College Bulletin* 1:2 (winter 1967): 3.
74. The article appears, for instance, in my course reader: Jonathan L. Friedmann, ed., *20th Century Synagogue Music: Essential Readings* (Woodland Hills, CA: Isaac Nathan), 92–94.
75. For example, Rabbiner-und Kantorenausbildung, Abraham Geiger Kolleg an der Universität Potsdam, Berlin (Winter semester 2012/2013).
76. Most recently, Tamar Heather Havilio, "(Re)Learning *L'Hitpaleil*: The Performance of Prayer as Spiritual Education," *CCAR Journal: The Reform Jewish Quarterly* (winter 2014): 190–206. Havilio erroneously refers to the essay as an unpublished, undated article from the 1970s. The fact that it has been reproduced and disseminated in this unspecified way is further testament to its popularity. It has attained "folk" status in the field.
77. In my own experience, mentioning William's name to rabbis and cantors often elicits references to the essay.
78. Abraham W. Binder, *Biblical Chant* (New York: Philosophical Library, 1959); Solomon Rosowsky, *The Cantillation of the Bible* (New York: Reconstructionist, 1957).
79. Irene Heskes, *Passport to Jewish Music: Its History, Traditions, and Culture* (New York: Tara, 1994), 39.

Notes. Chapter 5

80. Eric Werner, "Review of *The Cantillation of the Bible: The Five Books of Moses*, by Solomon Rosowsky," *The Jewish Quarterly Review* 41 (April 1959): 292.

81. Ibid., 289.

82. William Sharlin, "Review of *Biblical Chant*, by A. W. Binder," *Central Conference of American Rabbis Journal* (June 1960): 65–66. The trope systems in Ashkenazi custom include: (1) Torah (Shabbat and Weekday); (2) Haftarah; (3) Torah (High Holiday); (4) Esther; (5) Song of Songs, Ruth, and Ecclesiastes; (6) Lamentations.

83. Ibid., 66.

84. William took four courses with Abraham W. Binder at SSM: Cantillation (Spr. 1950); Worship (Spr. 1950); Jewish Musical Settings (Fall 1950); and Harmony and Counterpoint (Spr. 1951).

85. The published works of William Sharlin include, from Transcontinental: *Eil Na R'fa Na La*; *Elohai N'shama*; "May the Time Not Be Distant"; *Mi Barehev*; *Oseh Shalom*; *Shalom Aleychem*; *Shir Hashirim*; *T'fillah L'misrat Torah* (Gottschalk Service); *V'shamru*; *Yom Zeh L'Yisrael*. From Laurendale Associates: *Ani Ma'amim*; "Jacob's Dream"; *Shalom Rav*; *Sim Shalom*; *Tzor Te'udah*; *Va'ani T'filati*; *V'shamru no. 1*; *V'shamru no. 2*; *V'shamru no. 3*; *V'shamru no. 4*; "Will There Yet Come Days"; *Yesh Kochavim*.

86. Merel, Interview.

87. Sharlin, "Trust the Process," 117.

88. A compound chord symbol involves the root note letter followed by a slash and the base note letter or inversion (e.g., C/G).

89. Sharlin, "Trust the Process," 117.

90. For instance, William sang the Bloch *Sacred Service* with the Camerata Singers in a program commemorating the fiftieth anniversary of Temple Israel, Long Beach, in 1974. The event also included a lecture by Holocaust survivor and political activist Elie Wiesel. Kaelter, *From Danzig*, 222–223.

91. Ernest Bloch, quoted in Suzanne Bloch, program notes for the Symphonic Choral Society of New York's presentation of the *Sacred Service* (Philharmonic Hall, Lincoln Center, December 7, 1969).

92. Schachet-Briskin, "The Music of Reform Youth."

93. Joshua R. Jacobson, *Chanting the Hebrew Bible: The Complete Guide to the Art of Cantillation* (Philadelphia: Jewish Publication Society, 2002). The book's front matter lists William among those who donated funds for its completion.

94. The obligations of *Eilu D'varim*: "To honor father and mother; to perform acts of love and kindness; to attend the house of study daily; to welcome the stranger; to visit the sick; to rejoice with bride and groom; to console the bereaved; to pray with sincerity; to make peace when there is strife. And the study of Torah is equal to them all because it leads to them all."

95. Kol Echad filed Articles of Incorporation in the State of California on Tuesday, August 1, 1978.

96. Weiner, interview.

97. In addition to Jewish community centers, synagogues, and Jewish organizations, Kol Echad performed for the American Guild of Organists, the American Choral Directors Association, and the Schoenberg Institute at USC, among others.

98. For example, Gary Bachlund's "Essays on Peace," which Kol Echad premiered as part of the Jewish Music Commission of Los Angeles's "Celebration of Jewish Music II," held on March 3, 1984, at Valley Beth Shalom, Encino.

99. "American Composers: Synagogue Music of the New World" (Program Notes, Temple Beth Shalom, Santa Ana, and Gindi Auditorium, University of Judaism, March 26 and 29, 1994).

100. See, for instance, Daniel Cariaga, "Lane, Merrill with Kol Echad Chorale," *Los Angeles Times*, June 15, 1987.

101. Max Stern, "Kol Echad is holding auditions," *Chazzanut Online* (Mail Archive), Dec. 21, 1993. http://archive.chazzanut.com/jewish-music-old/msg00494.html

102. Weiner contributed three pieces to the 1994 "American Composers" concert:

"The Book of Life," "All the Vows," and "Peace."

103. Press release, "The Music of William Sharlin," undated. For concert details, see "Tradition and Modernity: The Music of William Sharlin" (Program Notes, Temple Bat Yahm, Newport Beach and Leo Baeck Temple, Los Angeles, June 2 and 4, 1991).

104. The orchestra included six violins, two violas, two celli, one bass, one flute, one oboe, one clarinet, one bassoon, and one French horn.

105. Weiner, interview.

106. For example, William's settings of *Yom Zeh L'Yisrael*, *Eilu D'varim*, *Shir Hashirim*, and *P'tach Lanu* were included in the "California Composers" program, co-sponsored by The American Conference of Cantors and The Guild of Temple Musicians (Wilshire Boulevard Temple, Los Angeles, June 26, 2000).

107. J. Sharlin, interview.

Chapter 6

1. Kaelter, *From Danzig*, 121.
2. *Ibid.*, 135.
3. Irwin I. Soref, "Samuel Kaminker," *Jewish Education* 34:4 (1964): 222.
4. Hillel Gamoran, "The Road to Chalutzim: Reform Judaism's Hebrew-Speaking Program," in *A Place of Their Own: The Rise of Reform Jewish Camping*, ed. Michael M. Lorge and Gary P. Zola (Tuscaloosa: University of Alabama Press, 2006), 135.
5. Soref, "Samuel Kaminker," 222.
6. J. Sharlin, interview.
7. Lisa Sharlin's *Yom Zeh L'Yisrael* is included in *Shireinu: The Complete Jewish Songbook*, ed. Joel N. Eglash (New York: Transcontinental, 2002), 380. The piece includes a round suggestive of her father's influence.
8. Schachet-Briskin, "The Music of Reform Youth."
9. *Ibid.*
10. *Ibid.*
11. Shlomo Carlebach's participation at Camp Saratoga was arranged by Bill Cutter. Cutter, interview.
12. Sam Weiss, "Carlebach, Neo-Hasidic Music and Liturgical Practice," *Journal of Synagogue Music* 34 (2009): 55–56.
13. William Sharlin, "Israel's Influence on American Liberal Synagogue Music," 122–127.
14. *Ibid.*, 125.
15. *Ibid.*
16. *Ibid.*, 126.
17. William Sharlin, "Hasidic Music" (presentation at Metivta: Center for Contemplative Judaism, Los Angeles, CA, February 9, 1998).
18. As time passed, the musical content of The Hasidic Song Festival strayed from its Hasidic roots. The shift owed in part to tensions between Hasidim and non-observant Jews in Israel, and a coinciding depletion of enthusiasm for all things "Hasidic-style," including music. The festival was discontinued after 1986. Marsha Bryan Edelman, *Discovering Jewish Music* (Philadelphia: Jewish Publication Society, 2003), 307, n. 32.
19. The *Vehaeir Eineinu* formula appears in most of Carlebach's songs, which some have numbered upwards of 1,000. Weiss, "Carlebach, Neo-Hasidic Music and Liturgical Practice," 56. See also Motti Regev and Edwin Seroussi, *Popular Music and National Culture in Israel* (Berkeley: University of California Press, 2004), 127–129.
20. The orchestrated setting of *Oseh Shalom* was part of the "Service of Inauguration for Alfred Gottschalk as the Fifth President of the Hebrew Union College-Jewish Institute of Religion" (Isaac Mayer Wise Temple, Cincinnati, Ohio, February 24, 1972). The second setting is an adaptation of the first.
21. Schachet-Briskin, "The Music of Reform Youth."
22. *Ashreinu/Sh'ma* and *Lo Yareyu* (as *Lo Yarei-u/V'chit'tu*) are included in Joel N. Eglash, ed., *The Complete Jewish Songbook:*

Notes. Chapter 6

The Definitive Collection of Jewish Songs (New York: Transcontinental, 2002). *Lo Yarei-u* is heard on *Shir Mi-libeinu: A Song From Our Heart; UAHC Camp Institutes for Living Judaism Camp Swig and Camp Newman*, Sounds Write, 2000, compact disc [originally recorded in 1984].

23. William Sharlin, *T'fillah L'Misrat Torah: A Service on the Receiving and Transmission of the Torah*; Composed and Arranged for the Service of Inauguration of President Alfred Gottschalk, Hebrew Union College—Jewish Institute of Religion (New York: CCAR, 1972; reprinted New York: Transcontinental, 1999).

24. "Los Angeles Cantor Leads Songfest at Jewish Service," *San Quentin News*, August 6, 1959, 3.

25. Kaelter, *From Danzig*, 146. With some exceptions, the Temple Israel quartet was a relatively steady group during Kaelter's tenure. Its longtime members were Anita Bard, Gloria Palacios, Dan Armistead, and Marvin Ekedal, under the direction of organist Lloyd Holzgraf.

26. Wolli Kaelter, quoted in Hanna Chu, "Kaelter, Temple Israel Rabbi," *Long Beach Press-Telegram*, Jan. 10, 2008. http://www.presstelegram.com/technology/20080111/kaelter-temple-israel-rabb

27. I witnessed this during my season with the Long Beach Camerata Singers, the resident choir of the Long Beach Bach Festival (2003–2004). At the conclusion of the Mass in B Minor, the eighty-nine-year-old Rabbi Kaelter immediately rose from his seat (Bethany Lutheran Church, Long Beach, California, November 1, 2003).

28. The *Long Beach Press-Telegram* ran this notice: "Wolli and Sarah Kaelter will be honored with a special, admission-free concert in honor of their 18th anniversary in Long Beach. The concert, which will be given at Millikan High School on Sept. 16, is the world premiere of composer-cantor William Sharlin's 'Shabbat Suite.' The idea was conceived by Mr. and Mrs. Gerald B. Bubis who asked friends at Temple Israel and others to underwrite the event. So far 197 families have responded. Contributions will be used for scholarships in the Kaelters' name at Long Beach State" (August 18, 1973).

29. The cantor-soloists were Lawrence Avery, Richard Botton, Ramon Gilbert, Paul Kwartin, Misha Alexandrovitch, and Harold Orbach.

30. Robert Sherman, "Cantica Hebraica Fuses Old and New," *New York Times*, Nov. 12, 1974.

31. The November 10, 2010, goodwill concert, "To God's Ears," was organized by the New York-based Interreligious Information Center in cooperation with Cardinal William Keeler, the emeritus archbishop of Baltimore. It included twenty Reform cantors from across the United States and took place at the Basilica of Santa Maria degli Angeli e dei Martiri in Rome, a cavernous church adapted by Michelangelo from the ancient Baths of Diocletian. Keeler is the basilica's cardinal priest.

32. William's *Mi Shebeirach* is listed in "Selected Acquisitions," *American Jewish Archives* 33:1 (1981): 164. The piece is not found in his complete catalog.

33. Sharlin, "Trust the Process," 123.

34. Guitar is a required course for cantorial students at Hebrew Union College's Debbie Friedman School of Sacred Music.

35. Pitesky, interview.

36. Sharlin, "Trust the Process," 132.

37. Bill Cutter, "Eulogy for William Sharlin" (presented at Leo Baeck Temple, Los Angeles, November 9, 2012).

38. Sharlin, "Trust the Process," 124.

39. *Ibid.*

40. Sharlin, "Comments Made to the Cantor."

41. William Sharlin, letter to Hans, Los Angeles, CA, March 20, 1967.

42. These chords are played beneath the words, "*Aleinu l'shabeiach la-adon ha-kol, la-tet g'dulah l'yotzeir b'reishit, she-lo asanu k'goyei ha-aratzot, v'lo samanu k'mishp'chot ha-adamah, she-lo sam chelkeinu kahem, v'goraleinu k'chol ha-monam.*"

"We must praise the Master of all, to ascribe greatness to the Maker of creation, for He has not made us like the other nations of the lands, and has not established us like the families of the Earth. For he has not assigned our portion like theirs, nor our lot like all the multitudes."

43. Sharlin, "The Musical World of Cantor William Sharlin."

44. This approach echoes the ideal of Erik Routley, a British minister, composer, and musicologist, who wrote: "Give us the best music we can have, but make it friendly to the people." Erik Routley, *The Church and Music: An Enquiry into the History, the Nature, and the Scope of Christian Judgment on Music* (London: Gerald Duckworth and Co., 1960), 161.

45. Bill Cutter, quoted in "HUC-JIR Mourns the Death of Cantor William Sharlin, *z"l*," Nov. 9, 2012. http://huc.edu/news/article/2012/huc-jir-mourns-death-cantor-william-sharlin-z

46. Patty Linsky, quoted in "ACC Mourns the Passing of Cantor William Sharlin," November 5, 2012. http://www.accantors.org/acc/node/931

47. Pitesky, interview.

48. John P. Marshall, *Jews in Nevada: A History* (Reno: University of Nevada Press, 2008), 192.

Epilogue

1. W. Sharlin, "Trust the Process," 129.
2. William Sharlin, letter to Leo Baeck Temple members (Los Angeles, CA, January 29, 1988).
3. Anonymous, "How Do We Say Good-Bye to William?" (presented at Cantor Sharlin's Retirement Weekend, Leo Baeck Temple, Los Angeles, October 7, 1988).
4. Richard N. Levy, "In Praise of William Sharlin" (presented at Cantor Sharlin's Retirement Weekend, Leo Baeck Temple, Los Angeles, October 7, 1988).
5. Alexander M. Schindler, letter to William Sharlin (New York, April 13, 1994).

6. About Us, The Milken Archive of Jewish Music http://www.milkenarchive.org/about

7. William Sharlin, *In Pursuit of the Sacred: The Music of William Sharlin*, Leo Baeck Temple, 2001, compact disc.

8. Of the scores used for the recording, Laurendale Associates published seven (*Sim Shalom*/Grant Us Peace; *Ani Ma'amim*; *Shalom Rav*; "Jacob's Dream"; *V'shamru* No. 1; *V'shamru* No. 4; and *Va-ani T'filati*), and Transcontinental published five (*Yom Zeh L'Yisrael I*; *Shir Hashirim*; *Elohai N'shama*; *Eilu D'varim*; and *Shalom Aleichem*). The ten unpublished works are: *Esa Enai*; *Eliyahu*; *Shiru Ladonai*; "March Lied"; "Der Fiddler"; *Yom Zeh L'Yisrael II*; *Amar Rabi Akiva*; "Trees"; and "Is That Not Glorious"?

9. Zephyr: Voices unbound consists of Karen Altabet-Freed, Dawn Brooks, Rich Brunner, Robert DeCarlo, Stan DeWitt, Elizabeth Derwing, James Drollinger, Sally Etcheto, Paul Gibson, Ken Neufeld, Cheryl Ann Roach, Susan Taylor Mills, and Daniel Wilson.

10. Schachet-Briskin, interview.

11. *Eliyahu* and *Shir Hashirim* are included on *Cycle of Life in Synagogue and Home; Volume 04: Digital Album 5*, Milken Archive of Jewish Music, New York, 2014, digital download.

12. The piece is dedicated in memory of Gerald Ruben, by his loving family.

13. William Sharlin, *Eil Na R'fa Na—O God, Pray Heal!* [2001] (New York: Transcontinental, 2003).

14. Multiple meter changes are found in several of William's compositions. For instance, there are eight time signature changes in his sixteen-measure setting of *V'shamru* (New York: Transcontinental, 1987), known as *V'shamru* No. 6, a setting for solo voice and keyboard or woodwinds.

15. William Sharlin, *Higid L'cha Adam* (Los Angeles: Multiview, 2006).

16. BT *Makkot* 23b-24a.

17. Sharlin Klein, comp., *Cantor William Sharlin: A Library of Original Scores*.

Notes. Epilogue

18. Friedmann and Stetson, ed., *Jewish Sacred Music and Jewish Identity*.
19. Sharlin, "Trust the Process."
20. Sharlin Klein, "William Sharlin."
21. Saltzman, interview.
22. I. Sharlin, "Eulogy for Dad."
23. William insisted on improvising the memorial prayer: "When I do *El Male Rachamim* at a funeral, I have no idea what I'm going to sing. I'm in my own world and the world of the mourner at that time, not outside." Quoted in Ellen Jaffe-Gill, "A Passion for Perfection: At 80, William Sharlin continues to contribute to the rich sound of Jewish music in Los Angeles," *Jewish Journal of Greater Los Angeles*, May 8, 2000, 11, 44.
24. Other participants included casket bearers Mark Wolfe Klein, Daniel Jaffee, Cantor Mark Saltzman, Cantor Sam Radwine, Elizabeth Beerman Rothbart, Matthew Anderson-Miller, Janet Miller, and Suzanne Segal, and honorary casket bearers Rabbi Leonard Beerman, Rabbi Sanford Ragins, Rabbi Bill Cutter, and Rabbi Richard Levy.
25. Saltzman, interview.
26. Stern, interview.
27. Sharlin, "Trust the Process," 131.

Bibliography

Adler, Cyrus, and Henrietta Szold, ed. *American Jewish Yearbook*. Philadelphia: Jewish Publication Society, 1904.
Alper, Robert A. Letter to William Sharlin. Cincinnati, OH, March 6, 1972.
"American Conference of Cantors Demonstration: On the Performance of Schoenberg's *A Survivor from Warsaw*, op. 46, with William Sharlin." *Journal of the Arnold Schoenberg Institute* 14:1 (1991): 38.
Anker, Perryne. Telephone interview by author. June 5, 2014.
Beerman, Leonard. "From Rabbi Beerman." *Leo Baeck Temple College Bulletin* 1:2 (winter 1967): 2.
———. Interview with Robert Corsini. Interfaith Communities United for Justice and Peace, Los Angeles, CA, September 2013.
———. Letter to William Sharlin. Los Angeles, CA, June 11, 1954.
———. Letter to William Sharlin. Los Angeles, CA, May 25, 1954.
Belskin-Ginsburg, W. "The Cantors Assembly: Its Creation and Growth." *Proceedings of the Cantors Assembly* (1972): 13–19.
Berenbaum, Michael. "Sharlin, William." *Encyclopedia Judaica*, 2nd ed., vol. 18. Detroit: Macmillan Reference, 2007. 414–415.
Bernheimer, Martin. "Tilson Thomas Closes 'Made in L.A.' Festival." *Los Angeles Times*, December 15, 1981.
Binder, Abraham W. *Biblical Chant*. New York: Philosophical Library, 1959.
Blinder, Robert. Letter to William Sharlin. St. Louis, MO, February 25, 1972.
Boston Symphony. *Beethoven—Symphony No. 9; Schoenberg—A Survivor From Warsaw*. RCA, 2000, compact disc.
"Cantor William Sharlin: Composer, Conductor, Soloist, Scholar-in-Residence." Congregation B'nai Jehudah, Kansas City, MO, March 7–9, 1986.
Cariaga, Daniel. "Lane, Merrill With Kol Echad Chorale." *Los Angeles Times*, June 15, 1987.
Chu, Hanna. "Kaelter, Temple Israel Rabbi." *Long Beach Press-Telegram*, January 10, 2008.
Cohen, Janece Erman. "The Life and Music of Cantor William Sharlin." M.S.M. thesis, Hebrew Union College–Jewish Institute of Religion, New York, 1990.
Cohen, Judah M. *The Making of a Reform Jewish Cantor: Musical Authority, Cultural Investment*. Bloomington: Indiana University Press, 2009.

Bibliography

———. "Singing Out for Judaism: A History of Song Leaders and Song Leading at Olin-Sang-Ruby Union Institute." In *A Place of Their Own: The Rise of Reform Jewish Camping*, edited by Michael M. Lorge and Gary P. Zola. Tuscaloosa: University of Alabama Press, 2006. 173–208.

———. "Transplanting the Cantorate: Eric Werner and the Founding of the School of Sacred Music." Building Sacred Bridges: Conference and Concert in Memory of Dr. Eric Werner. Hebrew Union College–Jewish Institute of Religion, New York. November 24, 2002.

Cook, Ray M. *Sing for Fun*. New York: UAHC, 1955.

Cutter, Bill. "Eulogy for William Sharlin." Funeral of William Sharlin. Leo Baeck Temple, Los Angeles, November 9, 2012.

———. Interview by author. Los Angeles, CA, September 15, 2014.

Cycle of Life in Synagogue and Home; Volume 04: Digital Album 5. Milken Archive of Jewish Music, New York, 2014, digital download.

Davis, D. J. "Funny, It Didn't Sound Jewish." *Washington Jewish Week*, April 9, 1992, 38.

Edelman, Marsha Bryan. *Discovering Jewish Music*. Philadelphia: Jewish Publication Society, 2003.

Eisenstein, Judith K. "The Professor in Room 202." *Shalshelet: The Chain* 2:2 (1976): 3–4.

Engel, Rose, Judith Berman, and Lita Greenberg. *My Sabbath Prayer Book*. Los Angeles: self-published, 1977.

Friedmann, Jonathan L. "Cantor Reuben Rinder, Frederick Jacobi and Temple Emanu-El of San Francisco: Commissioning the Sacred." *Western States Jewish History* 45:4 (2013): 321–332.

———. "A Conversation with Cantor William Sharlin." In *Jewish Sacred Music and Jewish Identity: Continuity and Fragmentation*, edited by Jonathan L. Friedmann and Brad Stetson. St. Paul, MN: Paragon House, 2008. 39–48.

———, ed. *Quotations on Jewish Sacred Music*. Lanham, MD: Hamilton, 2011.

———, ed. *20th Century Synagogue Music: Essential Readings*. Woodland Hills, CA: Isaac Nathan, 2010.

Friedmann, Jonathan L., and Brad Stetson, ed. *Jewish Sacred Music and Jewish Identity: Continuity and Fragmentation*. St. Paul, MN: Paragon House, 2008.

Friedmann, Jonathan L., and Seth Marlon Ettinger. "Chuck Feldman: Music Director of Wilshire Boulevard Temple, Los Angeles," *Western States Jewish History* 47:2 (2015): 65–83.

Gamoran, Hillel. "The Road to Chalutzim: Reform Judaism's Hebrew-Speaking Program." In *A Place of Their Own: The Rise of Reform Jewish Camping*, edited by Michael M. Lorge and Gary P. Zola. Tuscaloosa: University of Alabama Press, 2006. 124–150.

Gash, Eugene. *Memoir*. New York: Vantage, 1995.

Gertler, Judith. Interview with William Sharlin. "Leo Baeck Oral History Project: 1947-1963." Leo Baeck Temple, Los Angeles, CA, April 23, 1990.

Glaser, Joseph. Letter to William Sharlin. New York, February 24, 1972.

Glass, Herbert. "Dance and Music Reviews: A Vienna-to-Los Angeles Concert at Gindi." *The Los Angeles Times*, May 30, 1992.

Goldberg, Geoffrey. "Maier Levi of Esslingen, Germany: A Small-Town *Hazzan* in the Time of the Emancipation and His Cantorial Compendium." Ph.D. diss., Hebrew University of Jerusalem, 2000.

Goldman, Ari L. "As Call Comes, More Women Answer." *New York Times*, October 19, 1986.

Gottlieb, Jack. *Funny, It Doesn't Sound Jewish: How Yiddish Songs and Synagogue Melodies Influenced Tin Pan Alley, Broadway, and Hollywood*. New York: SUNY Press, 2004.

Bibliography

Gottschalk, Alfred. Letter to William Sharlin. Jerusalem, March 6, 1972.
Guest, John F. "Commissioning Émigré Composers in Los Angeles, 1938–1945: Rabbi Jacob Sonderling's Contributions to Jewish Musical History." M.J.S.M. thesis, Academy for Jewish Religion California, Los Angeles, 2018.
"Hadassah Menorah Marks 5th Birthday." *New York Post Home News,* April 1, 1951.
Havilio, Tamar Heather. "(Re)Learning *L'Hitpaleil*: The Performance of Prayer as Spiritual Education." *CCAR Journal: The Reform Jewish Quarterly* (winter 2014): 190–206.
Henken, John. "Raccoons Join Institute Orchestra at Bowl." *Los Angeles Times,* July 28, 1987.
Heskes, Irene. *Passport to Jewish Music: Its History, Traditions, and Culture.* New York: Tara, 1994.
Jacobson, Joshua R. *Chanting the Hebrew Bible: The Complete Guide to the Art of Cantillation.* Philadelphia: Jewish Publication Society, 2002.
Jaffe, Kenneth. *Solo Vocal Works on Jewish Themes: A Bibliography of Jewish Composers.* Lanham, MD: Scarecrow, 2011.
Jaffe-Gill, Ellen. "A Passion for Perfection: At 80, William Sharlin continues to contribute to the rich sound of Jewish music in Los Angeles." *Jewish Journal of Greater Los Angeles,* May 8, 2000, 11, 44.
Jeffrey, Peter. "*The Sacred Bridge, Volume 2*: A Review Essay." *Jewish Quarterly Review* 77:4 (1987): 293–298.
Kaelter, Wolli. *From Danzig: An American Rabbi's Journey,* with Gordon Cohn. Malibu, CA: Pangloss, 1997.
Kahn-Harris, Keith. "Jews United and Divided by Music: Contemporary Jewish Music in the UK and America." In *Religion and Popular Music in Europe: New Expressions of Sacred and Secular,* edited by Thomas Bossius, Andreas Häger, and Keith Kahn-Harris. London: I. B. Tauris, 2011. 71–91.
Kaplan, Mordecai. *Judaism as a Civilization: Toward a Reconstruction of American-Jewish Life.* New York: Macmillan, 1934.
Katchko, Adolph. *A Thesaurus of Cantorial Liturgy,* three volumes. New York: HUC School of Sacred Music, 1986.
Katz, Israel J. "Eric Werner (1901–1988): A Bibliography of His Collected Writings." *Musica Judaica* 10:1 (1987–88): 1–36.
Kol Echad Chorale. "American Composers: Synagogue Music of the New World." Program Notes. Temple Beth Shalom, Santa Ana and Gindi Auditorium, University of Judaism, March 26 and 29, 1994.
———. "Tradition and Modernity: The Music of William Sharlin." Program Notes. Temple Bat Yahm, Newport Beach and Leo Baeck Temple, Los Angeles, June 2 and 4, 1991.
Krakower, Dora B. *Trusting the Song That Sings Within: Pioneer Woman Cantor.* Santa Monica, CA: Azure, 1994.
Landeck, Beatrice, ed. *"Git on Board": Collection of Folk Songs Arranged for Mixed Chorus and Solo Voice.* New York: Edward B. Marks, 1950.
Leneman, Helen. "Teaching Trope: The Hows, Whys, and Whens." In *Bar/Bat Mitzvah Education: A Sourcebook,* ed. Helen Leneman. Denver, CO: A.R.E., 1993. 141-152.
Levin, Neil. Interview with William Sharlin. Milken Archive of American Jewish Music, undated.
———. "Music at JTS." In *Tradition Renewed: A History of the Jewish Theological Seminary,* vol. 1, edited by Jack Wertheimer. New York: Jewish Theological Seminary, 1997. 717–782.
Levy, Richard N. "In Praise of William Sharlin." Cantor Sharlin's Retirement Weekend. Leo Baeck Temple, Los Angeles, October 7, 1988.

Bibliography

A Life of Sacred Music: In Honor of Cantor William Sharlin. Los Angeles: Leo Baeck Temple, 2000.

"Los Angeles Cantor Leads Songfest at Jewish Service." *San Quentin News*, August 6, 1959, 3.

Marshall, John P. *Jews in Nevada: A History*. Reno: University of Nevada Press, 2008.

Maslow, Abraham. *The Farther Reaches of Human Nature*. New York: Viking Press, 1971.

Merel, Marcie. Liner notes to *Standing Ovation: Cantor Sheldon F. Merel, Tenor, Live in Concert*. Music Lab, 2000, compact disc.

Merel, Sheldon. "Memories of My Friend Cantor William (Bill) Sharlin." Unpublished. November 26, 2012.

Merel, Sheldon, and Marcie Merel. Interview by author. Encinitas, CA, August 10, 2014.

Moore, Deborah Dash. *To the Golden Cities: Pursuing the American Dream in Miami and L.A.* Cambridge: Harvard University Press, 1994.

Moses, I. "The Cantor as a Religious Functionary." *Annual Report of the Society of American Cantors* (1904).

"Mrs. Krakower Earns Silverman Music Award." *B'nai B'rith Messenger*, July 16, 1971.

Newman, Harry. *Thirty-Four Years on the Bimah: Vignettes of My Life as a "Professional" Jew*. Bloomington, IN: Author House, 2007.

Olitzky, Kerry M., Lance J. Sussman, and Malcom H. Stern, ed. *Reform Judaism in America: A Biographical Dictionary and Sourcebook*. Westport, CT: Greenwood, 1993.

Ouseley, F. A. Gore. "Canon." In *Grove's Dictionary of Music and Musicians, Vol. 1*, edited by H. C. Colles. New York: Macmillan, 1939. 548.

Perlmutter, Donna. "Heady Dose of Modern Masters." *Los Angeles Herald Examiner*, December 15, 1981.

Pinnolis, Judith S. "'Cantor Soprano' Julie Rosewald: The Musical Career of a Jewish American 'New Woman.'" *The American Jewish Archives Journal* 62:2 (2010): 1–53.

Pitesky, Shirl Lee. Interview by author. Los Angeles, CA, September 6, 2014.

Raphael, Marc Lee. *The Synagogue in America: A Short Story*. New York: New York University Press, 2011.

Regev, Motti, and Edwin Seroussi. *Popular Music and National Culture in Israel*. Berkeley: University of California Press, 2004.

Rosowsky, Solomon. *The Cantillation of the Bible*. New York: Reconstructionist, 1957.

Routley, Eric. *The Church and Music: An Enquiry into the History, the Nature, and the Scope of Christian Judgment on Music*. London: Gerald Duckworth and Co., 1960.

Ruben, Bruce. "A History of the School of Sacred Music at Fifty: The Franzblau Years." Fiftieth Anniversary of the School of Sacred Music, Hebrew Union College- Jewish Institute of Religion, Cincinnati, OH, 1999.

Sager, Sarah J. Letter to William Sharlin. Cleveland, Ohio, April 9, 1985.

Saltzman, Mark. Interview by author. Pasadena, CA, October 20, 2014.

Schachet-Briskin, Paul Henry (Wally). "The Music of Reform Youth." M.S.M. thesis, HUC School of Sacred Music, New York, 1996.

Schenck, Janet D. *Adventure in Music: A Reminiscence; Manhattan School of Music, 1918–1960*. New York: Manhattan School of Music, 1961.

Schiller, Benji-Ellen. "The Hymnal as an Index of Musical Change in Reform Synagogues." In *Sacred Sound and Social Change: Liturgical Music in Jewish and Christian Experience*, edited by Lawrence A. Hoffman and Janet R. Watson. Notre Dame: Notre Dame University Press, 1992. 187–212.

Schindler, Alexander M. Letter to William Sharlin. New York, April 13, 1994.

"Selected Acquisitions." *American Jewish Archives* 33:1 (1981): 158–165.

Bibliography

Sharlin, Ilana. "Eulogy for Dad." Funeral of William Sharlin. Leo Baeck Temple, Los Angeles, November 9, 2012.
Sharlin, Jacqui. Interview by author. Los Angeles, CA, July 5, 2014.
Sharlin, William. "The American Synagogue in Search of Its Musical Idiom." *Shalshelet: The Chain* 2:2 (1976): 6–8.
_____. *Ashreinu/Sh'ma*. In *The Complete Jewish Songbook: The Definitive Collection of Jewish Songs*, edited by Joel N. Eglash. New York: Transcontinental, 2002. 48.
_____. "Comments Made to the Cantor." Leo Baeck Temple, Los Angeles, CA, 1985.
_____. "Davening and Congregational Song." In *Emotions in Jewish Music: Personal and Scholarly Reflections*, edited by Jonathan L. Friedmann. Lanham, MD: University Press of America, 2012. 45–53.
_____. *Eil Na R'fa Na—O God, Pray Heal!* New York: Transcontinental, 2003.
_____. "The Ever-Changing Musical Tradition of the Jewish People: Diversity Through the Ages." Congregation Beth Am, Los Altos Hills, California, April 3–5, 1981.
_____. "Hasidic Music." Metivta: Center for Contemplative Judaism, Los Angeles, CA, February 9, 1998.
_____. *Higid L'cha Adam*. Los Angeles: Multiview, 2006.
_____. *In Pursuit of the Sacred: The Music of William Sharlin*. Leo Baeck Temple, 2000, compact disc.
_____. "Israeli Music at 37: Those Were the Days." *The Jewish Newspaper*, April 27, 1985, 6.
_____. "Israel's Influence on American Liberal Synagogue Music." In *Gates of Understanding*, edited by Lawrence A. Hoffman. New York: Central Conference of American Rabbis, 1977. 122–128.
_____. "L'dor V'dor: From Generation to Generation." In *Jewish Sacred Music and Jewish Identity*, edited Jonathan L. Friedmann and Brad Stetson. St. Paul, MN: Paragon House, 2008. 87–88.
_____. Letter to Hans. Los Angeles, CA, March 20, 1967.
_____. Letter to Leo Baeck Temple members. Los Angeles, CA, January 29, 1988.
_____. *Lo Yarei-u/V'chit'tu*. In *The Complete Jewish Songbook: The Definitive Collection of Jewish Songs*, edited by Joel N. Eglash. New York: Transcontinental, 2002. 218.
_____. "Mozart Mounts the *Bimah*—What a Mass!" *The Jewish Newspaper*, March 14, 1985.
_____. "Music of the Synagogue: When the *Chazzan* 'Turned Around.'" *CCAR Journal* (winter 1962): 43–44.
_____. "The Musical World of Cantor William Sharlin." Oneg Shabbat Program, UAHC Western Region Biennial. Los Angeles, 1989.
_____. "On Turning Around; Or, Can You Achieve Privacy in public?" *Leo Baeck Temple College Bulletin* 1:2 (winter 1967): 3.
_____. "The Purim Theme in Jewish Music." *The Jewish Newspaper*, February 28, 1985.
_____. Review of *Biblical Chant*, by A. W. Binder. *Central Conference of American Rabbis Journal* (June 1960): 65–66.
_____. *T'filat L'misrat Torah: A Service on the Receiving and Transmission of the Torah on the Occasion of the Inauguration of President Alfred Gottschalk, Hebrew Union College–Jewish Institute of Religion*. New York: CCAR, 1972.
_____. "Trust the Process: My Life in Sacred Song." In *Perspectives on Jewish Music: Secular and Sacred*, edited by Jonathan L. Friedmann. Lanham, MD: Lexington, 2009. 97–136.
_____. *V'shamru*. New York: Transcontinental, 1987.
_____. "When Religious Music Turns 'Cultural.'" *The Jewish Newspaper*, April 11, 1985.
_____. "Why Can't a Woman Chant Like a Man?" *The Jewish Newspaper*, date unknown.

Bibliography

Sharlin Klein, Lisa, comp. *Cantor William Sharlin: A Library of Original Scores.* Los Angeles: Pacific Southwest Region of the American Conference of Cantors, 2007. CD-ROM.

———. "William Sharlin." Funeral of William Sharlin. Leo Baeck Temple, Los Angeles, November 9, 2012.

———. *Yom Zeh L'Yisrael.* In *Shireinu: The Complete Jewish Songbook,* edited by Joel N. Eglash. New York: Transcontinental, 2002. 380.

Sherman, Robert. "Cantica Hebraica Fuses Old and New." *New York Times,* November 12, 1974.

Shir Mi-libeinu: A Song From Our Heart; UAHC Camp Institutes for Living Judaism Camp Swig and Camp Newman. Sounds Write, 2000, compact disc.

Skirball, Jack. Letter to William Sharlin. Los Angeles, CA, February 29, 1972.

Slobin, Slobin. *Chosen Voices: The Story of the American Cantorate.* Urbana: University of Illinois Press, 1989.

Songbook for The American Conference of Cantors, Twelfth Annual Convention. Sportsmen's Lodge, Los Angeles, CA, June 28–July 1, 1965.

Soref, Irwin I. "Samuel Kaminker." *Jewish Education* 34:4 (1964): 222.

Special Songster of New Materials for Congregational and Solo Singing; prepared for The First Institute on Sacred Music of the American Conference of Certified Cantors, June 8–11, 1953 in New York City. New York: Hebrew Union School of Sacred Music, 1953.

Stein, Erwin, ed. *Arnold Schoenberg Letters.* Berkeley: University of California Press, 1987.

Steinberg, Paul M. "School of Sacred Music of The Hebrew Union College–Jewish Institute of Religion." In *The Cantorial Art,* edited by Irene Heskes. New York: National Jewish Music Council, 1966. 81–88.

Stern, Joel. Interview by author. Los Angeles, CA, May 11, 2014.

Streeter, Kurt. "At 93, Rabbi Leonard Beerman still stirs passions with pacifist views." *Los Angeles Times,* November 26, 2014.

Strimple, Nick. *Choral Music in the Twentieth Century.* New York: Hal Leonard, 2005.

"Sunday Morning Service." *The Temple Bulletin* 43:12, December 23, 1956, 1.

Thal, Leonard. Untitled Speech. Evening of Tribute to Cantor William Sharlin. New York, October 8, 1988.

Thal, Linda Rabinowitch. Introduction to "The Musical World of Cantor William Sharlin." UAHC Western Region Biennial, Los Angeles, CA, 1989.

"Tri-Culture Music Concert at Leo Baeck Wednesday Eve." *B'nai B'rith Messenger,* October 18, 1963, 32.

Vinaver, Chemjo. "Out-of-Print Classics of Cantorial Liturgy." *Commentary,* January 1, 1957. 556–558.

Weiner, Alan. Interview by author. Agoura Hills, CA, December 8, 2014.

Weiss, Sam. "Carlebach, Neo-Hasidic Music and Liturgical Practice." *Journal of Synagogue Music* 34 (2009): 55–75.

Werner, Eric. "The Common Ground in the Chant of Church and Synagogue." *Congresso Internazionale di Musica Sacra* (1952): 134–148.

———. "The Conflict Between Hellenism and Judaism in the Music of the Early Christian Church." *Hebrew Union College Annual* 20 (1947): 407–470.

———. "De quibusdam relationibus inter accentus Masoretarum et neumas liquescentes." Ph.D. diss., University of Strasbourg, 1928.

———. "Die jüdischen Wurzeln der christlichen Kirchenmusik." In *Geschichte der katholis-*

Bibliography

chen Kirchenmusik, Vol. 1, edited by Karl Gustav Fellerer. Kassel: Bärenreiter, 1972. 22–30.

———. "The Doxology in Synagogue and Church: A Liturgico-Musical Study." *Hebrew Union College Annual* 19 (1945–56): 275–351.

———. "Felix Mendelssohn—Gustav Mahler: Two Borderline Cases of German Jewish Assimilation." *Yuval* 4 (1982): 240–64.

———. *From Generation to Generation: Studies on Jewish Musical Tradition.* New York: American Conference of Cantors, 1967.

———. "Gustav Mahlers Symphoniethemen: Eine typologische Untersuchung der ersten vier Symphonien." *Musicologica Austriaca* 7 (1987): 69–127.

———. "Gustav Mahlers Weg (Zu seinem Todestag am 18. Mai)." *Jüdische Rundschau* 39:40 (1934): 13.

———. "Hebrew and Oriental Christian Metrical Hymns: A Comparison." *Hebrew Union College Annual* 23:2 (1950–51): 397–432.

———. "The Influence of Jewish Music on the Gregorian Chant." *Proceedings of the Music Teachers National Association* 68 (1944): 241–247.

———. "The Lost Chords: Notes About Synagogue and Church Music." *Hebrew Union College Monthly* 29:2 (1942): 8.

———. *Mendelssohn: A New Image of the Composer and His Age.* New York: Free Press, 1963.

———. "Meyerbeer, Mendelssohn, Mahler: Ein Crescendo des Judentums." *B'nai B'rith Mittelungen für Österreich* 36 (1926): 188–122.

———. "O, Once There Was a Magic-Kabalistic Song." *Sh'ma: A Journal of Jewish Responsibility* 11:210 (1981): 73–74.

———. "The Origin of the Eight Modes of Music." *Hebrew Union College Annual* 21 (1948): 211–255.

———. Preface to *Services for Sabbath Eve and Morning and Three Festival,* by Adolph Katchko. New York: HUC School of Education and Sacred Music, 1952.

———. "Preface to the Out-of-Print Classics Reissue by the Hebrew Union School of Sacred Music" (various volumes). New York: Sacred Music Press, 1953.

———. "Preliminary Notes for a Comparative Study of Catholic and Jewish Musical Punctuation." *Hebrew Union College Annual* 15 (1940): 335–366.

———. "Review of *The Cantillation of the Bible: The Five Books of Moses,* by Solomon Rosowsky." *The Jewish Quarterly Review* 41 (April 1959): 287–292.

———. *The Sacred Bridge: Liturgical Parallels in Synagogue and Early Church.* New York: Columbia University Press, 1959.

———. "The True Source of Jewish Music." *Commentary* 7:4 (1949): 382–387.

———. Untitled message. *Shalshelet: The Chain; Publication of the School of Sacred Music Alumni Association* 2:3 (Fall 1976): 16.

———. *A Voice Still Heard: The Sacred Songs of the Ashkenazic Jews.* University Park: Pennsylvania State University Press, 1976.

———. "What Function Has Synagogue Music Today?" *CCAR Journal* 13:4 (1966): 35–40.

"Women Lead Jewish Services." *Los Angeles Times,* November 22, 1970.

Zeldin, Isaiah. Letter to William Sharlin. Los Angeles, CA, May 25, 1954.

Index

Adler, Hugo Ch. 43
Ahavah Rabah (prayer-song) 116–117, 125
Ahavah Rabbah (melodic mode) 45–46, 84
Ahavat Olam 30–31
Aleinu and *Vene'emar* 132–133
Alexandrovitch, Misha 171*n*29
All Saints Episcopal Church, Pasadena 67
Aloni, Aminadav 119
Alper, Robert A. 74
Altschuler, Saul 30
American Conference of Cantors (ACC) 7, 44, 88, 97, 99, 104, 136, 139, 167*n*38
American Conference of Certified Cantors 43–44
Anderson-Miller, Matthew 173*n*24
Anker, Perryne 3, 102, 167*n*29
Anshe Chesed Congregation–Fairmount Temple, Cleveland 85
Arafat, Yasser 67
Armistead, Dan 171*n*25
Ashreinu/Sh'ma 126
Avery, Lawrence 171*n*28

Ba'al Tefillah 34
Bach, Johann Sebastian 8, 56, 62, 107, 111, 128, 141, 171*n*27
Baeck, Leo 44–45, 53
Baer, Abraham 34
Bamberger, Bernard 157*n*8
Barash, Jack 27
Bard, Anita 171*n*25
Bardin, Shlomo 94
Beerman, Leonard 50–51, 53–54, 57, 59, 65, 66–70, 82, 112, 141, 162*n*48–51, 164*n*81, 173*n*24
Beerman Rothbart, Elizabeth 173*n*24
Beethoven, Ludwig van 8
Ben Uri, Meir 163*n*60
Benjamin Platt Award 108
Berlin 44, 121, 124
Bernstein, Leonard 119, 151, 165*n*93
Bet Midrash L'Morim Mizrachi 14
Biggs, John 71–72, 163*n*59
Binder, Abraham W. 43, 115–116, 118, 128, 151, 157*n*8
Birnbaum, Edward 34, 37
Blank, Sheldon H. 74
Blinder, Robert 74, 174*n*69
Bloch, Ernest 61, 117–118, 119, 129, 148
Bloom, Sidney 163*n*58
Blumstein, Robert 157*n*21
B'nai B'rith Youth Organizations 122
Bordeaux 9
Bornstein, Jacob 30
Boston Symphony Orchestra 86
Botton, Richard 104, 171*n*29
Brahms, Johannes 8, 165*n*108
Brandeis Arts Institute 57, 94–95
Braun, Yechezkiel 129
Broadway 8, 19, 42, 81–82, 165*n*93
Bronx 12, 14, 15, 18, 27, 35
Brooklyn 12, 30, 124
Brostoff, Neal 166*n*121
Brown, Samuel 163*n*58
Bureau of Jewish Education 122

Cage, John 166*n*108
Camp Avodah 122

Index

Camp Roosevelt 63
Cantica Hebraica 128
cantillation 25, 36, 46, 79, 95, 96, 103, 115–116, 118, 150–151
Cantor William Sharlin: A Library of Original Scores 139
The Cantor William Sharlin Award for Excellence in Liturgy 136
Cantorial Training Institute 25
Cantors Assembly 22–23, 43
Cantors Institute 25
Cardozo, David 22
Carlebach, Shlomo 123–125, 131, 170n11
Carnegie Hall 61–62
Castelnuovo-Tedesco, Mario 165n108
Catskills 27, 29
Center Theatre Group 82
Central Conference of American Rabbis 29, 50, 112, 114, 128
Central Park 11
Chajes, Julius 129
Chanukah 83, 111
Chicago Board of Jewish Education 122
Chihara, Paul 165n108
A Chorus Line 81
Cincinnati Conservatory 49
City College of New York 28
Cohen, Hermann 143
Cohen, Minnie 157–158n22
Cohn, Eli H. 164n70
Cohon, Samuel L. 159n2
College of Jewish Studies (Spertus) 56–57
Congregation Beth Israel, San Diego 32
Congregation Shearith Israel, New York 22
Congregation Tifereth Israel, Cleveland 48–49
Cook, Ray 42
Cook, Samuel 39–40, 42
Cordy, Henry 157n21
Croen, Laura 119
Cutter, Bill 3, 111–112, 133, 141, 170n11, 173n24

Dahl, Ingolf 165n108
Danzig 121, 128
Daugherty-Alonzo, Deborah 137
Davidson, Charles 163n60
Davidson, Gordon 82
Davidson, Walter 43, 160n29
Desby, Frank 71–72, 163n59
Dessau, Paul 166n120
Dixson, Terri 137

Dorothy Chandler Pavilion 87
Dunajewsky, Abraham 34
Durbin, Deanna 62
The Dybbuk 83

Eilu D'varim 118, 137
Eisendrath, Maurice 93
Eisler, Hans 165n108
Ekedal, Marvin 171n25
El Maleh Rachamim 141, 143n23
Eliyahu 19, 172n8
Ephros, Gershon 19, 29, 157n16
Epstein, Elias L. 159n2
Erlich, Larry 31
Erman Cohen, Janece 107, 167n17
Esa Einai (Enai) 19, 156n30, 137, 172n8
Essrig, Harry 108

Feldman, Chuck 57
Fiddler on the Roof 81
Fleisher, Leon 60
Foss, Lukas 165n108
Frailich, Jay 137
Franzblau, Abraham N. 24, 26, 43, 49, 157n14
Freed, Isadore 157n8
Freelander, Dan 126
Freund, Iser L. 126
Friedman, Debbie 103–104, 156n31, 167n31
Friedmann, Elvia 3
Fulton, Richard 157n21

Gabbai, Ezra 127
Ganchoff, Moshe 30
Gates of Prayer 147–148
Gerovitsch, Eliezer 34, 129
Gershwin, George 166n108
Giannini, Vittorio 17
Gilbert, Ramon 171n29
Glaser, Joseph 40, 49, 74–75, 112–113
Gluck, Gerhard 157n21
Glueck, Nelson 24, 26, 49, 73, 93
Gold, Maurice 119
Goldberg, Janet 158n22
Goldfarb, Israel 26, 157n8
Goldman, Maurice 183n60
Gordon, Louis 157n21
Gottlieb, Jack 57, 160n9, 168n67
Gottschalk, Alfred 33, 73–75, 96, 127
Gottschalk Service 73–75, 169n85, 170n20, 171n23
Greenfield, Morris 30

Index

Grimm, Stephen 137
Groveman, Felix 163*n*58
Guide, Leon H. 57
guitar 5, 7, 38, 39, 41, 52, 74, 75, 79, 110, 124, 127, 129–133
Guthrie, Woody 123

Hadassah 28, 31
Haganah 15, 51
Hambro, Leonid 88, 168*n*60
Harlem 9–10, 11, 12
Harris, Roy 166*n*108
Hashomer Hatzair 122
Hasidic Song Festival 111, 125, 170*n*18
Hasidism (Chasidism) 19, 45–46, 71, 85, 111, 122, 144, 145, 148, 149, 161*n*33
Havilio, Tamar Heather 168*n*76
Hazzanim Farband 22, 43
hazzanut 10, 19, 25, 28, 30, 77, 96, 106–107, 114, 150, 152, 153, 154
Hebrew Congregation, Washington, D.C. 83
Hebrew University of Jerusalem 27, 51
Hebron 9
Hecker, Wolf 32, 33, 157*n*21
Helfman, Max 44, 57, 94, 95, 127, 129, 157*n*8, 164*n*76
Heller, James 157*n*8
Henken, John 87
Herman, Henry 157*n*21
Hershman, Morris 52
Hess Kramer 57
High Holy Days (Holidays) 1, 54, 58, 81, 72, 99, 100, 131
Higid Lecha Adam 138–139
Hirsch, John 82–83
Hirsch, Nurit 125
Holocaust 23, 36, 44, 53, 86–88, 129, 169
Holy Blossom Temple, Toronto 32
Holzgraf, Lloyd 171*n*25
Horowitz, Vladimir 61
Hyams, Barry 108

Idelsohn, Abraham Z. 36, 37, 113, 115
In Pursuit of the Sacred: The Music of Cantor William Sharlin 136–137
International Jewish Music Library 128
Israeli music 41, 71, 97, 123, 148, 155

Jacobson, Joshua 118
Jaffee, Daniel 173*n*24
Janowski, Max 56
Jassinoswky, Pinchas 43, 157*n*8

Jerusalem 7, 9, 13–15, 48, 51, 71, 95, 97, 121, 124, 161*n*45
Jerusalem Conservatory 7, 15
Jerusalem Riots 14
Jewish Institute of Religion 23
Jewish Music Forum 22
Jewish Sacred Music and Jewish Identity 139
Jewish Theological Seminary 22–23, 25, 92, 110, 115, 156*n*33, 166*n*2
Juilliard 102

Kaelter, Sarah 122
Kaelter, Wolli 26, 127–129, 133, 156*n*28
Kagen, Sergius 102
Kaiser, Alois 21
Kaiser, Shirley 59
Kallis, Mischa 64–66
Kallis House 64–66
Kaminker, Samuel 122–123
Kaplan, Mordecai 92, 102
Kaplan Eisenstein, Judith 37, 156*n*33
Katchko, Adolph 32–34, 43
Katchko, Theodore 32
Kaufman Shelemay, Kay 48
Kazansky, Boris 119
Keeler, William 171*n*31
Kelemer, Samuel 43, 160*n*29
Kent, Peter 137
Kingsley, Gershon 57
Kingston Trio 123
Klein, Mark Wolf 173*n*24
Klepper, Jeff 126
Kligman, Mark 48
Kol Echad Chorale 100, 119–120, 169*n*95–101
kol isha 105–106
Kol Nidre (Schoenberg) 88
Kopland, S.L., Jr. 164*n*68
Korngold, Erich Wolfgang 166*n*108
Kosakoff, Reuben 72
KPFK 88, 168*n*60
Kraft, William 166*n*108
Krakower, Dora 107–109
Krenek, Ernst 166*n*108
Kutz Camp 126
Kwartin, Paul 171*n*29

Lehrerseminare 24
Leinsdorf, Erich 86
Lerner, Harold 119
Levant, Oscar 166*n*108
Levin, Neil 23, 136, 166*n*21

Index

Levy, Richard N. 135, 173*n*24
Lewandowski, Louis 34, 129
Lewis, Robert 137
Liberty Ships 28
Lincoln Center 99, 128
Linsky, Patti 107, 133
Liszt, Franz 62
Lo Yareyu 127
Long Beach Camerata Singers 129, 169*n*90, 171*n*27
Los Angeles Master Chorale 140
Los Angeles Philharmonic 85–87

Magnin, Edgar 92–93, 95
Mahler, Gustav 36, 84, 128
Mailamm 22
El Maleh Rachamim 141, 143*n*23
Manhattan School of Music 1, 7, 15, 16–17, 19, 35, 36, 62, 88, 155*n*18, 156*n*25
Manischewitz Company 63
Ma'oz Tzur 83, 111
Marcus, Jacob Rader 74
Mark Taper Forum 82
Maslow, Abraham 68
Meisels, Saul 102
Menuhin, Yehudi 60
Merchant Marines 28
Merel, Marcie 3, 31
Merel, Maynard 29
Merel, Sheldon 3, 27–32, 35, 43, 57, 110, 119, 158*n*43
Merel Brothers Recording Studio 29
Michalsky, Donal 166*n*108
Mihaly, Eugene 74
Milhaud, Darius 61, 119, 129
Milken Archive of Jewish Music 136
Miller, Janet 173*n*24
Millikan High School 128, 171*n*28
Milnes, Sherrill 86–87
minhag 32, 34
Mirkovic, Leo 157*n*21
Moddel, Philip 163*n*60
Morris Evening High School 16
Mount of Olives 14
Mount Sinai Memorial Parks and Mortuaries 140
Mozart, Wolfgang Amadeus 8, 83

Nathanson, Moshe 43
National Federation of Temple Sisterhoods 39
National Federation of Temple Youth (NFTY) 39–40, 121, 126–127, 129–130

Naumbourg, Samuel 34
Neo-Hasdisim 123–124
niggun 46, 101, 124–125, 144
Norris, Kathleen 121
North American Prize Contest 61
Nowakowsky, David 34, 119
nusach 25, 32, 95, 96, 100, 144, 146, 150

Oconomowoc, WI 38–42
Oheb Shalom, Baltimore 21
Olsen, David 157*n*21
Orbach, Harold 43, 75, 140*n*29, 171*n*29
organ 23, 31, 56, 57, 62, 72, 73, 74, 75, 78, 88, 118, 130–132
Ostfeld-Horowitz, Barbara 109–110
"Out-of- Print Classics of Cantorial Liturgy" 33–34

Pacific Area Reform Rabbis 46
Pacific Chorale 88
Palacios, Gloria 171*n*25
Palestine 9, 14, 16
Papiercyzk, Pinkus 157*n*21
Pentagon 17
Perlmutter, Donna 87
Picket, Frederick 43, 129
Pitesky, Shirl Lee 3, 56–59, 73, 120, 133
Polish, David 164*n*70
Portnoy, Joseph 43, 157*n*21, 160*n*29
Priesand, Sally J. 74, 109
Putterman, David 157*n*8

Rabinowitch Thal, Linda 77–78
Rachmaninoff, Sergei 61
Radwine, Samuel 173*n*24
Ragins, Sanford 69–70, 112
Rapaport, Jacob 129
Ravel, Maurice 128
Reider, Louise 63
Reider, Maurice 63
Renaissance music 19, 75, 97, 129, 136
Resnick, Hyman 56
Rinder, Reuben 60–61
Robbins, Betty 161*n*31
Robinson, Irving 157*n*21
Robson, Mark 88, 166*n*119
Rodeph Shalom, Philadelphia 119
Roger Wagner Chorale 119
Rosenbloom, Aviva 101, 107
Rosewald, Julie 161*n*31
Rosowsky, Solomon 115–116
Rossi, Salamone 19, 34, 97
Roth, Max 163*n*58

Index

Routley, Erik 172*n*44
Royce Hall (UCLA) 85–86, 87
Rubardt, Peter 87
Rye Street Synagogue, New York 32

Sachs, Curt 37, 157*n*8
Sacred Bridge 36, 37, 47, 71
SAFAM! 119
Safran, B. 164*n*70
Sager, Sarah J. 85
Saltzman, Mark 3, 100–101, 140–141, 165*n*93
Saminsky, Lazar 25
San Quentin State Prison 126–127
Sanders, Saul 30–31
Saul Silverman Award 100, 108, 137, 167*n*26
Schachet-Briskin, Wally 126, 137, 165*n*93
Schindler, Alexander M. 136
Schindler, Rudolph 64–65
Schliefer, Eliyahu 48
Schmitz, E. Robert 60–62, 68
Schmitz, Germaine 60, 63
Schoenberg, Arnold 85–88, 165–166*n*108
School for Nursery Years 59
Schoolman, Leonard A. 164*n*70
Schubert, Franz 128
Schumann, Robert 88, 128, 163*n*31, 168*n*30
Sebran, Harry 157*n*21
Secunda, Sholom 167*n*29
Segal, Suzanne 173*n*24
Senesh, Hannah 141
Se'u She'arim Rosheichem 118
Shabbat Suite (Sabbath Suite) 128–129, 171*n*28
Shalom Aleychem 19, 129, 141, 156*n*28, 169*n*85
Shalshelet 27, 160*n*9
Shapiro, Marc 41
Sharlin, Chaya 9, 10, 13–14
Sharlin, Edward 9, 13, 14, 59, 89
Sharlin, Hillel 9, 10, 11–12, 13, 14, 15, 16, 58
Sharlin, Ilana 66, 90, 91, 141
Sharlin, Isaac 9–10, 12, 13, 14, 15, 89–90
Sharlin, Jacqui 3, 58–66, 73, 88, 90–91, 98, 101, 110, 120, 123, 136, 140, 162*n*21, 167*n*33, 168*n*60
Sharlin, Rachel
Sharlin Klein, Lisa 3, 66, 90, 91, 107, 123, 137, 139, 140
Shemer, Naomi 72

Sherman, Robert 129
Silberman, Kurt 157*n*21, 158*n*29
Silver, Abba Hillel 48–49
Silver, Daniel 48
Silverman, Myron 164*n*70
Silverman, Richard 102
Silverman, Saul 163*n*58
Simon, Murray E. 160*n*9
Simon-Weiner, Amy 3, 119
Singer, Carole 63
Singer Sewing Machine 63
Skirball, Jack 50, 54, 74, 94, 161*n*45–46
Skirball Cultural Center 50
Smolover, Raymond 57
Society for the Advancement of Judaism 102
Society of American Cantors 21
Solel Unit 122
Song and Dance Leaders' Institute 126
Sores, Irving 122
Southern California Choral Society 88
Spector, Johanna 156*n*33, 158*n*22
Stahl, Howard 74
Stein, Leonard 88, 166*n*119
Steinberg, Paul M. 160*n*9
Stephen S. Wise Temple 81, 96, 102, 107, 109
Stern, Isaac 60, 62
Stern, Joel 3, 99–100
Stetson, Brad 139
Stevens, Delores 137
Still, William Grant 166*n*108
Stravinsky, Igor 60, 86, 165–166*n*108
Strimple, Nick 88
Sulzer, Salomon 21, 34, 132
A Survivor from Warsaw 85–88, 166*n*108
Swados, Elizabeth 119
Swig, Ben 121
Switzerland 9

Tabatsky, Israel 157*n*21
Talma, Louise 61
Temple Beth El, South Bend 32
Temple Beth Sholom, Santa Monica 102
Temple B'nai Emet, Montebello 99
Temple Emanu-El, San Francisco 60, 62, 160*n*29, 161*n*31
Temple Israel, Hollywood 101, 107, 137, 167*n*26
Temple Israel, Long Beach 1, 127–129, 133, 156*n*28, 169*n*90, 171*n*25–27
Temple of the Arts 102
Temple Sinai, Oakland 32

Index

Thal, Loenard 158*n*43
Theresienstadt 44
Thesaurus of Cantorial Liturgy 32–34
Thomas, Diane 137
Thomson, Virgil 61
Tilson Thomas, Michael 86
Toch, Ernst 166*n*108
"Trust the Process: My Life in Sacred Song" 140
Tucker, Richard 30, 102, 167*n*29

Union Hebrew High School 122
Union Hymnal 21, 152, 156*n*2
Union of American Hebrew Congregations 7, 44, 50, 57, 59, 74, 93, 96, 112, 118, 121, 122, 136, 164*n*70, 167*n*4
Union Prayer Book 78, 153
Union Songster 123
United States Army 17–18
United States Marine Corps 51
United Synagogue of America 43
Universal Studios 64
University of California, Los Angeles (UCLA) 56, 57, 85–86, 128
University of Judaism 92–93, 95, 96, 107–108, 166*n*121, 166*n*2
University of Southern California (USC) 63, 71, 96, 98, 169*n*97
University Synagogue, Los Angeles 57, 108

Va-ani T'filati 137
Verdi Restaurant 88
Victory Gardens 122
Vienna 21, 36, 88, 166*n*121
Vietnam War 67
Vinaver, Chemjo 34

Wagner, Richard 36
Wald, George 157*n*21
Walz, John 141

Warsaw Ghetto Uprising 85
Weavers 123
Weigand, Angela 137
Weinberg, Jacob 26, 157*n*8, 163*n*60
Weiner, Alan 3, 100, 104, 119–120, 168*n*67
Weiner, Lazar 43, 129
Weinflash, George 43, 160*n*29
Weintraub, Hirsch 34
Werner, Elisabeth 36
Werner, Eric 22–27, 32–34, 35–37, 45–48, 71, 83, 84, 113, 114–116, 128, 143–144, 157*n*8, 159*n*5, 160*n*9, 164*n*69
Wiesel, Elie 129, 169*n*90
Wilshire Boulevard Temple 57, 92, 93, 95
Wise, Stephen 23
WKXR 88
Wohlberg, Max 163*n*60
Wolf, Alfred 57, 93
Woodward, Ty 120
World War I 60
World War II 17, 23, 28, 29, 61, 122, 159*n*1
Wyner, Yehudi 57

Yasser, Joseph 157*n*8
Yesh Kochavim 141
Yeshiva D'Bronx 12
Yeshiva D'Harlem 11
Yeshiva University 22, 25, 99
Yeshiva University High School 13, 15–16
Yih'yu L'ratzon 78
YMHA 28
Yom Zeh L'Yisrael 19, 137, 156*n*30, 169*n*85, 170*n*70, 172*n*8

Zamir Chorale, New York 100
Zeldin, Isaiah 59, 81–82, 93–95, 96, 102
Zephyr: Voices Unbound 137, 172*n*9
Zuill, Paul 165*n*93

www.ingramcontent.com/pod-product-compliance
Lightning Source LLC
Chambersburg PA
CBHW032103300426
44116CB00007B/864